Cascading Style Sheets

CASCADING STYLE SHEETS

Designing for the Web

Håkon Wium Lie

Bert Bos

 **Addison Wesley Longman**

Harlow, England • Reading, Massachusetts • Menlo Park, California • New York
Don Mills, Ontario • Amsterdam • Bonn • Sydney • Singapore • Tokyo • Madrid
San Juan • Milan • Mexico City • Seoul • Taipei

© Addison Wesley Longman 1997

Addison Wesley Longman Limited
Edinburgh Gate
Harlow
Essex CM20 2JE
England

and Associated Companies throughout the World.

Cover designed by Designers & Partners, Oxford, UK
Text design by Sally Grover Castle
Line illustrations by the authors and by Margaret Macknelly, Tadley, UK
Typeset in 9/13pt Helvetica by 42
Printed and bound in The United States of America

First printed 1997

ISBN 0-201-41998-X

British Library Cataloguing-in-Publication Data
A catalogue record for this book is available from the British Library

Library of Congress Cataloging-in-Publication Data is available

Foreword

When the Web was in its infancy, five years ago or so, I felt greatly relieved at the final removal of all the totally unsolvable problems of fixed format presentation. In the young Web, there were no more pagination faults, no more footnotes, no silly word breaks, no fidgeting the text to gain that extra line that you sorely needed to fit everything on one page. In the window of a Web page on the NeXTStep system, the text was always clean. Better than that: I decided what font it came out in, how big I wanted the letters, what styles I chose for definition lists and where tabs went.

Then we descended into the Dark Ages for several years, because the Web exploded into a community that had no idea that such freedom was possible, but worried about putting on the remote screen exactly what they thought their information should look like. I've read recommendations against using structured markup because you have no control over what comes out the other side. Sad.

You will by now have understood that I'm firmly in the camp of those who think that quality of content comes first, and presentation comes later. But of course, I'm not entirely right here: presentation is important. Mathematical formulae are always presented in a two-dimensional layout.

Fortunately, SGML's philosophy allows us to separate structure from presentation, and the Web DTD, HTML, is no exception. Even in the NeXTStep version of 1990, Tim provided for style sheets, though at a rudimentary level (we had other things to do then!).

Today, style sheets are becoming reality again, this time much more elaborate. This is an important milestone for the Web, and we should stop for a minute to reflect on the potential benefits and pitfalls of this technology.

I followed the CSS effort from its inception – mostly over cups of coffee with Håkon at CERN – and I've always had one concern: is it possible to create a powerful enough style sheet "language" without ending up with a programming language?

The CSS described in this book shows that you can create some quite stunning presentations without programming. While the programmer in me may be a little disappointed, the minimalist in me is comforted. In fact, I'll never need this much freedom and special effects, but then I'm not a graphic artist. Anything that needs more complication effectively becomes an image, and should be treated as such. I feel therefore that the middle part of the spectrum between pure ASCII text and full images is effectively covered by the power of CSS, without introducing the complexity of programming.

You have here a book on presentation. But it is presentation of information that should also remain structured, so that your content can be effectively used by others, while retaining the specific visual aspects you want to give it. Use CSS with care. It is the long-awaited salt on the Web food: a little is necessary, too much is not good cooking.

The efforts of the authors have finally brought us what we sorely needed: the author's ability to shape the content without affecting the structure. This is good news for the Web!

Robert Cailliau
CERN, Geneva
February 1997

Preface

This book is about a new way to design Web pages. It's called Cascading Style Sheets (CSS) and it will revolutionize the way authors design Web pages and how users see them. CSS lets authors specify how they want their documents to appear on screens or paper, for example what fonts and colors to use.

Ever since the first Web document was written, Web authors have been yearning for more control over their documents. That desire has been so strong that every possible means to influence other people's screens – making text bold, have it blink, being pushed off five pixels to the right or scrolling across your screen – have gathered a following. No matter how stupid the effect, as long as the most popular browsers support it, it gets added to the ever-increasing list of accepted HTML extensions. When developing CSS, we made sure it offers people some neat new toys – to satisfy the immediate desires. Also, we were able to sneak in some features that we think will actually help the Web remain a publishing arena for documents beyond sales brochures.

This book is written for people who design Web pages. You will learn how CSS can make your work easier and your pages look better. CSS has been created to give Web designers the influence they want while retaining the Web's interoperability and accessibility – and a few other "abilities":

- CSS has been developed in a vendor-neutral consortium (the World Wide Web Consortium, directed by the same Tim Berners-Lee that invented the Web and HTML).

- CSS will soon come to a browser near you.

- CSS does not break current documents, it augments them.

- CSS allows readers, as well as authors, to define style sheets.

- CSS uses common desktop publishing terminology that you probably already know.

- CSS allows organization-wide style sheets: you only need to change one file when your site style changes.

This book will tell you all you need to know to start using CSS.

Website accompanying this book

On the Web, things change quickly and CSS is no exception. There will no doubt be new developments to report in just a few months: more browsers that support CSS, more features to use in your Web pages, more software to help you write CSS. For that reason, we have set up a special Website to keep you up to date with the latest developments. Its address is **http://www.awl.com/css/**

The Website contains updates to the text of the book as well as many additional CSS-related hyperlinks. You can also find all the book's examples there, ready to be cut and pasted into your own pages. And should there be any errata to the book, they will also be posted there.

Acknowledgments

Creating a lasting specification for the Web is not a job for one person. That's why the two authors joined forces. Then we found out two wasn't enough – the help we have gotten from the Web community has been tremendous. Especially, we would like to thank the following people: Terry Allen, Murray Altheim, Glenn Adams, Walter Bender, Tim Berners-Lee, Scott Bigham, Steve Byrne, Robert Cailliau, James Clark, Daniel Connolly, Donna Converse, Adam Costello, Todd Fahrner, Todd Freter, Roy Fielding, Neil Galarneau, Wayne Gramlich, Phill Hallam-Baker, Kevin Hughes, Scott Isaacs, Tony Jebson, William Johnston, Phil Karlton, Evan Kirshenbaum, Murray Maloney, Lou Montulli, Henrik Frystyk Nielsen, David Perrell, William Perry, Scott Preece, Paul Prescod, Liam Quin, Vincent Quint, Jenny Raggett, Thomas Reardon, Cécile Roisin, Michael Seaton, David Seibert, David Siegel, David Singer, Benjamin Sittler, Jon Smirl, Charles Peyton Taylor, Irène Vatton, Daniel Veillard, Mandira Virmani, Greg Watkins, Mike Wexler, Lydja Williams, Brian Wilson, Chris Wilson, Lauren Wood and Stephen Zilles. Each of these people changed the CSS1 specification in one way or the other.

INRIA (The French National Institute for Research in Computer Science and Control) has been a productive environment for W3C and the development of CSS. Among the people who have been vital in establishing and sustaining this environment are: Jean-François Abramatic, Anselm Baird-Smith, Yves Bertot, Daniel Dardailler, Philipp Hoschka, Gilles Kahn, Philippe Kaplan, Yves Lafon, Jean-Michel Leon and Colas Nahaboo. All along, Stephane Boyera kept the disks spinning and the software running.

Sally Khudairi and Rohit Khare, W3C's I/O processors, deserve thanks for sharing their up-to-date information.

Publishing a book is much more than writing it: the people at Addison Wesley Longman have patiently accepted our changes of schedule while adhering to their own. Our thanks go to Nicky McGirr, Dylan Reisenberger and Karen Mosman.

Three people deserve special mention: Dave Raggett (for his encouragement and work on HTML3), Chris Lilley (for his continued contributions, especially in the area of colors and fonts) and Steven Pemberton (for his organizational as well as creative skills).

And a final word of thanks to family members Siri, Julie and Anniken whose structure and style always inspired and supported the project.

Håkon Wium Lie
Bert Bos
Nice, March 1997

Contents

Publisher's acknowledgments

The publishers wish to thank the following for permission to reproduce the material listed.

Figure 3.2, clipping from TIME magazine, © 1997 TIME Inc. Reprinted by permission.

Thanks to Netscape Communications Corp. whose Navigator browser is featured, with permission, on the cover. This cover image may not be reprinted or copied without the express written permission of Netscape. Netscape Communications Corporation has not authorized, sponsored, or endorsed, or approved this publication and is not responsible for its content. Netscape and the Netscape Logos are trademarks and trade names of Netscape Communications Corporation.

We are grateful to Microsoft Corporation, whose browser Internet Explorer is used to display several of the screen shots in this book, and is featured on the cover.

Thanks also to the many contributors listed in Chapters 9 and 10 for their examples of web page design; and to the World Wide Web Consortium (W3C), whose Arena browser and Amaya editor are featured in Appendix B.

Trademark notice

AltaVista is a trademark or registered trademark of Digital Equipment Corporation

FrameMaker and Portable Document Format are trademarks or registered trademarks of Adobe Incorporated.

Internet Explorer, Word and Windows are trademarks or registered trademarks of Microsoft Corporation.

Java is a trademark or registered trademark of Sun Microsystems Inc.

Les Pages Jaunes is a trademark of France Telecom.

NCSA Mosaic is copyrighted © 1993, 1994 by the Board of Trustees of the University of Illinois

Panorama and Panorama Pro are trademarks or registered trademarks of SoftQuad

UNIX is a trademark or registered trademark of X/Open Company Ltd

Chapter 1

The Web and HTML

Cascading Style Sheets, CSS for short, represent a major breakthrough in how Web page designers work, by expanding their ability to improve the appearance of their Web pages – the documents that people publish on the Web.

Since the World Wide Web (the Web, for short) was created in 1990, people who want to put pages on the Web have had little control over what those pages will look like. In the beginning, authors could only specify structural aspects of their pages, for example that some piece of text would be a heading or some other piece would be straight text. Also, there were ways to make text **bold** or *italic*, among a few other effects. But that's where their control ended.

In the scientific environments where the Web was born, people are more concerned with the content of their documents than the presentation. In a research report, the choice of type faces (or fonts, as we call them in this book) is of little importance compared to the scientific results that are reported. However, when authors outside the scientific environments discovered the Web, the limitations of HyperText Markup Language (HTML) became a source of continuing frustration. These authors often came from a paper-based publication environment where they had full control of the presentation. They wanted to be able to change the color of text, make it look more s p a c e d   o u t or more squeezed, to center it or put it against the right margin – or anywhere else they want. Many Web designers come from a desktop publishing background, in which they can do all of these things, and more, to improve the appearance of printed material. They want the same capabilities when they design Web pages. However, such capabilities have been slow to develop – slow by Internet speed standards, that is. So designers have devised techniques to sidestep these limitations, but these techniques have unfortunate side effects. We discuss them and their side effects later in the chapter.

This book is about a new method for designing Web pages – CSS – that works with HTML, the means by which users of the Web exchange information on the Web. HTML describes the document's *structure*; that is, the roles that the various parts of a document play. For example, a piece of text may be designated as a heading or a paragraph. HTML doesn't pay much attention to the document's *appearance*, and in fact it has only very limited capability to influence appearance. CSS, however, describes how these elements are to be presented to the reader of the document. Using CSS, you, the designer, can better specify the appearance of your HTML pages as well as make your pages more available to Web users worldwide. Even though HTML has limited capabilities to influence appearance, as we explain later in the chapter, without style sheet capabilities, it has been a half-baked publishing environment. The release of CSS greatly enhances the potential of HTML and the Web.

Cascading Style Sheets – CSS – is a simple mechanism for adding style to HTML documents. With CSS, you can specify such styles as the size, color, and spacing of text, as well as the placement of text and images on the page. Plus a whole lot more. This is done via the use of style sheets. A **style sheet** is a set of stylistic rules that describe how HTML documents are presented to users.

A key feature of CSS is that style sheets can **cascade**. That is, several different style sheets can be attached to a document and all of them can influence the presentation of the document. In this way, the author can create a style sheet to specify how the page should look, while the reader can attach a personal style sheet to adjust the appearance of the page for human or technological handicaps, such as poor eyesight or a personal preference for a certain font.

CSS is a simple language that can be read by humans – in contrast to some computer languages. Perhaps even more important, however, is that CSS is easy to write. All you need to know is a little HTML and some basic desktop publishing terminology: CSS borrows from desktop publishing terminology when expressing style. So those of you who have experience in desktop publishing should be able to grasp CSS very quickly. But if you're new to HTML, desktop publishing, and/or Web page design, don't despair. You, too, will likely find CSS surprisingly easy to grasp. The book includes a brief review of basic HTML as well as information on page design.

To understand how revolutionary CSS is, you first need to understand Web page design as it has been up to now and the design problems that CSS can help solve. In this chapter, we begin with a brief tour of the Web and the problems Web page designers and others have faced prior to the introduction of CSS. Then we quickly review the basics of HTML. For those of you who are already publishing on the Web, this all may be old news. For those of you who are new to the idea of designing Web pages, this should help put things in perspective. In Chapter 2 we step you through the basics of how to use CSS. In subsequent chapters, we delve more deeply into CSS, covering how you can specify the text, background, color, spacing, and more in the design of your Web pages.

THE WEB

The Web is a vast collection of documents on the Internet that are linked together via hyperlinks. The **Internet** consists of millions of computers worldwide that communicate electronically. A **hyperlink** is a predefined linkage between two documents. The hyperlinks allow a user to access documents on various Web servers without concern for where they are located. A **Web server** is a computer on the Internet that serves out Web pages on request. From a document on a Web server in California, the user is just one mouse click away from a document that is stored, perhaps, on a Web server in France. Hyperlinks are integral to the Web. Without them, there would be no Web.

Users gain access to the Web through a **browser**. A browser is a computer program that lets users "surf" the Web by fetching documents from Web servers and displaying them to the user. To move from one document to another, the user clicks on a <u>highlighted</u> word or image that represents a hyperlink. The browser then retrieves the document that is at the other end of the hyperlink and displays it on the screen. For example, a user could be in a document about baroque music and click the highlighted words <u>Johann Sebastian Bach</u> which are linked to "Bach's home page" (on the Web, all celebrities – as well as everyone else who wants one – have a home page). When the browser has fetched Bach's home page (instantly in the best case) it will appear on the user's screen.

Development of the Web

The Web was invented around 1990 by Tim Berners-Lee and Robert Cailliau. Tim was then working at CERN, the European Laboratory for Particle Physics. A graduate of Oxford University and a long-time computer and software expert, he is now Director of the World Wide Web Consortium – W3C – an organization that coordinates the development of the Web. He also is a Principal Research Scientist at Massachusetts Institute of Technology's Laboratory for Computer Science (MIT LCS). He's also our boss. Robert is a 20-year veteran at CERN. It was Robert who organized the first Web conference in Geneva in 1993. Both Tim and Robert were awarded the ACM Software System Award in 1995 because of their work on the Web. Robert wrote the Foreword to this book.

Tim created the language – HTML – that is used by people to exchange information on the Web. We discuss what HTML is in the next section and give a brief review of its basics later in the chapter. Tim also began work on style sheets soon afterward, but when the Web really started taking off in 1993 the work on them was not complete.

The "world" discovered the Web around 1994. Since then, the Web's growth has been tremendous. Had style sheets been available on the Web from its beginning, Web page designers would have been spared much frustration. However, the release of CSS now, three years later, has some advantages. First, in the interim we have learned much about the kind of visual effects that Web designers want to achieve on their pages. Second, we learned that users also want their say in how documents are presented on their computer screens; for example, visually impaired people may want to make fonts bigger so that they can read documents more easily. As a result, we were able to provide functionality to meet as many of these needs of designers and users as possible. (We'll add even more in forthcoming releases of CSS.) Hence, the CSS of 1997 is a better solution than a style sheet solution years earlier would have been.

MARKUP LANGUAGES

HTML is a markup language. A **markup language** is a method of indicating within a document the roles that the document's pieces are to play. Its focus is on the structure of a document rather than its appearance. For example, you can indicate that one piece of text is a paragraph, another is a top-level heading, and a third is a lower-level heading. You indicate these by placing codes, called **tags**, into the document. HTML has around 30 commonly used tags which are reviewed later in this chapter. You could, for example, use a tag that says, in effect, "Make the text coming up a heading."

In contrast, desktop publishing (DTP) programs emphasize the presentation of a document rather than its structure. Authors can select font families, text colors and margin widths and thereby accurately control what the final product – which normally ends up on paper – looks like.

The distinction between structural and presentational systems isn't always as clear-cut as described above. HTML, while having its roots in structured documents, has some tags that describe presentation rather than structure. For example, you can specify that a text should be presented in **bold** or *italic*. Also, some DTP programs let you describe the structure – in addition to the presentation – of a document. When you create a new document in applications like Microsoft Word or Adobe FrameMaker, there is a standard set of "styles" available. A style is a group of stylistic characteristics that you can apply to a piece of text. For example, you may have a style called "title1" that has the stylistic characteristics that set the text to "18 point Helvetica bold italic." (If you're not familiar with what "18 point Helvetica bold italic" means, don't worry; we explain it in Chapter 4.) By applying the style "title1" to selected parts of your document you are effectively marking it up. At the same time, you are also specifying how those pieces of text should be presented. Here is what "18 point Helvetica bold italic" looks like:

18 point Helvetica bold italic

Conceptually, this is very similar to HTML and CSS. In HTML, "title1" would be a tag, and the stylistic characteristics (namely "18 point Helvetica bold italic") would be written in a CSS style sheet. If you already know a DTP program that supports this notion of styles, the transition to HTML and CSS will be easy.

DODGING THE LIMITATIONS OF HTML

The HyperText Markup Language – HTML – is a simple, easy-to-learn markup language designed for hypertext documents on the Web. In fact, a computer-literate person can learn to write basic HTML in less than a day. This simplicity is one reason for the huge success of the Web.

From the beginnings of HTML, Web page designers have tried to sidestep its stylistic limitations. While their intentions have been good – to improve the presentation of documents – the techniques for doing so have unfortunate side effects. These techniques work for some of the people some of the time but never for all of the people all of the time. They include the following:

- Using proprietary HTML extensions
- Converting text into images
- Placing text into tables
- Writing a program instead of using HTML

We discuss these techniques, and their side effects, in the next sections.

Proprietary HTML extensions

One way to sidestep HTML's limitations has been for browser vendors to create their own tags that give designers who use their browser a little more control over the appearance of a Web page. At some point, it seemed that every new version of a browser introduced a few new tags that designers could play with. Doing this may sound like a good idea. However, it creates it own problem; namely, these browser-specific tags are not universal, at least not when they are first created.

For example, in 1994, Netscape – the company that makes the popular Navigator browser – introduced the CENTER tag for centering text on the screen and the FONT tag to indicate the font size. But the effect worked only in Netscape's Navigator browser. In 1995, Microsoft introduced the MARQEE tag, which enabled text to slide across the screen. But it worked only in Microsoft's Internet Explorer browser. While the browser for which these tags were written knows what to do with them, there is no guarantee that any other browser will. So no matter how terrific your page looks, the impact will likely be lost if your page, full of browser-specific tags, is displayed to a user who is using a different browser. The only way you can know how your page will appear on all the various browsers is if you test the page on each one. In short, you, the Web page designer, are at the mercy of browser software developers. To take advantage of the latest browser capabilities, you have to change the documents that form your pages. As you will see, by using CSS in such cases, you need not change your document; you need only change your style sheets. This is a much easier and less costly way to update your pages.

Converting text into images

A second way by which designers have sought to get around the limitations of HTML has been to make text into images. With an image, the designer can fully control colors, spacing, and fonts, among other features. Then the designer simply inserts in the document the appropriate hyperlink where the image is to appear on the page, thereby linking the image to the page. When the browser displays the page, the text – in the form of an image – appears on the page.

This method, too, has downsides. First, you compromise accessibility to your page. Easy accessibility is one of the guiding principles of the Web. Second, you make your readers wait longer for your documents to display. At the same time, you also slow down the Web in general.

Compromised accessibility
Accessibility of your page to Web users is compromised in two ways when you use images to hold text. First, certain types of software called *robots* (also known as *crawlers* or *spiders*) roam the Web (so to speak) seeking what's out there and then creating and updating indexes that users can use to find Web pages. Indexing services like AltaVista, Hotbot, and Lycos use robots to build their indexes.

Robots work by loading a Web page and then automatically loading all of the pages that are linked from that page, and then loading all of the pages that are linked from those pages, and so on, usually for the purpose of creating a database of all the words on all of the pages. When a user searches for a particular word or set of words, all the pages containing that selection are made available to the user. Robots, however, cannot read images. So they just skip them. Hence, they simply miss text that is in images.

Accessibility of your page to Web users is compromised in a second way. Not all users have a browser that provides a GUI – graphical user interface – such as that provided by Navigator and Explorer. Some browsers can display only text, not images. So the content of your images is lost to the user.

Currently, the only way around these accessibility problems is to enclose a textual description of the image that robots and text-only browsers can use. In the latter, for example, the user would receive this textual description of the image rather than the image – not a great substitute for the real thing but better than nothing.

Longer download time

The second downside to using images to hold text is that images take longer to load and draw on the screen. The user may become impatient and back out of your page before it's had time to completely load. Also, the preponderance of images as a substitute for attractive type can account for much of the reputed slowness of the Web to respond when drawing pages on screens.

Placing text into a table

A third technique designers have used to bypass the limitations of HTML is to put text into a table. Doing this enables the designer to control the layout of the text. For example, to add a margin of a certain width on the left side of a page, you would put the whole document inside a table and then add an empty column along the left side to create the "margin."

The downside (you knew there would be one): not all browsers support tables, so pages that use tables do not display well on those browsers. Depending on how you use tables, the result on such browsers can be somewhere between "weird" and "disastrous."

The use of tables also complicates the writing of HTML. You have to add a lot more tags even for a simple table. The more complex the table or table structure – you can create tables within tables to any depth you want – the more complex your code becomes.

Used with care, tables can sometimes be the right solution. CSS does not fully replace tables. But, if you use tables, you must be prepared to cope with the extra complexity and the inability of some browsers to display them properly.

Writing a program instead of using HTML

A fourth technique designers use to bypass the limitations of HTML is to create a program that displays pages. Although much more complex than any other alternative, this technique has the advantage of giving designers control over every pixel on the screen – something not even CSS style sheets can do. However, this technique shares some of the drawbacks of the previous three discussed. A program cannot be searched by robots, and it cannot be used by text-only browsers. Further, because it is an actual programming language (which HTML is not), it is more difficult to learn. It may contain a computer virus. And it is questionable whether 15 years from now there will be computers that can execute the program. Examples of programming languages for creating Web documents are Java and JavaScript.

Why should all of this matter?

HTML has become a universal data format for publishing information. Due to its simplicity, anyone with a computer and Internet connection can publish in HTML without expensive DTP applications. Likewise, on the user side, HTML documents can be shown on a variety of devices without the user having to buy proprietary software. Also, perhaps the strongest point in HTML's favor of all: it allows for electronic documents that have a much higher chance of withstanding the years than proprietary data formats. The methods of dodging the limitations of HTML described above are undermining these benefits: HTML is in danger of turning into a compli-cated proprietary data format that cannot be freely exchanged. CSS, by allowing authors to express their desire for influence over document presentation, will help HTML remain the simple little language it was meant to be.

This is why we developed CSS.

Also, there are esthetic and commercial reasons for why the Web needs a powerful style sheet language. Today, placing a page on the Web is no longer just a matter of putting up some text and hoping someone will stumble across it. Web pages have become an important means whereby people around the world can get together to share ideas, hobbies, interests, and much more. It also is becoming an increasingly important medium for advertising products and services. Today, a page needs to attract and stimulate as well as inform. It needs to stand out among the enormous and rapidly growing repertoire of pages crowding onto the Web. Esthetics have become more important. The current HTML tools simply aren't enough for the Web page designer who wants to make good-looking pages.

Let's get started. In the next section, we review the basics of writing HTML. In Chapter 2 we introduce CSS and show you how it works with HTML. From there, we lead you on an exploration of CSS and what you can do with it.

HTML BASICS

CSS was designed to work along with HTML. To take advantage of CSS, you need to know a little HTML. As we said in the Preface, we assume most readers of this book will have had some exposure to HTML. However, to ensure we all are talking about the same thing, we review here the basics of HTML.

Elements

HTML is simple to write. It's essentially a series of elements that define the structure of your document. An element normally has three parts:

• Start tag

• Content

• End tag

The diagram below illustrates the three parts of an element:

```
<SENTENCE>This is a very simple element.</SENTENCE>
```
Start tag   Content   End tag

All tags in HTML start with a '<' and end with a '>'. Between these comes the name of the element. In the above example, the name of the element is "SENTENCE." The content of the above element is a string of characters (but we will soon see that the content of an element can be another element). After that comes the end tag. End tags look like the start tag, except they have a '/' before the tag name.

Building a simple HTML document

HTML has around 30 commonly used elements. "SENTENCE" isn't one of them; in fact, sentence isn't an HTML element at all. We just used it as an example to show the basic structure of all elements. Let's look at a real HTML element.

```
<HTML></HTML>
```

One of the elements in HTML is called "HTML." The HTML start tag (<HTML>) marks the beginning of an HTML document, and the HTML end tag (</HTML>) marks the end. Everything between these two tags is the content of the HTML element. In the above example there isn't anything between the start and the end tag. In the next example we have added some content:

```
<HTML><TITLE>Bach's home page</TITLE></HTML>
```

What we added from the last example is marked in bold letters (this is a convention we will use throughout this chapter). Unlike the "SENTENCE" example, the content of the HTML element is not just a string of characters – it's actually another element. The title element contains the title of an HTML document. The title of the document we will be building in this chapter is "Bach's home page." Figure 1.1 maps out the two elements we have so far:

```
                       HTML element
             _____|_____
            |                                       |
<HTML><TITLE>Bach's home page<TITLE/><HTML>
             _____|_____
                              |
                        TITLE element
```

Figure 1.1 Diagram of an element.

To make it easier to see where elements start and end, we will show the HTML examples over several lines and indent elements that are inside others. We do this because it makes the code easier to read. The browser will ignore the extra space as well as the line breaks that separate one line from another.

```
<HTML>
   <TITLE>Bach's home page</TITLE>
</HTML>
```

When a browser displays an HTML document in a window on the screen, the content of the TITLE element will go into the title bar of the window. The title bar is at the top of the window. Below that is often the browser's control panel. Further below is the most interesting part of the browser window: the **canvas**. The canvas is that part of the window in which documents are actually displayed. See Figure 1.2.

As you can see, we have yet to put anything in our document that will be displayed in the canvas. To have something actually show up on the canvas, you must place it in the BODY element. The BODY element is inside the HTML element:

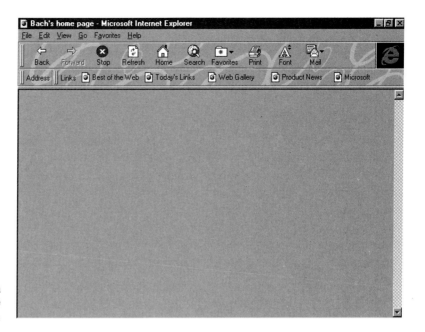

Figure 1.2 The parts of a browser's window. Notice the title bar on top.

```
<HTML>
   <TITLE>My own site</TITLE>
   <BODY>
   </BODY>
</HTML>
```

By themselves, the BODY tags do not add anything to the canvas; we need to give the BODY element some content. Let's start by adding a first-level heading to the sample document. The standard HTML tag for a first-level heading is H1. Here's the HTML code:

```
<HTML>
   <TITLE>Bach's home page</TITLE>
   <BODY>
      <H1>Bach's home page</H1>
   </BODY>
</HTML>
```

(Above, the title of the document is the same as the first-level heading. This will often be the case in an HTML document, but doesn't have to be.)

The above code will actually result in text appearing on the canvas. See Figure 1.3.

Figure 1.3 Adding text on the canvas.

HTML also has other headings you can use: H2, H3, H4, H5, and H6. The larger the number, the lower the level of heading. Typically, the lower the level, the smaller the font size. Here's our document with a couple of extra headings added (the result is shown in Figure 1.4):

```
<HTML>
    <TITLE>Bach's home page</TITLE>
    <BODY>
        <H1>Bach's home page</H1>
        <H2>Bach's compositions</H2>
        <H3>The keyboard music</H3>
    </BODY>
</HTML>
```

Bach's home page

Bach's compositions

The keyboard music

Figure 1.4 Three levels of heading.

However, we don't need those two extra headings right now, so we delete them and add a paragraph of text instead. We do this using the paragraph element, P (the result is shown in Figure 1.5):

```
<HTML>
  <TITLE>Bach's home page</TITLE>
  <BODY>
  <H1>Bach's home page</H1>
    <P>Johann Sebastian Bach was a prolific composer.
  </BODY>
</HTML>
```

Bach's home page

Johann Sebastian Bach was a prolific composer.

Figure 1.5 Adding a paragraph of text.

Note that we left out the ending paragraph tag, </P>. Normally, an element begins with a start tag and ends with an end tag. However, sometimes the end tag may be omitted. In the above example, the end tag is there to notify the browser when the element ends. In some cases, the browser can figure this out for itself without the help of an end tag, so the end tag may be omitted. For example, the P element cannot exist outside of the BODY element. So, when the browser encounters the BODY end tag (</BODY>), it knows that the P element also has ended. Still, including the P end tag is perfectly legal.

Next, suppose we want to emphasize a word relative to the surrounding text. Several HTML elements can express this; among them we find STRONG and EM (EM stands for emphasis). The names of these elements do not say anything about how they are to be displayed, but there are some conventions: STRONG elements are normally displayed in **bold**, and EM elements are displayed in *italic*.

The following code shows the use of the STRONG element:

```
<HTML>
  <TITLE>Bach's home page</TITLE>
  <BODY>
    <H1>Bach's home page</H1>
    <P>Johann Sebastian Bach was a <STRONG>prolific</STRONG>
      composer.
  </BODY>
</HTML>
```

This is displayed as shown in Figure 1.6.

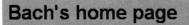

Bach's home page

Johann Sebastian Bach was a **prolific** composer.

Figure 1.6 An example of using the STRONG element.

Notice how the word "prolific" stands out relative to the surrounding text. Also note that while the H1 and P elements start on a new line, the STRONG element continues on the same line where the P element started. H1 and P are examples of "block-level" elements, while the STRONG element is an "inline" element. We discuss block-level and inline elements next.

Block-level and inline elements

In the previous section, the STRONG element was placed in the middle of another element, P, while the P and H1 elements both began and ended a line. You can't insert a P element in the middle of another element, say an H1 element, or vice versa. But you can insert an element like STRONG in the middle of any other element. This is because the P and H1 elements are *block-level* elements, while the STRONG element is an *inline* element.

Elements can be divided into three groups:

- Block-level

- Inline

- Invisible

A **block-level element** is an element that begins and ends a line or, put another way, that has a line break at its beginning and end. Examples of block-level elements that you've seen so far in this chapter are H1 and P. Others are given in Table 1.1.

An **inline element** is an element that does not begin and end a line, although it may be placed at either end. Examples of inline elements are STRONG, which you saw in the earlier example, and EM. Others are given in Table 1.1.

An **invisible element** is an element whose content isn't displayed on the canvas. We have seen only one invisible element so far: TITLE. It's not really an invisible element since it appears in the title bar of the window, but it is not displayed on the canvas. HTML only has a few invisible elements and you will find them in Table 1.1.

Element overview

Confused about the different elements? Don't worry. Table 1.1. gives you an overview of the most common HTML elements. We've introduced you to

Element name	Abbreviation for	Block, inline or invisible	Typical effect	End tag can be omitted?	Empty? Replaced?
A	Anchor	Inline	Highlighted	No	
BLOCKQUOTE		Block-level	Indented	No	
BODY		Block-level	Inside canvas	Yes	
BR	Break	Block-level	Breaks the line	–	Empty
DD	Definition Description	Block-level		Yes	
DL	Definition list	Block-level		No	
DIV	Division	Block-level		No	
DT	Definition term	Block-level		Yes	
EM	Emphasis	Inline	Italic	No	
H1, H2 ... H6	Heading levels	Block-level	Large fonts	No	
HR	Horizontal rule	Block-level	Horizontal rule	–	Empty
HTML		Block-level		Yes	
I	Italic	Inline	Italic	No	
IMG	Image	Inline	As an image	–	Empty, replaced
LI	List item	Block-level	With a list item marker in front	Yes	
LINK		Invisible		–	Empty
OBJECT		Block-level		No	Replaced
OL	Ordered list	Block-level		No	
P	Paragraph	Block-Level		Yes	
PRE	Preformatted	Block-level	Monospace font	No	
SPAN		Inline		No	
STRONG		Inline	Bold	No	
STYLE		Invisible	Content interpreted as style sheet	No	
TITLE		Invisible	Shown in title bar, not on canvas	No	
TT	Teletype	Inline	Monospace font	No	
UL	Unordered list	Block-level		No	

Table 1.1 Common HTML tags. You may have noticed that we have put the names of elements in all capital (uppercase) letters. This is not necessary. HTML tags are not case-sensitive. That is, any combination of uppercase and lowercase letters can be used. Hence, "TITLE", "Title", and "title" are all the same. We use all uppercase letters to help distinguish element names from the rest of the text.

several of these already and will discuss others shortly. We talk about others as appropriate throughout the rest of the book and use them in a lot of examples. Also, we suggest you refer to the table as needed as you work your way through the book.

Among the elements that are not included in Table 1.1 are the elements used to create forms and tables. Also, the HTML extension elements have been left out.

In the next several sections, we add to your repertoire of HTML tags by discussing elements that you can use to create lists, add a horizontal rule, force a line break, and link to text and images.

Comments

Most of your document will consist of elements. However, you also can insert HTML comments into the document. A **comment** is anything you want to say about what is going on with your document that you don't want the user to see. The user can't see the contents of a comment because browsers ignore comments; that is, they do not display a comment's contents. Comments can be a helpful way of communicating something about your document to other designers who will see your code.

To ensure the comment really is not viewable by the user, you enclose the comment between a special string that the browser will recognize as enclosing a comment. You begin the comment with the string <!-- and end it with the string -->. (That's two hyphens in both cases.) Here's a sample comment:

```
<!--CSS is the greatest thing to hit the Web since hyperlinks-->
```

Lists

Lists are very common in HTML documents. HTML has three elements that create lists:

- OL, which creates an *ordered* list. In an ordered list, each list item has a label that indicates the order, for example a digit (1, 2, 3, 4 or I, II, III, IV) or letter (a, b, c, d). In desktop publishing terminology, ordered lists are often called numbered lists.

- UL, which creates an *unordered* list. In an unordered list, each list item has a mark that does not indicate order, e.g. a bullet symbol. In desktop publishing terminology, unordered lists are often called "bulleted" lists.

- DL, which creates a *definition* list. A definition list is a list of terms with their corresponding definitions. For example, a dictionary is a (long!) definition list.

Bach's home page must surely include a list of some of his compositions. Let's add an ordered list:

```
<HTML>
  <TITLE>Bach's home page</TITLE>
  <BODY>
    <H1>Bach's home page</H1>
    <P>Johann Sebastian Bach was a <STRONG>prolific</STRONG>
       composer. Here are his best works:
```

```
<OL>
  <LI>the Goldberg Variations
  <LI>the Brandenburg Concertos
  <LI>the Christmas Oratorio
</OL>
</BODY>
</HTML>
```

Notice that an LI doesn't need an end tag, but a OL does. Figure 1.7 shows the result.

Figure 1.7 An ordered list.

The ordered list above is unfair to all the other great compositions by Bach. Let's change the ordered list into an unordered list. To do this, we simply change the OL to UL:

```
<HTML>
  <TITLE>Bach's home page</TITLE>
  <BODY>
    <H1>Bach's home page</H1>
    <P>Johann Sebastian Bach was a <STRONG>prolific</STRONG>
      composer. Among his works are:
    <UL>
      <LI>the Goldberg Variations
      <LI>the Brandenburg Concertos
      <LI>the Christmas Oratorio
    </UL>
  </BODY>
</HTML>
```

Notice that we do not have to change the LI elements to change the list from unordered to ordered: both UL and OL use LI as the list item element. But since the LI elements are now inside the UL element, they will look different (Figure 1.8).

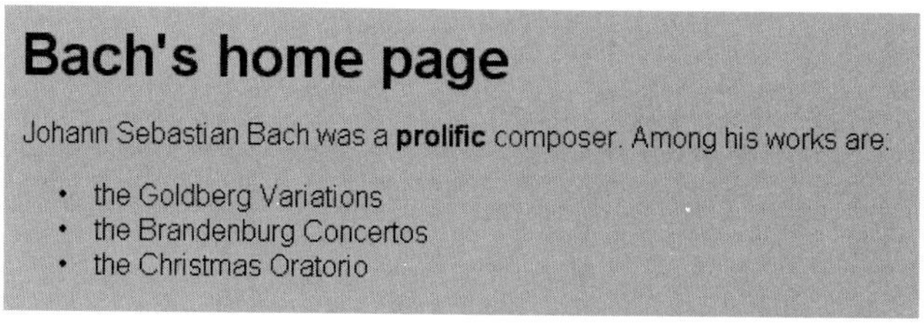

Figure 1.8 An unordered list.

A DL, or definition list, is used for lists that have terms – each contained in a DT element – and their corresponding definitions – each contained in a DD element. An example of a DL is a dictionary or glossary. In the next example, we change our OL to a DL. Notice how the LIs change to DTs and that like the LIs, they do not require end tags. Figure 1.9 shows the result.

```
<HTML>
    <TITLE>Bach's home page</TITLE>
    <BODY>
        <H1>Bach's home page</H1>
        <P>Johann Sebastian Bach was a <STRONG>prolific</STRONG>
            composer. Among his works are:
        <DL>
            <DT>the Goldberg Variations
            <DD>composed in 1741, catalog number BWV988
            <DT>the Brandenburg Concertos
            <DD>composed in 1713, catalog numbers BWV1046-1051
            <DT>the Christmas Oratorio
            <DD>composed in 1734, catalog number BWV248
        </DL>
    </BODY>
</HTML>
```

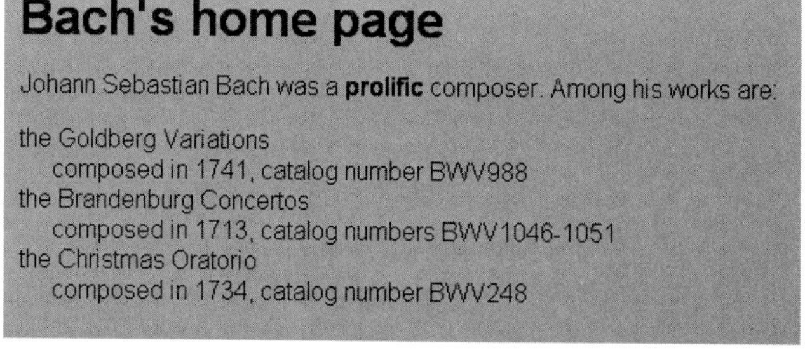

Figure 1.9 A definition list.

Empty elements

All HTML elements we have discussed so far have had content. HTML also has some elements that do not have content – they are **empty elements**. One example is the HR element which inserts a horizontal rule in the document. It doesn't need any content. Also, there is the BR element whose sole purpose is to force a line break. Since empty elements do not have any content they don't need any end tags either.

Adding a horizontal rule

We can add a horizontal rule to a document by using the HR (horizontal rule) element. HR is an empty element, so you should omit its end tag.

Here's the code for adding an HR element.

```
<HTML>
    <TITLE>Bach's home page</TITLE>
    <BODY>
        <H1>Bach's home page</H1>
        <P>Johann Sebastian Bach was a <STRONG>prolific</STRONG>
            composer. Among his works are:
        <UL>
            <LI>the Goldberg Variations
            <LI>the Brandenburg Concertos
            <LI>the Christmas Oratorio
        </UL>
        <HR>
    </BODY>
</HTML>
```

The result is shown in Figure 1.10.

Figure 1.10 Adding a horizontal rule.

Adding a line break

We can force a line break in the middle of an element by using the BR (break) element. The browser normally ignores line breaks in the HTML document and will automatically break a line when needed when it displays the document. However, if you want to enforce a line break at a certain spot in the document, BR lets you do this. BR is an empty element, so you should omit its end tag.

Here's the code for a BR element (note, we reverted to our example that included the UL).

```
<HTML>
   <TITLE>Bach's home page</TITLE>
   <BODY>
      <H1>Bach's <BR>home page</H1>
      <P>Johann Sebastian Bach was a <STRONG>prolific</STRONG>
         composer. Among his works are:
      <UL>
         <LI>the Goldberg Variations
         <LI>the Brandenburg Concertos
         <LI>the Christmas Oratorio
      </UL>
      <HR>
   </BODY>
</HTML>
```

The result is shown in Figure 1.11.

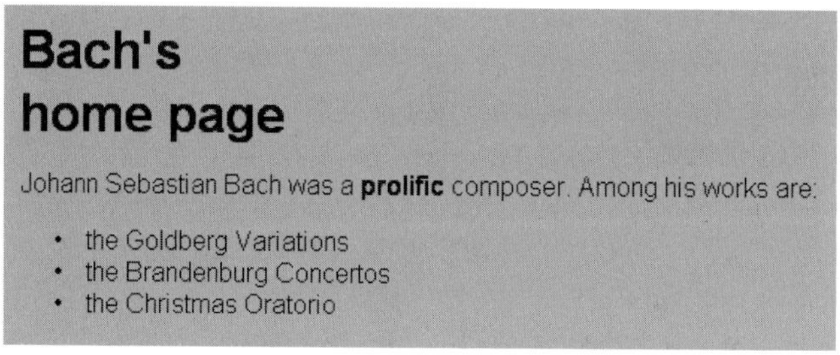

Bach's home page

Johann Sebastian Bach was a **prolific** composer. Among his works are:

- the Goldberg Variations
- the Brandenburg Concertos
- the Christmas Oratorio

Figure 1.11 Adding a line break.

Forcing line breaks is generally not a good idea, so we'll take out the BR element as we move on.

Maintaining preformatted text

In the previous example, we mentioned that a browser generally ignores line breaks, except for those that you enter using the BR element. The browser also ignores tabs and extra white space. Tabs are converted to single space characters, while extra space characters – any more than one – are collapsed into one space character. Generally, this is what we want. This feature enables us to space out our code so that it is more readable and reflects the structure of the document, secure in the knowledge that the browser will ignore all the extra spaces.

Sometimes, however, you may want to insert white space and have the browser display your text exactly as you formatted it. The PRE (preformatted) element allows you do this. Simply enclose within <PRE> tags the information whose formatting you want to preserve. The PRE element is often used for simple tables where columns need to align vertically:

```
<HTML>
   <TITLE>Bach's home page</TITLE>
   <BODY>
      <H1>Bach's <BR>home page</H1>
      <P>Johann Sebastian Bach was a <STRONG>prolific</STRONG>
         composer. Among his works are:
      <PRE>
COMPOSITION                    YEAR    CATALOG#
Goldberg Variation             1741    BWV988
Brandenburg Concertos          1713    BWV1046-1051
Christmas Oratorio             1734    BWV248
      </PRE>
   </BODY>
</HTML>
```

Notice that the content of the PRE element cannot be aligned with the other elements since the extra white space would appear on the canvas. Figure 1.12 shows the result of the above code.

Figure 1.12 Preserving preformatted text.

Adding hyperlinks

We can make our document more interesting by adding hyperlinks to it. When hyperlinks are in place, users can click on links to access related documents from somewhere else on the Web. Hyperlinks are integral to HTML and the Web. Without hyperlinks, there would be no Web.

To make a hyperlink, you use the A (anchor) element. When the user clicks on the A element, the browser fetches the document in the other end of the hyperlink. The browser needs to be told where it can find the other document, and this information goes into an attribute on the A element. An **attribute** is a characteristic quality of the element, other than the type or content of an element. The A element uses an attribute called HREF (hypertext reference) to add a hyperlink:

```
<HTML>
  <TITLE>Bach's home page</TITLE>
  <BODY>
    <H1>Bach's home page</H1>
    <P>Johann Sebastian Bach was a <STRONG>prolific</STRONG>
      composer. Among his works are:
    <UL>
      <LI>the <A HREF="goldberg.html">Goldberg</A> Variations
      <LI>the Brandenburg Concertos
      <LI>the Christmas Oratorio
    </UL>
    <HR>
  </BODY>
</HTML>
```

Let's take a closer look at the newly added A element. Figure 1.13 shows the different parts of the A element.

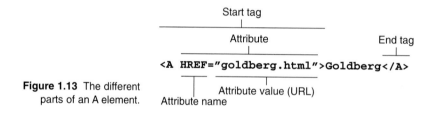

Figure 1.13 The different parts of an A element.

The A start tag is a bit more complicated than the other start tags we have
seen so far; in addition to the element name it includes an attribute. Different
element types have different attributes; among the most common ones is
the HREF attribute on the A element. Attributes can only go into the start tag
of the element, after the element name. Most attributes need a value: the
HREF attribute always takes a URL as a value. A URL, Universal Resource
Locator, is a Web address that the browser uses to locate the hyperlinked
document. When URLs are used as values on the HREF attribute, they
should always be quoted (" . . . ").

URLs come in two flavors:

- A *relative URL* gives the location of the document relative to the document
where it's referenced (that is, the document where the A element is). You
can only use relative URLs when you link to a document on the same Web
server as the document you are linking from.

- An *absolute URL* gives the location of the document independent of any
other document. You must use absolute URLs when you link to a document
on a different server. Absolute URLs can be typed into any machine on the
Internet and the browser will find it. That's why you see absolute URLs on
T-shirts, in TV commercials etc.

In the previous example, the HREF attribute had a relative URL
("goldberg.html") as value. If the user clicks on the word "Goldberg," the
browser will fetch the document called "goldberg.html" from the location
where our sample document is found.

We can also put an absolute URL into our document:

```
<HTML>
  <TITLE>Bach's home page</TITLE>
  <BODY>
    <H1>Bach's home page</H1>
    <P>Johann Sebastian Bach was a <STRONG>prolific</STRONG>
      composer. Among his works are:
    <UL>
      <LI>the <A HREF="goldberg.html">Goldberg</A>
        Variations
      <LI>the Brandenburg Concertos
      <LI>the <A HREF="http://www.noel.org/christmas.html">
        Christmas</A> Oratorio
    </UL>
    <HR>
  </BODY>
</HTML>
```

As you can see above, absolute URLs are slightly more complicated than relative ones. In fact, when Tim Berners-Lee invented the URL scheme, they were only meant to be seen by machines. Dissected into a diagram, the above URL looks as shown in Figure 1.14.

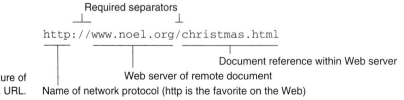

Figure 1.14 The structure of a URL.

The details of URLs are not the main topic of this book and as long as you are aware of the two types of URLs you can safely proceed.

Adding images

Images proliferate on the Web. It wasn't until the Mosaic browser added support for images in 1993 that a critical mass of people realized the potential of the Web. You can add images to your documents with the IMG element – IMG is short for image.

IMG is a peculiar element. First, it's empty. That's not so strange, we've see those before (quick reminder: an empty element is an element without content, e.g. HR, BR). Second, it's a *replaced* element. A replaced element is a placeholder for some other content that is being pointed to from the element. In the case of IMG, it points to an image that is fetched by the browser when the IMG element is encountered. Unlike the A element, which gives the user the option of jumping to a link or not, the browser will automatically fetch the image IMG points to. Also, unlike the A element, IMG uses an attribute called SRC to point to the image.

Let's add an image to the sample document. Not many portraits of Bach are known, but those that exist are on the Web:

```
<HTML>
  <TITLE>Bach's home page</TITLE>
  <BODY>
    <H1><IMG SRC="jsbach.gif" ALT="Portrait of J.S.Bach">
      Bach's home page</H1>
    <P>Johann Sebastian Bach was a <STRONG>prolific</STRONG>
      composer. Among his works are:
    <UL>
```

```
          <LI>the <A HREF="goldberg.html">Goldberg</A> Variations
          <LI>the Brandenburg Concertos
          <LI>the <A HREF="http://www.noel.org">Christmas</A>
              Oratorio
      </UL>
      <HR>
   </BODY>
</HTML>
```

Let's take a closer look at the attributes on the IMG element (Figure 1.15).

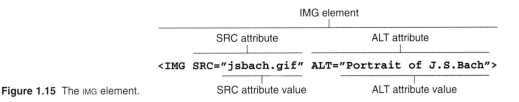

Figure 1.15 The IMG element.

The SRC on IMG is similar to the HREF attribute on A: they both take a URL as a value. The ALT attribute is new. The purpose of ALT is to provide an alternative (from which it gets its name) textual description of the image in case the browser cannot show it. Sometimes a browser cannot fetch the image (perhaps the Web server is broken?) or it may be configured to ignore images, for example, in the case of a text-only browser. In these cases, the browser will look for the alternative textual description and display that instead of the image. Therefore, you should always try to include a textual description of the image so users still can get a sense of what is going on.

Figure 1.16 illustrates how Microsoft Internet Explorer shows the page while the image is being fetched.

Figure 1.16 Waiting for an image to be fetched.

When the image is ready, the page looks as shown in Figure 1.17.

Figure 1.17 After the image has been fetched.

DOCUMENT TREES

In this chapter, we have demonstrated how elements in HTML are placed inside one another. We did this by indenting the code, as shown in all the previous code examples. The HTML element itself is the outermost element that encompasses all the other elements. Inside the HTML element are the TITLE and BODY elements, with the latter encompassing all the other elements, such as H1 and P. And within some of those elements are other elements. For example, within the UL element are the LI elements. If you were to diagram this idea of elements within elements, the result might be as shown in Figure 1.18.

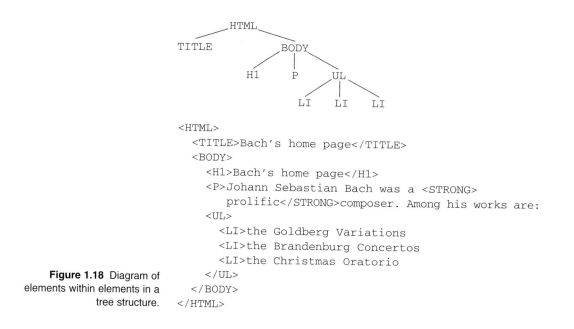

```
<HTML>
    <TITLE>Bach's home page</TITLE>
    <BODY>
        <H1>Bach's home page</H1>
        <P>Johann Sebastian Bach was a <STRONG>
            prolific</STRONG>composer. Among his works are:
        <UL>
            <LI>the Goldberg Variations
            <LI>the Brandenburg Concertos
            <LI>the Christmas Oratorio
        </UL>
    </BODY>
</HTML>
```

Figure 1.18 Diagram of elements within elements in a tree structure.

Notice how the diagram resembles a person's genealogical chart, with parents and children spread out in a top-to-bottom fashion, where parents can also be children. This is called a *tree structure*. In the tree structure of an HTML document, the HTML element is the earliest ancestor – the top parent. All other elements are children, grandchildren, and great-grandchildren – in short, descendants – of the HTML element. An element can have from zero to many children, but it always has only one parent, with the exception of the HTML element, which is an orphan. In this diagram, note that TITLE and BODY are children of HTML. TITLE has no children, but BODY has three: H1, P, and UL. In turn, UL has three children: the LIs. (Actually, family charts are more complex since each person has two parents.) Also note that in this example, BODY is both a child and a parent, as is UL.

We encounter tree structures in many situations outside HTML and genealogy. Trees – real trees such as spruce and pine – are (not surprisingly) tree structures. Organizational charts for companies are often set out in a tree structure. Books and technical documents, too, are usually set out in a tree structure, where sections and subsections are branches of the whole. (The fact that books are made from trees has nothing to do with this!) The last example is the reason why HTML documents always have a tree structure.

Nested elements

In HTML, there are some restrictions on which elements can be children of which elements. Usually, an element cannot contain children of its own type. That is, a P, for example, cannot be a child element of another P. You would not typically want to put a paragraph inside another paragraph, anyway. Similarly, an H1 cannot be a child element of another H1.

Some elements, however, may contain children of their own type. One example is BLOCKQUOTE, the element used to position quoted material within a document. This element can have nested within it quoted material that is the content of another BLOCKQUOTE element; that is, you can put a quote within a quote. This ability of an element to have children of its own type is called **nesting**.

Following is an example using first one BLOCKQUOTE element (shown in bold italic) and then two nested BLOCKQUOTE elements (shown just in bold):

```
<HTML>
  <TITLE>Fredrick the Great meets Bach</TITLE>
  <BODY>
    <H1>Fredrick the Great meets Bach</H1>
    <P>In his book "Gödel, Escher, Bach", Douglas Hofstadter
      writes:
```

```
<BLOCKQUOTE>Johann Nikolaus Forkel, one of Bach's
            earliest biographers, tells the story as
            follows:
    <BLOCKQUOTE>One evening, just as he was getting his
              flute ready, and his musicians were
              assembled, an officer brought him a list of
              the strangers who had arrived. With his
              flute in his hand he ran over the list, but
              immediately turned to the assembled
              musicians, and said, with a kind of
              agitation:
        <BLOCKQUOTE>Gentlemen, old Bach is come.
        </BLOCKQUOTE>
    </BLOCKQUOTE>
</BLOCKQUOTE>
  </P>
 </BODY>
</HTML>
```

This can be displayed as shown in Figure 1.19.

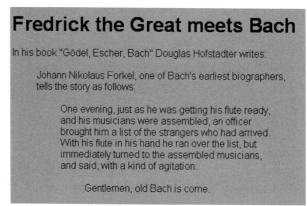

Figure 1.19 Nested BLOCKQUOTE elements.

Notice how with the nested elements, the second element is indented even more than the first is. This is a visual indication that it is a child of the first BLOCKQUOTE.

BLOCKQUOTE has been a much-used element, first because it marks content as a quote. When you use it for all quotes in your document, you or others, such as robots, can easily extract all of the quotes. It is much used also as a means of indenting material other than quotes. It is common to see stacks of BLOCKQUOTE elements, not because there are so many levels of quotes but because designers think indentation looks good. Here's an example:

```
<HTML>
  <BODY>
    <BLOCKQUOTE>
      <BLOCKQUOTE>
        <BLOCKQUOTE>
          <BLOCKQUOTE>
            Indentation is great!
          </BLOCKQUOTE>
        </BLOCKQUOTE>
      </BLOCKQUOTE>
    </BLOCKQUOTE>
  </BODY>
</HTML>
```

Figure 1.20 Using BLOCK-
QUOTE for indentation.

Indentation is great!

Unfortunately, when robots or other programs search for quotes, they find not only quotes but also everything else tagged as quotes.

With the arrival CSS, this misuse of BLOCKQUOTE should not be necessary. CSS provides easy-to-use methods for indenting text and images, as we will show you in subsequent chapters.

Well, there you have it. The elements we described in this chapter, plus a few others we discuss later where appropriate, form the basics of HTML. With these, you can write and publish many literary gems. Of course, they may not look all that great. But we will fix that in the next chapter.

Chapter 2

Enter CSS

As we explained in Chapter 1, HTML elements enable a Web page designer to mark up a document to indicate its structure. The HTML specification lists some guidelines on how browsers should display these elements. For example, you can be reasonably sure that the contents of a STRONG element will be displayed bold. Also, you can pretty much trust that most browsers will display the content of an H1 element using a big font size … at least bigger than the P element and bigger than the H2 element. But beyond trust and hope, you don't have any control over how your text appears.

CSS changes that. CSS puts you, the designer, in the driver's seat. We devote much of the rest of this book to explaining what you can do with CSS. In this chapter, we begin by introducing you to the basics of how to write CSS and how CSS and HTML work together to affect both the structure and appearance of your document.

RULES AND STYLE SHEETS

CSS is based on rules and style sheets. A **rule** is a statement about one stylistic aspect of one or more elements. A **style sheet** is one or more rules that apply to an HTML document.

An example of a simple style sheet is a sheet that consists of one rule. In the following example, we add a color to all first-level headings (H1). Here's the line of code – the rule – that we add:

```
H1 { color: red }
```

Let's take a closer look at the anatomy of a rule.

Anatomy of a rule

A rule consists of two parts:

- Selector – that part before the left curly brace
- Declaration – that part within the curly braces

```
H1 { color: red }
└┬┘   └────┬────┘
Selector  Declaration
```

The **selector** is the link between the HTML document and the style. It specifies what element(s) are to be affected by the declaration. The **declaration** is that part of the rule that sets forth what the effect will be. In the previous example, the selector is H1 and the declaration is "color:red." Hence, all H1 elements will be affected by the declaration, that is, they will be shown in red.

The above selector is based on the *type* of the element: it selects all elements of type 'H1'. This kind of selector is called a **type selector**. Any HTML element type can be used as a type selector. (It doesn't make sense to use invisible (see Table 1.1) element types as selectors though.) Type selectors are the simplest kind of selector and the only one we will use in this chapter. We discuss other kinds of selectors in Chapter 3.

Anatomy of a declaration

A declaration has two parts separated by a colon:

- Property – that part before the colon

- Value – that part after the colon

```
H1 { color: red }
     └─┬─┘  └┬┘
    Property Value
```

CSS1 refers to "Cascading Style Sheets, level 1", the W3C recommendation for CSS. Currently CSS1 is the only specification in what we expect will be a family of CSS specifications. You can read more about these efforts in Chapter 15. For now, we use CSS1 when we refer specifically to the first-level specification and CSS in statements that apply to forthcoming specifications as well.

The **property** is a quality or characteristic that something possesses. In the previous example, it is "color." (the color property is discussed in Chapter 8.) CSS1 defines more than 50 properties and we can assign values to all of them.

The **value** is a precise specification of the property. In the example, it is "red," but it could just as easily be blue, green, yellow, or some other color.

Figure 2.1 shows the diagram of a rule using as an example the H1 element whose contents we turned red. The curly braces ({ }) and colon (:) make it possible for the browser to distinguish between the selector, property, and value.

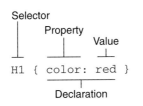

Figure 2.1 Diagram of a rule.

Grouping selectors and rules

In designing CSS, brevity was a goal. We figured that if we could reduce the size of style sheets, we could speed up the development of style sheets that were written "by hand," that is, without an authoring tool (a computer program that helps you author HTML documents). Also, short style sheets load faster than longer ones. CSS therefore includes several mechanisms to shorten style sheets by way of grouping selectors and declarations.

For example, consider these three rules:

```
H1 { font-weight: bold }
H2 { font-weight: bold }
H3 { font-weight: bold }
```

All three rules have exactly the same declaration – they set the font to be bolder. (This is done using the font-weight property, which we discuss in Chapter 4.) Since all three declarations are identical, we can group the selectors into a *comma-separated list* and only write the declaration once, like this:

```
H1, H2, H3 { font-style: bold }
```

This rule will produce the same result as the first three will.

A selector may have more than one declaration. For example, we could write a style sheet with these two rules:

```
H1 { color: red }
H1 ( text-align: center }
```

In this case, we set all H1s to be red and to be centered on the canvas. (This is done using the text-align property, discussed in Chapter 6.)

But we can achieve the same effect faster by grouping the declarations that relate to the same selector into a *semicolon-separated list*, like this:

```
H1 {
  color: red;
  text-align: center }
```

All declarations must be contained within the pair of curly braces. A semicolon separates the declarations and may – but doesn't have to – also appear at the end of the last declaration. Also, to make your code easier to read, we suggest you place each declaration on its own line, as we did here. (Browsers won't care. They'll just ignore all the extra whitespace and line breaks.)

Now you have the basics of how to create CSS rules and style sheets. However, you're not done yet. You can't simply write the style sheet, stick it wherever you want in the document, and expect it to work. It won't. You have more work to do. Next, you have to "glue" your style sheet to your HTML document.

GLUING STYLE SHEETS TO THE DOCUMENT

For any style sheet to affect the HTML document, it must be "glued" to the file. That is, the style sheet and the HTML document must be combined so that they can work together to produce the whole document. This can be done in any of four ways:

- Apply the basic, document-wide style sheet for the document by using the STYLE element.

- Apply a style sheet to an individual element using the STYLE attribute.

- Link an external style sheet to the document using the LINK element. This method is used to reference alternative style sheets that the browser can select if a previous one cannot be displayed.

- Import a style sheet using the CSS @import notation. This method is used to automatically import and merge an external style sheet with the current style sheet.

In the next section, we discuss the first method: using the STYLE element. We discuss using the STYLE attribute in Chapter 3, and using the LINK element and the @import notation in Chapter 12.

Gluing by using the STYLE element

You can glue the style sheet and HTML document together by putting the style sheet inside a STYLE element at the top of your document. The STYLE element was introduced in HTML specifically to allow style sheets to be inserted inside HTML documents. Here's a style sheet (shown in bold) glued to a sample document by using the STYLE element. The result is shown in Figure 2.2.

```
<HTML>
  <TITLE>Bach's home page</TITLE>
  <STYLE>
    H1 { color: red }
  </STYLE>
  <BODY>
    <H1>Bach's home page</H1>
    <P>Johann Sebastian Bach was a prolific composer. Among
      his works are:
    <UL>
```

```
      <LI>the Goldberg Variations
      <LI>the Brandenburg Concertos
      <LI>the Christmas Oratorio
   </UL>
   <H1>Historical perspective</H1>
   <P>Bach composed in what has been referred to as the
      Baroque period.
   </BODY>
</HTML>
```

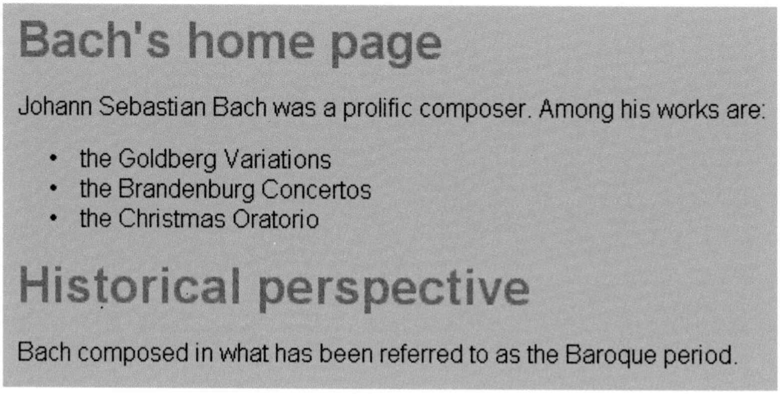

Bach's home page

Johann Sebastian Bach was a prolific composer. Among his works are:

- the Goldberg Variations
- the Brandenburg Concertos
- the Christmas Oratorio

Historical perspective

Bach composed in what has been referred to as the Baroque period.

Figure 2.2 The result of adding to a style sheet a rule to turn H1s red and then gluing the style sheet to the document using the STYLE element.

Notice that the STYLE element is placed after the TITLE element and before the BODY element. The title of a document does not show up on the canvas, so it is not affected by CSS styles.

The content of a STYLE element is a style sheet. However, whereas the content of such elements as H1, P, and UL appears on the canvas, the content of a STYLE element does not show on the canvas. Rather, it is the *effect* of the content of the STYLE element – the style sheet – that appears on the canvas. So you don't see "{ color: red }" displayed on your screen; you see instead two H1s colored red. No rules have been added that affect any of the other elements, so those elements appear in the browser's default color.

BROWSERS AND CSS

For CSS to work as described in this book, you must use a CSS-enhanced browser, that is, a browser that supports CSS. A CSS-enhanced browser will recognize the STYLE element as a container for a style sheet and present the document accordingly. At the time of this writing, the most widely available CSS-enhanced browser is Microsoft's Internet Explorer 3.0 (MSIE3), but when you read this, more and newer browsers should support CSS1.

See Appendix B for a list of the software that currently supports CSS1 and check the book's Web site (http://www.awl.com/css) for an updated list. Note that throughout this book when we display examples of CSS usage, those examples appear as they would on a CSS-enhanced browser.

Some browsers, such as Netscape's Navigator (version 2.x and 3.x) don't support style sheets but they know enough about the STYLE element to fully ignore it. Next to supporting style sheets, this is the preferred behavior.

However, other browsers that do not know the STYLE element, such as Navigator 1.x and MSIE2, will ignore the STYLE *tags* but display the *content* of the STYLE element. Thus, the user will end up with the style sheet printed on the top of the canvas.

At the time of writing, roughly 10% of Web users will experience this problem. To avoid this, you can put your style sheet inside an *HTML comment*, which we discussed in Chapter 1. Because comments don't display on the screen, by placing your style sheet inside an HTML comment, you prevent the oldest browsers from displaying the STYLE element's content. CSS-enhanced browsers are aware of this trick, and will treat the content of the STYLE element as a style sheet.

Recall that HTML comments start with '<!--' and end with '-->'. Here's an excerpt from the previous code example that shows how you write a style sheet in an HTML comment. The comment encloses the STYLE element content only:

CSS also has its own set of comments that you can use within the style sheet. A CSS comment begins with '/*' and ends with '*/'. (Those of you familiar with the C programming language will recognize these.) CSS rules put inside a CSS comment will not have any effect on the presentation of the document.

```
<HTML>
  <TITLE>Bach's home page</TITLE>
  <STYLE>
    <!--
    H1 { color: red }
    -->
  </STYLE>
  <BODY>
    ..
  </BODY>
</HTML>
```

The browser also needs to be told that you are working with CSS style sheets. Currently, CSS is the only style sheet language on the Web, but this could change. Just as there is more than one image format (GIF, JPEG and PNG come to mind), there could be more than one style sheet language. So the browser needs to be told which style sheet language is being used. This is done via the TYPE attribute on the STYLE element. The value of TYPE indicates which style sheet is being used; for CSS, that value is "text/css." Following is an excerpt from our previous sample document that shows you how you would write this:

```
<HTML>
  <TITLE>Bach's home page</TITLE>
  <STYLE TYPE="text/css">
    <!--
    H1 { color: red }
    -->
  </STYLE>
  <BODY>
    ..
  </BODY>
</HTML>
```

When the browser loads a document, it checks to see if it understands the style sheet language. If it does, it will try to read the style sheet, otherwise it will ignore it. The TYPE attribute (see Chapter 1 for a discussion on HTML attributes) on the STYLE element is a way to let the browser know which style sheet language is being used. We don't know for sure if it will be necessary to declare that you are using CSS, but including a TYPE attribute will never hurt.

To make examples easier to read, we have chosen not to wrap style sheets in HTML comments, but we do use the TYPE attribute throughout this book.

TREE STRUCTURES AND INHERITANCE

Recall from Chapter 1 the discussion about HTML representing a document with a tree-like structure and how elements in HTML have children and parents. There are many reasons for having tree-structured documents. For style sheets, there is one very good reason: inheritance. Just like children inherit from their parents, so do HTML elements. Instead of inheriting genes and money, HTML elements inherit stylistic properties.

Let's start by taking a look at the sample document:

```
<HTML>
  <TITLE>Bach's home page</TITLE>
  <BODY>
    <H1>Bach's home page</H1>
    <P>Johann Sebastian Bach was a <STRONG>prolific</STRONG>
      composer. Among his works are:
    <UL>
      <LI>the Goldberg Variations
      <LI>the Brandenburg Concertos
      <LI>the Christmas Oratorio
    </UL>
  </BODY>
</HTML>
```

The tree structure of this document is:

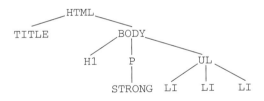

Through inheritance, CSS property values set on one element will be transferred down the tree to its descendants. For example, our examples have up to now set the color to be red for elements like H1 and P. Now, say, you would like to set the same color on all elements in your document. You could do this by making one rule for each element type:

```
<STYLE TYPE="text/css">
  H1 { color: red }
  P { color: red }
  LI { color: red }
</STYLE>
```

However, most HTML documents are more complex than our sample document, and your style sheet would soon get long. You could shorten it by grouping selectors, but there is an even better – and shorter – way. Instead of setting the style on each element type, we set it on their common ancestor, the BODY element:

```
<STYLE TYPE="text/css">
  BODY { color: red }
</STYLE>
```

Since other elements inherit properties from the BODY element, they will all inherit the color red:

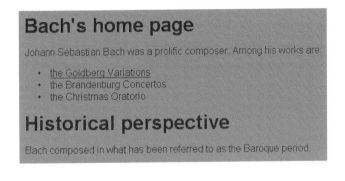

As you have seen above, inheritance is a transport vehicle that will distribute stylistic properties to descendants of an element. Since the BODY element is a common ancestor for all visible elements, 'BODY' is a convenient selector.

OVERRIDING INHERITANCE

In the previous example, all elements were given the same color through inheritance. Sometimes, however, children don't look like their parents. Not surprisingly, CSS also accounts for this. Say you would like H1 elements to be blue while the rest should be red. This is easily expressed in CSS:

```
<STYLE TYPE="text/css">
    BODY { color: red }
    H1 { color: blue }
</STYLE>
```

Since H1 is a child element of BODY (and thereby inherits from BODY), the two rules in the above style sheet are conflicting. The first one sets the color of the BODY element – and thereby also the color of H1 through inheritance – while the second one sets the color specifically on the H1 element. Which rule will win? Let's find out:

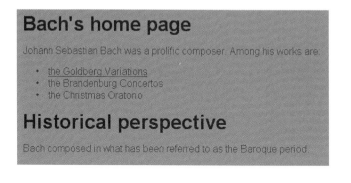

The reason why the second rule wins is that it is more *specific* than the first. The first rule is very general – it affects all elements on the canvas. The second rule only affects H1 elements in the document and is therefore more specific.

If CSS had been a programming language, the order in which the rules were specified would determine which of them would win. CSS is not a programming language, and in the above example, the order is irrelevant. The result is exactly the same if we use this style sheet:

```
<STYLE TYPE="text/css">
   H1 { color: blue }
   BODY { color: red }
</STYLE>
```

CSS has been designed to resolve conflicts between style sheet rules like the one above. The exact rules for how to do this are quite complicated, but are described in detail in Chapter 11.

PROPERTIES THAT DON'T INHERIT

As a general rule, properties in CSS inherit from parent to child elements as described in the previous examples. Some properties, however, don't inherit and there is always a reason why.

We will use the background property as an example of a property that doesn't inherit.

Let's say you want to set a background image for a page – this is a common effect on the Web. In CSS, you can write:

```
<HTML>
   <TITLE>Bach's home page</TITLE>
   <STYLE TYPE="text/css">
     BODY { background: url(texture.gif) blue }
   </STYLE>
   <BODY>
     <H1>Bach's <EM>home</EM> page</H1>
     <P>Johann Sebastian Bach was a prolific composer.
   </BODY>
</HTML>
```

The background property has a URL ("texture.gif") that points to a background image as value. (Also, a color is specified for use when the image is not available.) When the image is ready, the canvas looks like:

As you can see, the background image covers the surface like a wallpaper – also the backgrounds of the H1 and P element have been covered. This is not due to inheritance, but to the fact that unless otherwise set, all backgrounds are transparent. So, since we haven't set the backgrounds of the H1 or P element to something else, the parent element, BODY, will shine through.

Visually, the effect of transparency is similar to inheritance: it looks like all elements have the same backgrounds. So if they are so similar, why don't we just use inheritance? There are two reasons: First, transparent backgrounds are faster to display (there is nothing to display!) than other backgrounds. Second, since background images are aligned relative to the element they belong to, you would otherwise not always end up with a smooth background surface.

We've given you some simple examples to get you started on understanding and using inheritance with CSS. We talk a lot more about inheritance in subsequent chapters, particularly when we discuss the various CSS properties that can be set on text and images. Chapter 11 is devoted to a more in-depth discussion of inheritance. In that chapter, we also discuss the concept of cascading, which we now introduce.

INTRODUCTION TO CASCADING

A fundamental feature of CSS is that more than one style sheet can influence the presentation of a document. This feature is known as *cascading* because the different style sheets are thought of as coming in a series. Cascading is a fundamental feature of CSS since we realized that any single document could end up with style sheets from multiple sources: the browser, the designer, and possibly the user.

Each browser will have a default style sheet that describes how it displays a document that doesn't have its own style sheet. The default style sheet contains all the presentation style rules that Web designers have come to expect; for example, that text inside the EM element is italicized. This style sheet is merged with any other style sheets the author or user has associated with the document. Since the default style sheet includes the common presentation rules, authors and users don't need to put them into their style sheets.

We have known for years that designers want to develop their own style sheets. However, we discovered that users, too, want the option of influencing the presentation of their documents. With CSS, they can do this by supplying a personal style sheet that will be merged with the browser's and the designer's style sheets. Any conflicts between the various style sheets are resolved by the browser. Usually, the designer's style sheet will have the strongest claim on the document, followed by the user's, and then the browser's default.

We go into details about cascading in Chapter 11. Before that, there is much to learn about fonts, space and colors.

Chapter 3

Selectors

In Chapter 2, we talked about *type* selectors – selectors that identify elements by their type, for example, H1 and P. These are the simplest and most-used selectors. However, CSS also offers other kinds of selectors.

In this chapter, we discuss the different kinds of selectors and how you work with them. Using the more advanced selectors allows you to carefully choose the parts of your document that are to be influenced by your style settings. If you are eager to learn more about the visual properties of CSS – which we describe in subsequent chapters – you might want to skim this chapter in the first reading and return to it when you need to know more about selectors.

SELECTOR SCHEMES

To give you more freedom to select which elements your style is applied to, CSS1 supports four selector schemes. Each is based on some aspect of an element:

- An element's type

- An element's attributes

- The context in which the element is used

- External information about the element

Also, CSS1 includes a way of attaching style rules to an element without using a traditional selector; the STYLE attribute effectively bypasses the whole selector mechanism. We also discuss the STYLE attribute in this chapter.

At the end of this chapter we discuss how the various schemes can be combined to form complex selectors.

TYPE SELECTORS

The simplest kind of selector in CSS is the name of an element type. Using this kind of selector – which is called a *type selector* – you apply the declaration to every instance of the element type. For example, the selector of the following simple rule is H1, so the rule affects all H1 elements in a document:

```
H1 { color: red }
```

We discussed type selectors in Chapter 2.

If you find yourself writing several style rules that are the same except for the selector, for example:

```
H1 { color: red }
H2 { color: red }
H3 { color: red }
```

Type selectors are case-insensitive. Therefore, the following four rules are equivalent:
```
BLOCKQUOTE
{ margin-left: 2em }
       BlockQuote
{ margin-left: 2em }
       blockquote
{ margin-left: 2em }
       BLockQUoTE
{ margin-left: 2em }
```
(For now, don't worry about the margin declarations – margins are explained in Chapter 6.)

you can shorten them by *grouping* the selectors in a comma-separated list:

```
H1, H2, H3 { color: red }
```

It is a matter of taste whether you want to use this grouping mechanism or not.

ATTRIBUTE SELECTORS

One of the most powerful aspects on which to base selection is an attribute. Recall from Chapter 1 that an attribute is a characteristic quality, other than the type or content of an element. In that chapter we discussed the attributes HREF, SRC, and ALT. In this chapter we will discuss two new attributes that have been added to all HTML elements to support style sheets:

• CLASS

• ID

Both these attributes can be used with any HTML element and we will see how they can be used to create powerful selectors.

The CLASS attribute

The CLASS attribute enables you to apply declarations to a group of elements that have the same value on the CLASS attribute. All elements inside BODY can have a CLASS attribute. Essentially, you **classify** elements with the CLASS attribute, create rules in your style sheet that refer to the value of the CLASS attribute, and then the browser will automatically apply those rules to the group of elements.

For example, say you are an actor rehearsing for the role of Polonius in Shakespeare's *Hamlet*. In your copy of the manuscript you would like all lines by Polonius to stand out. The first step to achieving this is to classify Polonius's lines – that is, set the CLASS attribute on all elements containing lines by Polonius. Here is how you set the CLASS value:

```
         Start tag                                        End tag
 _____|___                                            _|_
<P CLASS=POLONIUS>Polonius: Do you know me, my lord?</P>
             ___|___
            Class name
 _____|___
 Class attribute
```

An element whose start tag includes a CLASS attribute – like the one above – is called a *classed element*. In the above example, the class name chosen is "POLONIUS." Authors pick class names.

Currently, class names must be single words, although you can use digits and dashes. The following are all acceptable class names:

• POLONIUS

• name-10

• first-remark

But the following are not:

• The man   (contains space)

• item+12   (contains plus sign)

• last!!   (contains exclamation mark)

At the time of writing it's unclear if class names will be case-sensitive or case-insensitive. In some languages it's not trivial to convert between upper and lower cases, so good advice at this point is not to depend on case-insensitivity.

The next step is to write style rules with a selector that refers to the class name. A selector that includes a class name is called a *class selector*. Here is a rule with a selector that selects all of Polonius's elements:

```
Class selector          Declaration
_____|_____       _____|_____

.POLONIUS  {  font-weight:  bold  }
|_____|
|  Class name
Flag character
```

The class selector starts with a **flag character** (the period) which signals what type of selector follows. The period was chosen because it is associated with the term "class" in many programming languages. Translated into English, the flag character reads "elements with class name." The whole selector says: "elements with class name POLONIUS." Authors are free to choose class names. Assuming you have consistently classified elements containing lines by Polonius, they will be printed in a bold font.

Let's look at a complete example that introduces a second class:

```
<HTML>
  <TITLE>Hamlet, excerpt from act II</TITLE>
  <STYLE TYPE="text/css">
    .POLONIUS { font-weight: bold }
    .HAMLET { font-weight: normal }
  </STYLE>
  <BODY>
    <P CLASS=POLONIUS>Polonius: Do you know me, my lord?
    <P CLASS=HAMLET>Hamlet: Excellent well, you are a fishmonger.
    <P CLASS=POLONIUS>Polonius: Not I, my lord.
    <P CLASS=HAMLET>Hamlet: Then I would you were so honest a man.
  </BODY>
</HTML>
```

In the above example, two classes have been defined, HAMLET and POLONIUS. The style sheet in the STYLE element sets the font weight (the "thickness" of the fonts, see Chapter 4) to be different. The result can be seen below.

> **Polonius: Do you know me, my lord?**
>
> Hamlet: Excellent well, you are a fishmonger.
>
> **Polonius: Not I, my lord.**
>
> Hamlet: Then I would you were so honest a man.

As you can see, Polonius's lines stand out – an invaluable tool when you rehearse your role.

One could argue that the same result could be achieved without style sheets. By enclosing Polonius's lines in STRONG or B elements they would also come out bold. This is true, but consider the consequences when the actor who is scheduled to play Hamlet catches a cold and you have to replace him. Now you suddenly need Hamlet's lines to stand out and Polonius's lines to use the normal font weight. If you had been using STRONG elements to emphasize Polonius's lines, you'd have to remove them and add them to Hamlet's lines instead. But, since you are using CSS, you simply change two lines in the style sheet:

```
.POLONIUS { font-weight: normal }
.HAMLET { font-weight: bold }
```

This will reverse the effect and Hamlet's lines will stand out:

> Polonius: Do you know me, my lord?
>
> **Hamlet: Excellent well, you are a fishmonger.**
>
> Polonius: Not I, my lord.
>
> **Hamlet: Then I would you were so honest a man.**

The CLASS attribute is a very powerful feature of CSS. We recommend that you use the CLASS attribute to add more information about elements – information that can be used to enhance the presentation of your documents. We do not recommend that you use the CLASS attribute to totally change the presentation of an element. For example, you can easily change an LI element to look like an H1 element by classifying it. If you want an element to look like H1, we would rather recommend that you mark it up as H1. Do not let style sheets replace the structure of your documents; rather, let the style sheets enhance the structure.

The ID attribute

The ID attribute works like the CLASS attribute with one important difference: The value of an ID attribute must be unique throughout the document. That is, every element inside BODY can have an ID attribute, but the values must all be different. This makes the ID attribute useful for setting style rules on individual elements. A selector that includes an ID attribute is called an *ID selector*. The general form of an ID selector resembles that of the CLASS attribute in the previous section:

```
ID selector                    Declaration
___|___        _____|_____
#xyz34 { text-decoration: underline }
|__|__|
|  ID value
| Flag character
```

Notice that the flag character for ID selectors is a hash mark (#). The flag character alerts the browser that an ID value is coming up next. In English, the above selector says "the element with an ID value equal to xyz34." The entire rule reads: "The element with an ID value equal to xyz34 is to be underlined." The author is free to pick the value of the ID attribute, and the chosen value is case-insensitive.

The HTML syntax of the element on which you want to use the ID attribute resembles that of other elements with attributes; for example:

```
<P ID=xyz34>Underlined text</P>
```

Combined with the style sheet rule above, the content of the element will be underlined. Because the value of the ID attribute must be unique, you could not include another usage of it in the same document, such as:

```
<H1 ID=XYZ34>A HEADLINE</H1>
<P ID=XYZ34>UNDERLINED TEXT</P>
```

Rather, you would have to give the two elements different ID values:

```
<H1 ID=xyz34>A headline</H1>
<P ID=xyz35>Underlined text</P>
```

Here is a complete example using an ID selector:

```
<HTML>
  <TITLE>ID showoff</TITLE>
  <STYLE TYPE="text/css">
    #xyz34 { text-decoration: underline }
  </STYLE>
  <BODY>
    <P ID=xyz34>Underlined text</P>
  </BODY>
</HTML>
```

By using the ID selectors, you can set style properties on a per-element basis. Like CLASS, ID is a powerful feature. It carries the same cautions we set out in the previous section.

The STYLE attribute

The STYLE attribute is different from the other attributes described in this chapter. Whereas CLASS and ID attribute values can be used in selectors, the STYLE attribute is actually a replacement for the whole selector mechanism. Instead of having a value that can be referred to in a selector (which is what ID and CLASS have), the value of the STYLE attribute is actually one or more CSS declarations.

Normally, using CSS, a designer will put all style rules into a style sheet that goes into the STYLE element at the top of the document (or is LINKED externally as described in Chapter 12). However, using the STYLE attribute, you can bypass the style sheet and put declarations directly into the start tags of your document.

Here is one example:

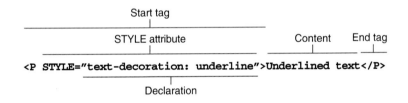

The example above attaches a declaration to a single element and results in the content of the element being underlined. You will recall from the example in the previous section that the ID attribute accomplishes the very same thing – setting style on a single element. Whereas the ID attribute involves an indirection, the STYLE attribute bypasses the style sheet and puts the declaration directly into the start tag of the element it applies to. Properties set using the STYLE attribute are treated exactly in the same manner as if the property had been set in a style sheet using an ID selector.

You could conceivably use the STYLE attribute to apply styles to just about anything and everything. For example, you could use the STYLE attribute this way (shown in bold):

```
<HTML>
  <TITLE>Hamlet, excerpt from act II</TITLE>
  <BODY STYLE="color: black; background: white">
```

```
    <P STYLE="font-weight: bold">Polonius: Do you know me,
                                      my lord?
    <P STYLE="font-weight: normal">Hamlet: Excellent well,
                                      you are a fishmonger.
    <P STYLE="font-weight: bold">Polonius: Not I, my lord.
    <P STYLE="font-weight: normal">Hamlet: Then I would you
                                      were so honest a man.
  </BODY>
</HTML>
```

This use of the STYLE attribute is legal, but there are two reasons why you should not – in general – use the STYLE attribute. First, it's the long way to go about setting styles. Since the declarations in the STYLE attribute only apply to the element where they are specified, there is no way to reuse your declarations and your documents will get longer. Also, if you later want to change the presentation of your document, you will have to make changes in more places. Second, by interleaving style and content, you miss out on an important advantage of style sheets: the separation of content and presentation. By putting all your style settings into a style sheet, you can make your style sheets apply to more than one document (see Chapter 12 for how the LINK element can be used for this).

The rather messy use of the STYLE attribute above can be rewritten into:

```
<HTML>
  <TITLE>Hamlet, excerpt from act II</TITLE>
  <STYLE TYPE="text/css">
    BODY { color: black; background: white }
    .POLONIUS { font-weight: bold }
    .HAMLET { font-weight: normal }
  </STYLE>
  <BODY>
    <P CLASS=POLONIUS>Polonius: Do you know me, my lord?
    <P CLASS=HAMLET>Hamlet: Excellent well, you are a
                    fishmonger.
    <P CLASS=POLONIUS>Polonius: Not I, my lord.
    <P CLASS=HAMLET>Hamlet: Then I would you were so
                    honest a man.
  </BODY>
</HTML>
```

So use the STYLE element to apply styles to all occurrences of a type of element. Save the STYLE attribute for those occasions when you want to make stylistic changes to a particular occurrence of an element while leaving alone the style of all others of the same element type.

COMBINING SELECTOR TYPES

Three kinds of selectors have been described in this chapter up to now: type selectors, ID selectors and class selectors. Often, different selector types are combined to form more complex selectors. By combining selectors you can more accurately target elements you want to give a certain presentation. For example, by combining a type selector and a class selector, an element must fulfill both requirements – it must be of the right type *and* the right class – in order to be influenced by the style rule. Let's look at one example:

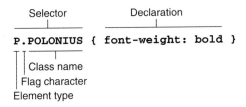

In English the selector above reads: "P elements with class name POLONIUS." That is, an element must be of the right type (P) *and* it must also be of the right class (POLONIUS). Compare the above example with this selector:

```
.POLONIUS { font-weight: bold }
```

The latter example omits the element type and starts off with the flag character. By doing so, it selects *all* elements with the right class – no matter what type the element is.

We will see more examples of how to combine different kinds of selectors later in this chapter.

CONTEXTUAL SELECTORS

A **contextual selector** is a selector that takes into account the context in which the style is to be applied. That is, the specified style is applied to an element only if the element is in the specified context. An element's *context* is its ancestor elements.

Suppose you were to write these rules:

```
H1 { color: red }
EM { color: red }
```

These rules will work fine. H1 headings will turn red, and so will EM elements. Now, suppose you have this code in your document:

```
<H1>This headline is <EM>very</EM> important.</H1>
```

You want to emphasize "very" but because both the EM and the H1 are set to red, you will lose the emphasis provided by EM. You want both EM and H1 to stay red for the document as a whole, but for EM elements inside H1, you're going to have to come up with some other way to emphasize "very." You still want to use the EM element. How do you do it?

Using a contextual selector, you can specify a rule that only applies to EMs that are inside H1 elements. No other EM elements will be affected. Consider this rule:

```
H1 EM { color: blue }
```

In English, this rule is saying, "For any EM that is inside H1, make it blue (and not red like the previous rule specified). Thank you." Thus the EM will be made blue only in the context of an H1. In all other contexts, it will be red as usual. Hence the name contextual selector.

Contextual selectors are made up of two or more *simple* selectors separated by white space. Any type, class or ID selector is a simple selector. Also, combinations of type and class selectors, as described in the previous section, are regarded as simple selectors.

You fine-tune your contextual selector by including more simple selectors. For example:

```
OL OL { list-style: upper-alpha }
OL OL OL { list-style: lower-alpha }
```

Here we have used two contextual selectors. The first selects all OL elements that appear inside another OL. The second selects all OL elements that have *two* other OLs as ancestors – they are the third level of OL lists. Figure 3.1 shows the result of these three rules.

Figure 3.1 Contextual selectors in action.

1. first level, first item
   A. second level, first item
      a. third level, first item
      b. third level, second item
   B. second level, second item
2. first level, second item

EXTERNAL INFORMATION: PSEUDO-CLASSES AND PSEUDO-ELEMENTS

In CSS, style is normally based on the tags and attributes as found in the HTML source. This works fine for many design scenarios, but it doesn't cover some common design effects designers want to achieve.

Pseudo-classes and pseudo-elements were devised to fill in some of these gaps. Both are mechanisms that extend the expressive power of CSS. In CSS1, using pseudo-classes, you can change the style of a document's links based on whether and when the links have been visited. Using pseudo-elements, you can change the style of the first letter and first line of an element. Neither pseudo-classes nor pseudo-elements exist in HTML, that is, they are not visible in the HTML code. Both mechanisms have been designed so that they can be further extended in future versions of CSS, to fill in more gaps.

The anchor pseudo-class

Currently only one element type in HTML uses pseudo-classes: the A (anchor) element. An **anchor pseudo-class** is a mechanism by which a browser indicates to a user the status of hyperlinks in a document the user is viewing.

A browser typically displays a link in a document in a different color than the rest of the text. Links that a user hasn't visited will be one color. Links the user has visited will be another color. Sometimes a browser will display an active link – the one currently mouse-clicked by the user – in a third color.

There is no way for an author to know whether a user has visited a link; this information is known only to the browser. However, you can set in your style sheet the colors used to indicate the status of links. This is done by including an anchor pseudo-class in the selector:

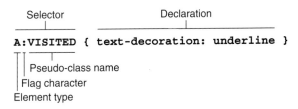

There are several things to note in the above example:

- The selector is a combination of a type selector and a pseudo-class selector. Since only A elements have pseudo-classes, this is strictly not necessary, but the selector arguably looks nicer.

- The flag character is a colon (:). Both pseudo-classes and pseudo-elements use the colon as the flag character.

All links in a document (that is, every A element with an HREF attribute) are automatically classified into one (and only one) of these three pseudo-classes:

- LINK

- VISITED

- ACTIVE

Normally, the link is in pseudo-class LINK; if the link has been visited recently, the browser will put it into pseudo-class VISITED. (How recent the visit has to be is up to the browser.) When the link is actively selected, that is, in the brief moment when the user clicks on a link, it will be in pseudo-class ACTIVE. The names of pseudo-classes and pseudo-elements are case-insensitive.

For each of these pseudo-classes, you can set style rules. Here are some examples:

```
A:link { color: red }       /* unvisited link */
A:visited { color: blue }   /* visited link */
A:active { color: lime }    /* active link */
```

The browser may only support a limited number of properties for the pseudo-classes. For example, you should not expect to be able to change the font size of the ACTIVE pseudo-class – this would mean the browser would have to reformat the whole document when the user clicks on a link. It's safe to assume that you can change colors and add/remove underlining, but any rule that may change the size of something (for example, font or margin) may be ignored by the browser.

Pseudo-elements

Pseudo-elements allow you to set style on a subpart of an element's content. Like pseudo-classes, pseudo-elements don't exist in the HTML code. Pseudo-elements have been introduced to allow for designs that would otherwise not have been possible.

CSS1 has two pseudo-elements: *first-letter* and *first-line*. The effects of these elements are not related to the structure of the HTML document. Rather, the effects are based on how the element is formatted. They enable you to set styles on the first letter of a word and on the first line of a para-graph, respectively, independent of any other styles. Both can be attached only to block-level elements.

These effects are not new. Traditional printers have been using them for centuries, and you will often find them in use in contemporary magazines. A common usage is to increase the size of the first letter or make the first line use uppercase letters. However, you can also set the properties color, background, text decorations and case transformation, among others.

According to the CSS1 specification, CSS1 browsers are not *required* to support pseudo-elements. At the time of writing, we do not know how widely pseudo-elements will be supported by browsers.

A pseudo-element has the following general form:

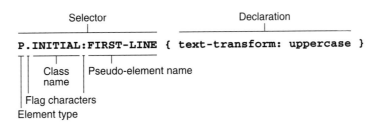

A pseudo-element selector will almost always be used in combination with other selectors. This is because you seldom want pseudo-element formatting on all elements in your document. Above, the pseudo-element selector is combined with two other selectors: a type selector (P) and a class selector (.INITIAL). The resulting selector reads: "the first line of P elements with class name INITIAL." The above rule is the first step on the way to creating a style sheet that replicates the style of articles in *TIME* magazine (see Figure 3.2).

than he barga

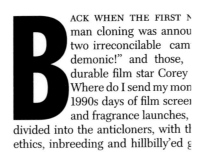

Figure 3.2 An example of typography from *TIME* magazine, which uses dropcap initials and small-caps letters on the first line. To achieve these effects in CSS, you need pseudo-elements.

Let's put the above rule into a complete document:

```
<HTML>
  <TITLE>The style of TIME magazine</TITLE>
  <STYLE TYPE="text/css">
    P.INITIAL:FIRST-LINE { text-transform: uppercase }
  </STYLE>
  <BODY>
    <H1>A sample article</H1>
    <P CLASS=INITIAL>The first line of the first paragraph
                    in a TIME magazine article is
                    printed in uppercase letters.
    <P>The text in the second paragraph has no special
       formatting.
  </BODY>
</HTML>
```

The above example will be displayed as shown in Figure 3.3.

THE FIRST LINE OF THE FIRST paragraph of a TIME magazine is printed in capital letters
   The text in the second line has no special formatting

It doesn't make any difference how long the line is or how many words are on it. Whatever text happens to fall on the first line will be displayed in upper-case. Because browser windows can be resized, there is no way for you to know how many words will be on the first line of a paragraph, so using a pseudo-element is the only way to achieve this effect.

The style sheet for *TIME* magazine is still missing a key design feature: the dropcap initial letter. A *dropcap initial* is a common trick in typography: the first letter of a text is enlarged and "dropped" into the formatted para-graph. We can attach style rules to the first letter of an element by using – you guessed it – the "first-letter" pseudo-element:

```
P.INITIAL:FIRST-LETTER { font-size: 200% }
```

The selector in the above example reads: "the first letter of P elements with class name INITIAL". That is, the style rule will apply to the first letter of lines that were affected in the example above. The whole rule says: "The first letter of P elements with class name INITIAL should have a font size twice as big as the surrounding text." Formatted, the text now looks like:

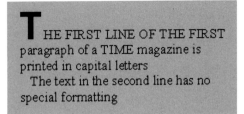

We're almost there! The first letter now has the right size, but not the right position; it's not "dropped" into the formatted paragraph. By making the first letter "float" (discussed in Chapter 7), we achieve the dropcap effect. The HTML example becomes:

```
<HTML>
    <TITLE>The style of TIME magazine</TITLE>
    <STYLE TYPE="text/css">
        P.INITIAL:FIRST-LINE { text-transform: uppercase }
        P.INITIAL:FIRST-LETTER { font-size: 200%; float: left }
    </STYLE>
    <BODY>
        <H1>A sample article</H1>
        <P CLASS=INITIAL>The first line of the first paragraph
                        in a TIME magazine article is
                        printed in uppercase letters.
        <P>The text in the second paragraph has no special
            formatting.
    </BODY>
</HTML>
```

Our sample document is formatted as:

THE FIRST LINE OF THE FIRST paragraph of a TIME magazine is printed in capital letters.
    The text in the second paragraph has no special formatting.

DIV AND SPAN

To round this chapter off we will introduce two new elements. DIV (division) and SPAN (to span over) have recently been added to HTML to support the introduction of style sheets. We have delayed describing them till now since they are mostly used in combination with the CLASS attribute.

By now you may have realized that the CLASS attribute is a very powerful feature of CSS. Using it, you can effectively create new elements in HTML. Creating new elements through the CLASS attribute is much easier than convincing browser vendors and maintainers of the HTML specification that a new tag is needed and beneficial for everyone.

Using the DIV and SPAN elements you can create your own elements. The reason there are two elements for this is that DIV is a block-level element, while SPAN is inline. For example, if you are a poet, you have no way to mark your products as poems in HTML. For this, you would like to have a new POEM tag. It's unlikely that POEM will become an HTML element in the near future, but the DIV element – in combination with the CLASS attribute – offers you an alternative:

```
<DIV CLASS=POEM>
  Roses are red, <BR>
  violets are blue, <BR>
  if you're into poetry, <BR>
  DIV is for you!
</DIV>
```

In this way, you can preserve semantics – the fact that the above text is a poem – through the use of the DIV element. In the style sheet, you can set a certain style for the "poem" element:

```
DIV.POEM { font-family: cursive }
```

Using the SPAN element you can make new inline elements:

```
<DIV CLASS=POEM>
  <SPAN CLASS=FLOWER>Roses</SPAN> are red, <BR>
  <SPAN CLASS=FLOWER>violets</SPAN are blue, <BR>
  if you're into poetry, <BR>
  DIV is for you!
</DIV>
```

The new "flower" element can be addressed in the style sheet:

```
SPAN.FLOWER { font-family: fantasy }
```

The complete HTML example thus becomes:

```
<HTML>
  <TITLE>A poem</TITLE>
  <STYLE TYPE="text/css">
    DIV.POEM { font-family: cursive }
    SPAN.FLOWER { font-family: fantasy }
  </STYLE>
  <BODY>
    <DIV CLASS=POEM>
      <SPAN CLASS=FLOWER>Roses</SPAN> are red, <BR>
      <SPAN CLASS=FLOWER>violets</SPAN are blue, <BR>
      if you're into poetry, <BR>
      DIV is for you!
    </DIV>
  </BODY>
</HTML>
```

Which can be displayed as:

ROSES are red,
VIOLETS are blue,
if you're into poetry,
DIV is for you!

Chapter 4

Fonts

Specifying the properties of type is one of the most common uses of style sheets. Such properties include the type's size, its width, its weight – such as whether it is light or bold – and its posture – whether it slants to the right (as in italics) or stands straight up.

Getting the look you want for your type is difficult with HTML, since HTML doesn't contain any information about fonts. The appearance of the page is the result of the browser's inserting styles it thinks are appropriate (and which ones it thinks are appropriate is determined by the browser's programmers). It does this using the HTML structural information in your document. CSS gives you more influence over how the type will look. Although even CSS cannot give you absolute control, it can enable you to give the browser fairly detailed hints about what the type should look like.

The control you have using CSS is still limited because there is no universally accepted system of classifying type. Conflicting terminology also creates difficulties. Traditional printing terminology and that used by the burgeoning desktop publishing and Web page design fields don't always agree. Further, much of the effect that appears on the user's screen depends on the resources available on the user's browser. So you may specify particular type only to discover that a browser doesn't know what you're talking about. However, the browser will do the best it can with all of your type specifications, attempting to find the best match according to its own resources.

In this chapter, we first discuss the basics of typography, always keeping in mind the lack of a universally accepted classification system and the inconsistent terminology. Then we discuss the properties that CSS allows you to specify so that your type can take on more of the character you want it to have.

INTRODUCTION TO TYPE

Before we do anything else, we need to establish some common understanding so that you and we are talking about the same thing. We first define certain terms common to traditional printing. Then we explain how some of those terms as used in desktop publishing and Web page design may differ. Next we set out the classifications of type. We end with a brief discussion of how to size type.

Type terminology

One of the most common misconceptions about type concerns the difference between a typeface and a font. Often, in the world of desktop publishing and Web page design, the two terms are used interchangeably. However, strictly speaking they are not the same. A typeface, sometimes called a face, is all type of a single design and style. That is, it is all the numbers, letters, punctuation, and special symbols that are of the same design and style.

Type can share the same basic design but vary in style by certain attributes, including weight (degree of boldness versus lightness), width (such as narrow versus expanded), and posture (straight versus slanted). Typefaces that essentially are the same design but vary in style by one or more attributes are considered to be part of the same type family. Type families are given names. Common names you may have heard are Helvetica, Arial, and Palatino. Times Roman (TR) is the name of another very popular type family. TR Regular, TR Italic, TR Bold, and TR Bold Italic are typefaces within the TR type family. Figure 4.1 shows a diagram of the TR family and a sample of each typeface.

Aa Bb Cc ....TR Regular

Aa Bb Cc ....TR Italic

Aa Bb Cc ....TR Bold

Aa Bb Cc ....TR Bold Italic

Figure 4.1 Four typefaces of the Times Roman type family.

The most common type families usually have at least these four styles: regular (also called "roman"), bold (aka boldface), italic, and bold italic. The roman style often forms the basic, most commonly used typeface within the family because in many type families it is very appropriate for running text. However, all type families have their own version of roman, even those whose appearance is inappropriate for running text. Further, not every type family has variations, while other families have many typefaces with these or other characteristics, such as being narrow, expanded or condensed.

The font

The traditional definition of a font is one typeface in one size and in one weight and style. For example, a 10-point TR Regular is one font, and a 12-point TR Regular is another font, as is a 14-point TR Regular. These differ only in their sizes and each is considered to be a font, by the traditional definition. Other fonts could be 10 pt TR Bold, 10 pt TR Italic, and 10 pt TR Bold Italic. These differ only in their style or weight or both. (Note, the term "point" is part of a system of measuring type. We talk about this shortly in the chapter.)

This definition of font comes from the time when each size and variation of a typeface had to be made specially and stored separately from other fonts so that they wouldn't get mixed up. This also meant the number of fonts was relatively limited (a typographer had just so much storage space). But this definition doesn't work in the world of desktop publishing and Web page design. In that world, type can be scaled (sized) by very small amounts very easily, thus the number of fonts is potentially much greater. Type no longer has to be stored in cabinets where different typefaces have little chance of getting mixed up; instead, what we think of as type is stored in computers. So the consideration of size in the definition of font no longer works, at least not for desktop publishing and Web page design.

The situation is further confused because software companies have generally referred to "font" when what was meant was "typeface." For example, a company may advertise that a certain package of fonts has hundreds of fonts. Using the traditional definition of font, you could expect to get perhaps a few typefaces, a couple of styles for each, and a wide variety of sizes for all; each style in a particular size would be a font. This is not usually how it works with fonts used in computers. That package of fonts may consist of dozens of typefaces, many of which have various styles and some of which have none. Size would never enter the picture.

Because of how fonts are considered in desktop publishing and Web page design, we think it is probably safe to say that the term font now means the same as typeface. This is the approach we take. By this, we consider TR Italic to be a font, TR Bold to be a font, and so on, with no consideration of the size of type. Similarly, you could say that a type family is a collection of all of the styles of one particular design, with no consideration of type size.

The name of a font often includes some reference to its weight or posture or width, such as TR Bold (a reference to weight), TR Italic (a reference to posture), and Helvetica Narrow (a reference to width). In these cases, you have some idea of what the font looks like. However, not all names of fonts are logical. You can't always be sure by the name that you're getting what you think you are. For example, is Quorum Book heavier than Quorum

Medium? The only way to tell is to look at them side by side. Doing this, you would find they are actually about the same weight. They differ mainly in that Medium is just a little more condensed (narrower).

CSS supports the most common styles. However, it does not yet support all possible styles; for example, expanded, condensed, and outline styles. We decided to limit the selection because the field of font definition is in flux. A **font definition** is all of the information about a font in as much detail as one cares to give, short of giving the actual character shape itself. This condition of flux is due in part to the Web and in part to the persistent incompatibility among the various common platforms – such as Windows PCs, Macintosh, and UNIX – that makes producing the same font on all systems very difficult. The Web connects all these platforms, and thus needs a single, unified way of describing typefaces. These font definitions need to be powerful enough to enable, eventually, a browser to download a font that it doesn't have.

We anticipate the current situation to change, of course, as font definitions become more unified and as they become independent of how the various platforms name fonts. CSS1 is part of the solution because it gives names for many aspects of a font (style, weight, and so on) in a manner that works on the Macintosh as well as on the PC. However, it doesn't yet have names for all aspects of fonts.

Classifying fonts

Nearly every country has one or more national standards for classifying fonts. These standards tend to differ somewhat from each other in the factors that are considered. Here are the factors that we considered when developing CSS1:

- Whether the font has serifs (defined shortly)

- Whether the font is proportional-spaced (variable-width) or monospaced (fixed-width)

- Whether the font was designed to resemble handwriting

- Whether the font was intended primarily for decorative purposes rather than for use in running text and headings

We discuss each of these in the next several subsections.

Whether the font has serifs

A serif is a short cross-stroke that some letters have. A font that has serifs is called serif. A font that has no serifs is called sans-serif (sans is French for "without"). Serifs can differ in appearance, ranging from short feathery strokes to slab-like square strokes. Figure 4.2 shows examples from several serif and sans-serif families. Both sans-serif and serif fonts work well for text and for headings.

(a)   *(b)*

Abc mn 123   Abc mn 123
Abc mn 123   Abc mn 123
Abc mn   Abc mn

serif

Figure 4.2 (a) Serif fonts; (b) sans-serif fonts.

Whether the font is proportional-spaced or monospaced

In a variable-width, or proportional-spaced, font each letter takes up just the amount of space it needs. An "I," being naturally skinny, takes up less space than the naturally fatter "M." In a fixed-width, or monospaced, font each letter takes up the same amount of space regardless of its width. For example, an "I" and an "M" take up the same amount of space even though they are obviously of different widths.

Proportional-spaced fonts may be either serif or sans-serif and may generally be used both for text and headings. Monospaced fonts are often called typewriter type. This is because, for a long time, typewriters could produce only monospaced type. Monospaced fonts may be used for both text and headings; however, it is usually reserved for special usages, such as to mimic the effects of a typewriter and to portray computer code. See Figure 4.3 for examples of (a) proportional-spaced fonts and (b) mono-spaced fonts.

(a)   Aa Bb Ii Mm 0123 !?

The quick brown fox jumps over the lazy dog

Figure 4.3 (a) Proportional-spaced fonts; (b) monospaced fonts.

(b)   Aa Bb Ii Mm 0123 !?

The quick brown fox jumps over the lazy dog

Whether the font resembles handwriting

A font designed to resemble handwriting is called cursive. Cursive characters are usually rounder than serif or sans-serif type, they do not have serifs, and they usually slant to the right. They also may be connected, like handwriting usually is, although this is not necessary. Many italic versions of serif fonts look cursive. They differ from cursive in that a serif font has a roman version, while a cursive form does not. Cursive fonts are often effective when you want to convey a personal touch, since much of it resembles handwriting. Figure 4.4 shows examples of cursive and italic fonts.

This is a cursive font (Lucida Handwriting)

This is a cursive font (Boulevard)

This is a cursive font (Brush Script MT)

This is an italic font (Times)

This is an italic font (Baskerville)

This is an italic font (Century Schoolbook)

(a)   (b)

Figure 4.4 (a) Cursive fonts; (b) italic fonts.

Whether the font is mainly for decorative purposes

Some fonts are seldom used for large amounts of text because their appearance is too unique to be read easily in large amounts. Typically they are reserved for display, and to some extent headline, purposes. Some don't even have full alphabets; they have just capital letters. They may be strangely decorated, irregular in shape, or very fancy. Figure 4.5 shows examples of fantasy font families.

Figure 4.5 Some fantasy font families.

On the basis of these factors, CSS1 classifies fonts into five categories, as follows:

• Sans-serif

• Serif

• Monospaced

• Cursive

• Fantasy

Figure 4.6 shows examples of these five categories.

serif	Ggm	Ggm	Ggm
sans-serif	Ggm	Ggm	Ggm
monospace	Ggm	Ggm	Ggm
cursive	*Ggm*	*Ggm*	*Ggm*
fantasy	**Ggm**	**GGM**	**Ggm**

Figure 4.6 Examples of the five categories of fonts.

The use of font categories is helpful in working with CSS. Each browser has a list of fonts that it can display. Those lists usually differ among browsers. However, all browsers must understand the previous five category names. Hence, when a requested font is not available on a particular browser, and you told the browser which category the font is in, the browser is expected to substitute a font from the same category. Although the resulting translation may be a bit rough, it will usually be a font that looks at least somewhat like the one intended. We talk more about this in the section, "Availability of fonts and font substitution."

Sizing type

Type is typically sized using a unit of measure specific to the printing industry called the point. Related to the point are the em, the ex, and the pica.

A point (abbreviated "pt") is the traditional typographer's unit for specifying the size of type, the spacing between adjacent lines of type, and the thickness of rules, among other things. It is still used a lot, although some countries and some publishers now prefer to use the metric system (specifically, the millimeter – mm – and centimeter – cm). There are three variants of the point:

- The continental European point (aka Didot point = 0.376065 mm)
- The Anglo–Saxon point (aka pica point = 0.351461 mm)
- Another Anglo-Saxon point (defined as 1/72 in. = 0.352778 mm)

CSS uses only the last one. It does so because that point's value is in between the other two values. Also, it conforms to the point size used in PostScript printers, the most common type of printer.

To understand how type is sized, you first need some information about what makes up a letter. The x-height is the size of the body, or main part, of the letter and is approximately equal to the height of the x of the font. The ascender is that part of the lowercase letter that extends above the x-height. The descender is that part of the lowercase letter that extends below the x-height.

Type sits on an imaginary horizontal line called the baseline. For example, notice this line of type you are now reading. All of it is sitting on the baseline.

Figure 4.7 shows the parts of a letter sitting on a baseline.

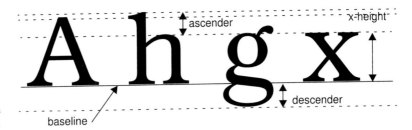

Figure 4.7 The parts of a letter.

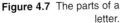

The size of type is usually obtained by measuring from the top of its ascenders to the bottom of its descenders. The measurement is expressed in points. The difference of a point is more noticeable in smaller sizes than in larger sizes. Text type, type used for running text, is generally 14 pt or less. Common sizes are 10 pt and 12 pt. Display type, type used for headings, generally is bigger than 14 pt.

Even though different fonts may be of the same point size, they may appear to be different sizes. This is typically because the x-heights of fonts vary. Some may have a large x-height, while others in comparison have a small x-height. Because type of one size has just so much height it can work with, a large x-height will often be combined with short descenders and ascenders, while a small x-height will be combined with long descenders and ascenders. So the visual impression of size that a font makes is largely due to the font's x-height in combination with the size of its ascenders and descenders. As Figure 4.8 shows, Times Roman has a relatively large x-height and therefore relatively short descenders and ascenders in comparison to Baskerville, which has a relatively small x-height and relatively long descenders and ascenders. Notice that the Times Roman sample appears bigger than the Baskerville sample even though both are the same point size.

Figure 4.8 Because of differences in x-heights, the Times Roman sample (a) looks bigger than the Baskerville sample (b) even though both are the same point size.

Because of the differences in x-heights, The Times Roman sample (a) looks bigger than the Baskerville sample (b), even though both are the same point size.

Because of the differences in x-heights, The Times Roman sample (a) looks bigger than the Baskerville sample (b), even though both are the same point size.

(a)

(b)

This relationship is important because it is one factor that affects the readability of your font on a user's screen. A font with a large x-height is often easier to read in smaller sizes than one with a small x-height. As the font size increases, this difference lessens.

The em unit

The em is a unit of measure that is relative to the font size. In CSS, it is exactly equal to the font size. For example, in a 12 pt font, the em is 12 pt wide, while in a 15 pt font, the em is 15 pt wide. (There are other slightly different definitions of em that we don't go into. We chose for CSS the one that appeared to be the most convenient.)

The em has the advantage of being scalable. That is, it increases or decreases in proportion to some other measure, in this case, the font's point size. The em is traditionally used for the indent of the first line of a paragraph and for indenting the left margin of a list. We recommend you use it also for other measures that should change proportionally if the font size changes, such as the spacing between paragraphs. We talk more about scalability in "Making your document scalable" later in this chapter.

The ex unit

The ex unit also is relative to the font size but in a different way. It is called "ex" because it is defined as the x-height. The em can be set explicitly in CSS1, but the ex is a characteristic of the font, so it cannot be set explicitly. This means you can determine how big it is only by inspecting the font. For example, Times Roman has a relatively large ex (x-height) compared to Baskerville. So even though a 12 pt Times Roman and a 12 pt Baskerville both have an em of 12 pt, their exs will vary because their x-heights vary. Times Roman's will be somewhat larger than Baskerville's. Figure 4.9 illustrates this.

1 em ⌈Abc　xyz⌶ 1 ex　　1 em ⌈Abc　xyz ⌶ 1 ex

　　　　1 em　　　　　　　　　　1 em

The ex is sometimes used in the values for vertical margins and the thickness of horizontal lines. For example, say you specify the thickness of a border as 1 ex. If you then specify Times Roman as the font, the border will be sized proportional to the Times Roman x-height and therefore will be approximately 5 pt thick. If you specify Baskerville, with its smaller x-height, the border's size will be closer to 4 pt.

The pica unit

A pica is 12 points. Six picas equal 1 in. The pica is commonly used, for example, to specify the width of a margin, the width of a line of type, and the size of an indent. It is often used in traditional paper publishing. Its use in Web documents is somewhat limited because it is an absolute unit and therefore does not scale. See also the section below, "Making your document scalable."

AVAILABILITY OF FONTS AND FONT SUBSTITUTION

Today there are thousands of fonts available. Hence, it is unlikely, if not impossible, for every computer to have every font. First, the typical computer hard disk can't hold them all. Second, you probably wouldn't want certain fonts on your computer because their quality is so poor. Third, buying all those fonts could be very expensive. Because of the limited number of fonts on any machine, if you send someone else a file in which you used various fonts, there is always a good chance that that person won't have the same fonts on his or her machine. Hence, the effect you sought by using those fonts will be lost. The same scenario applies to the Web. If you put up a page that contains fonts that few or no browsers have, users of those browsers will not be able to appreciate your handiwork.

What can you do? Well, you could send a copy of the font file along with the text file to whomever will be viewing the file. After all, fonts in computers are just files of information on how to build the font. As files, they should be easily copied, you may think. Technically, yes. A few clicks with the mouse, and you've copied the files. This is not a particularly practical solution when dealing with the Web, however. First, you'd have to somehow get that font file to every browser that users might use to view your page. Then there are legal issues to consider regarding the copying of font files; namely, copyright considerations. When you buy a font or a group of fonts, you typically are buying the right to use them on one machine. You are not usually given the right to let anyone else use them on a different machine. If you did so, you could be violating the copyright laws of various countries. So copying font files is not a viable solution.

Common software, including common browser software, usually will make a best effort at substituting another – default – font for a font it can't handle. Unfortunately, often that best effort isn't so great. The typical substitution font is Courier, Helvetica, or Times Roman, or clones of these such as Courier New, Arial, and Times New Roman. None of these may be anywhere near the font you really want. A related problem is when you use, say, Futura (a PostScript font) and the user's machine has a similar, but not exact, font match, such as Futuri (a TrueType font). How can the two be matched?

The problem of font matching and substitution is why you see so much Times Roman and Helvetica on the Web. Why bother to create fancy type effects that will just get dropped? Eventually, systems may be built into your computer that will automatically select the closest match for a font. Other systems may offer to download the font from somewhere for the duration of the Web session only, both to conserve space on your hard drive and to meet copyright requirements. Such systems may even be able to download only the letters you need so that you may view the page as the designer intended. Someday, we expect, you will be able to attach fonts to the document, with the help of a font definition as we described earlier. Someday. But not today.

As we explained in Chapter 1, this situation is one of the complaints designers have had about the Web. CSS can help with this problem. However, it can't solve it – yet. As solutions become available, we will certainly make them available to designers. Until then, however, you will have to do a little extra work to achieve as close to your desired effect as possible. Much of the rest of this chapter is devoted to telling you how to use CSS to specify font characteristics.

How CSS performs font substitution

In the absence of systems (such as operating systems) that do the font substitution, there is CSS. CSS enables you to specify those fonts you want the browser to try for substitution. Instead of specifying a single font, you specify a font set. A font set is a list of fonts, with the font names separated by commas. A browser checks whether it has the first font listed in the font set. If it does, it uses that font. If it doesn't, it moves to the next font in the list to see if it has that font, and so on until it finds a font that it has. If it doesn't have any of the listed fonts, it will use any font it does have.

Font sets also are helpful in documents that use different alphabets. A document that contains both English and Hebrew will likely require at least two fonts, one for each language. Listing both in the font set allows the browser to choose the right font: if the first font listed doesn't have the right letters, the browser will try the second font, and so on.

Specifying a font set for your document is essential. Most fonts contain only about 200 characters, enough for the letters, digits, punctuation marks, and perhaps some special symbols of the Latin alphabet, the one used, for example, in English, French, and Italian. Others contain many more characters, say a few thousand. With one of these alphabets, you could write, for example, most of Chinese with a single font. If you were to count all the characters in all the world's alphabets, however, you'd arrive at nearly 30 000 characters. No single font has that many characters. Using font sets helps you deal with these limitations.

HOW TO READ PROPERTY DEFINITIONS

Warning: This section and the next two are more difficult than the rest of the chapter. You can safely skip to "CSS FONT PROPERTIES" on page 80, where the explanation of fonts in CSS continues.

A CSS style sheet contains many different properties, such as font-size, margin and color. Each property has its own kind of value. A font-size is expressed as a length, such as 12 pt or 4 mm; a color is a certain color, such as red or blue. This chapter and ones following it define the possible values for each property.

The definitions start with five lines of data (some have only the first four) that summarize the property's values and the contexts in which the property is used. Here is an example of what the five lines look like (this is the summary definition of the font-style property):

Allowed values:	normal I italic I oblique
Initial value:	normal
Applies to:	all elements, except replaced elements
Inherited?:	yes
Percentages?:	N/A

Allowed values

Gives the possible values of the property. You may find one or many values, depending on the definition. If a property offers many possible values or many possible complex combinations of values, you may find square brackets, vertical bars, and other symbols in this area. We discuss what they mean in the next section, "Syntax for complex combinations of values." The example above says that this particular property accepts one of three keywords as value: "normal," "italic" or "oblique." The meaning of the vertical bar (|) is explained below.

Initial value

Gives the initial (default) value of the property. If the property is inherited, this is the value that is given to the first element of the document, which is HTML. Otherwise, it is the value that the property will have if there are no style rules for it in either the user's or the designer's style sheet.

The initial value can be either a specific value for a property or "UA-specific," which means that CSS does not define an initial value. Instead, it leaves that definition to the "UA." UA means *User Agent*, that is, the browser (or other program) that processes CSS on behalf of the user.

Applies to

Tells the kinds of elements to which the property applies. All elements have all properties, but some properties have no effect on some types of elements. For example, font-style has no effect if the element is an image.

Inherited?

Indicates whether the value of the property is inherited from a parent element.

Percentages?

Indicates how percentages should be interpreted, if they occur in the value of the property. We talk more about how percentages work in the following section, "Using percentages as values." If the line reads "N/A" (Not Applicable), this means that the property does not accept percentages as values.

Syntax for complex combinations of values

When the value for a property can be a combination of values, the syntax is defined in a shorthand notation using certain symbols:

- Angle brackets: < and >

- Vertical bars: | and ||

- Regular brackets: [ ]

- Question mark: ?

- Asterisk: *

Also used are keywords. A *keyword* is a word that appears in a value. Keywords must appear literally, without quotes, angle brackets, or other marks. Examples are "italic," "oblique," "thick," "thin," and "medium." The slash and comma also must appear literally when used in a value. (In this book, we add quotation marks around types of values and keywords when they are used in the text to help distinguish them from the text. You do not include these marks when writing your code.)

When the above symbols are used in this shorthand, they have special meanings. All other characters that appear in a value stand for themselves. Note, spaces may be inserted between all values; they also can often be omitted, as long as the result is unambiguous. Below is an explanation of what each symbol means.

Angle brackets < >

The words between the angle brackets < and > specify a type of value. The most common types of values are "length" (*<length>*), "percentage," "color," "number" and "url." We discuss most of these in this chapter. We talked about "url" in Chapter 1, and we deal with "color" in Chapter 8.

More specialized types include some you've already seen: "font-weight," "text-align," "font-style," "text-decoration," and "background." We describe these under the properties to which they apply in Chapters 4–8. For example, if the definition of a property (let's take the <u>color</u> property as an example) includes this line:

Allowed values: *<color>*

This means that the property accepts values of type "color," for example "red." As a result, in the style sheet you might find:

```
H2 { color: red }
```

The "url" value is handled a little differently from others. Instead of simply typing in the URL, you type "url" followed by the actual URL in parentheses, with no space between the two: `url(images/tree.png)`, or `url(http://www.w3.org/pub/WWW)`. Example usage:

```
BODY { background: url(bg/marble.png) }
```

Multiple values

If multiple values must occur in a certain order, they are given as a list. The following example could be used in the definition of a property that always required a color and a number (there is no such property in CSS1, this is just an example):

Allowed values: *<color> <number>*
Example: red 7.5
Example: #CECECE 25

Vertical bars | and ||

A single vertical bar | is used to separate alternative values. For example, in A|B, the | separates A and B; either A or B will be used. You may have any number of alternatives. *One and only one of the alternatives must occur.* In the following examples, exactly one of the listed values must occur:

Allowed values:	normal | italic | oblique
Example:	`normal`
Example usage:	`P { font-style: normal }`

Allowed values:	left | right | center | justify
Example:	`right`
Example usage:	`H1 { text-align: right }`

A double vertical bar || also separates alternative values; for example, A || B. However, the || means that *either A or B or both must occur.* Further, they may occur in any order. In the following example, there may be a color or a URL or both and their order is not important:

Allowed values:	*<url>* || *<color>*
Example:	`red url(logos/logo.png)`
Example:	`url(logos/logo.png) black`
Example:	`#00FF00`
Example:	`url(logos/logo.png)`
Example usage:	`DIV { background: url(wave.jpg) #11E }`

(The "#00FF00" and "#11E" are ways of writing colors, see Chapter 8.) Another example, slightly more complicated, is taken from the definition of the <u>border</u> property, which has a value defined as follows. The types "border-width" and "border-style" are defined in Chapter 6.

Allowed values:	*<border-width>* || *<border-style>* || *<color>*
Example:	`1pt dotted blue`
Example:	`dotted`
Example:	`black 0.5pt`
Example usage:	`P.note { border: red double 2px }`

Curly braces { }

Curly braces { } are used to indicate that the preceding *value may occur at least A and at most B times.* This is written as {*A, B*}. For example, in the following example, a "length" value may occur 1, 2, 3, or 4 times:

Allowed values:	*<length>* {1,4}
Example:	`2em`
Example:	`2em 3em`
Example:	`2em 3em 4em`
Example:	`2em 3em 4em 5em`
Example usage:	`P { margin: 2em 3em 4em 5em }`

In this example, we used the <u>margin</u> property to set a different margin for each of the four sides of a P element. See Chapter 6 for a complete definition of <u>margin</u>.

Question marks ? asterisks * and plus +

Any type or keyword may be followed by one of the modifiers +, * or ?. A plus (+) indicates that the preceding item may be repeated. The item must occur *one or more times*.

Allowed values:	*<percentage>*+
Example:	`0% 50% 50% 11% 0.1%`
Example:	`37.5%`

An asterisk (*) indicates that the preceding item may be repeated, but it may also be omitted. It may occur *zero or more times*.

Allowed values:	*<length>**
Example:	`12pt 12ex 3.5mm 12pt 12pc 3.6mm`
Example:	`1.1in`
Example:	

Note that the last example has no value at all.

A question mark (?) indicates that the preceding type or keyword is *optional*. For example:

Allowed values:	*<url>*? *<color>*
Example:	`url(http://www.w3.org/pub/WWW) black`
Example:	`white`

In this example, the available values are a URL and a color. <url> is followed by a ?, while <color> is not. Hence, the URL may be omitted, but the color may not. The background property has a value similar to that and in that property the presence of both values means that the color is displayed with the image on top of it. If the image pointed to by the URL is unavailable, then just the color will be displayed.

Square brackets [ ]

Square brackets are used to group parts of the definition together. A question mark, asterisk or other special symbol that follows the closing bracket applies to the whole group. The example below shows a group with a vertical bar inside and curly braces on the outside, to indicate that the whole group may be repeated between one and four times:

Allowed values:	[*<length>*	*<percentage>*]{1,4}
Example:	`12pt 10pt 12pt 5pt`
Example:	`10%`
Example:	`10% 10% 1px`
Example usage:	`ADDRESS { padding: 5% 1em }`

In each case, there are between one and four values, and each of the values is either a "length" or a "percentage."

Here is another, more complex example; it is a simplification of the definition of <u>font-family</u>:

Allowed values:	[*<family-name>* ,]* *<generic-family>*
Example:	`helvetica, arial, sans-serif`
Example:	`serif`
Example usage:	`EM { font-family: Helvetica, Arial, sans-serif }`

The group has an asterisk, to indicate that it can occur zero or more times. The group itself consists of a "family-name" and a comma. In the first example, the group occurs twice – there are two families and two commas – while in the second example the group is completely absent; just the "generic-family" appears.

Tying it all together

Following are examples of how to use the syntax shorthand. The first example is of the <u>line-height</u> property:

Allowed values:	normal	*<number>*	*<length>*	*<percentage>*

In this case, there is only one value, but it can be either the keyword "normal" or a number, a length or a percentage. Here are some example style rules that use the property:

```
P.intro { line-height: 14pt }
DIV.warning { line-height: normal }
H1, H2, H3 { line-height: 1.0 }
H4 { line-height: 120% }
```

The second example comes from the underline{text-decoration} property, which we discuss at the end of this chapter. This example uses the single vertical bar, the double vertical bar, and the regular brackets:

Allowed values: none | [underline || overline || line-through || blink]

This is interpreted as follows:

1 The value is either the keyword, "none," or one or more of the keywords in the group within the regular brackets.

2 If you choose "none," you're done. If you choose the bracketed group, you have other choices. The group has four keywords. The double vertical bars indicate that one or more of these must occur. If you choose more than one, the order in which they are used doesn't matter.

There is thus a large number of possible values. Here are some of them:

- underline overline
- overline underline
- none
- underline blink line-through
- blink

Since the order of the keywords doesn't matter for the underline{text-decoration} property, there are really only 15 different decorations you can set with it, but you can write some of them in more than one way.

UNITS OF MEASURE USED FOR VALUES

Many properties accept values that are numbers or a certain number of units of a particular measure. A number that is a value can be a whole number (0, 1, 2, . . .) or a fractional number (0.5, 2.57, 1.04, . . .). It also can be a negative number (–1,–3.14, –0.25, . . .). When the value is a length, a unit of measure is added directly after the number with no space between the number and the unit of measure. All units are two-letter abbreviations, with no period at the end. Examples are `0.5px`, `1.3cm`, and `0.1in`. The following units are available:

- millimeter :   `mm`
- centimeter: `cm` (1 cm = 10 mm)
- inch: `in` (1 in. = 25.4 mm)

- point: pt (72 pt = 1 in.)
- pica: pc (1 pc = 12 pt)
- em: em (1 em = the point size of the particular font)
- ex: ex (the x-height)
- pixel: px

These units fall into three categories:

1 Absolute – mm, cm, in, pt, pc

2 Relative – em, ex

3 Device-dependent – px

Although not units of measure, percentages and keywords are other relative forms of specifying values.

Properties may restrict the numbers and lengths they accept. For example, the font-size property cannot be set to a negative length. All CSS properties that accept lengths also accept the number 0 without a unit of measure. (If a length is 0, it doesn't matter whether it is points or inches.)

An *absolute unit* is a unit of measure that specifies a value that is fixed. For example, 3in, 4mm, and 5pt. Absolute values have limited usefulness because they cannot be scaled. We discuss scaling shortly. If the specified dimensions cannot be supported, the browser will attempt to display the element as closely as possible to your specifications.

A *relative unit* is a unit of measure that specifies a value that is relative to the font size, usually the font size of the element itself. (The only exception is the font-size property, which we discuss later in the chapter, where the value scales to the font size of the element's parent. We give an example of how this works when we discuss that property.) Relative units have the advantage over absolute units in that they scale automatically. When you choose a different font, all properties that were expressed in em or ex don't have to be changed.

A *device-dependent unit* is a unit of measure that depends on the device on which it is used. The pixel is the only device-dependent unit CSS1 uses (see the sidebar). It is relative to the resolution of the "canvas," which is most often the computer's display and sometimes the computer's printer. If the pixel density of the output device, such as a laser printer, is very different from that of the typical computer display, the browser should rescale the pixel values. Because of the low resolution of a computer screen, you can never be sure that 4 pt will be twice as large as 2 pt (one may round to five pixels, the other to three, for example), but 4 px will always be twice the size of 2 px.

Pixels

The term *pixel* is derived from Picture Element. The pixel is the smallest element on a video display screen, such as a computer monitor or a television. It also applies to the output from certain types of printers, such as laser printers. A screen is broken up into thousands of little dots that may appear singly or in groups. A pixel is one of these dots.

Different output media will have differently sized pixels. For example, a typical computer screen will have pixels of between 0.25 mm and 0.35 mm (0.010 in. to 0.013 in.). Pixels are a useful unit of measure because on any medium it is guaranteed that a difference of 1 pixel will actually be visible. On the other hand, the difference between 0.5 pt and 1.0 pt may disappear on a computer screen because the screen is not able to show differences smaller than 1 pixel.

The size of pixels should not vary too much, though. If the resolution of the output device is much higher than that of a typical computer screen, several pixels will be combined to form one "px." For example, a 600 dpi laser printer has six times more pixels per inch than a typical computer monitor does. On the other hand, the paper that it prints is held closer to the eyes than a computer screen, so to get the same perceived effect on screen and on paper, the laser printer could use a square of 4×4 pixels to emulate one screen pixel.

Percentages as values

Many properties that accept a number or a length as a value also accept a percentage, such as 50%, 33.3%, and 100%. Although not a unit of measure, percentages offer similar advantages to those of relative units, that is, they automatically scale.

What the percentage is a percentage of – that is, what it is relative to – depends on the property. Usually, it is a percentage of the value that the property has in the parent element. For example, an H1 with a font size of 80% means the font is 80% of the font size of its parent (often the BODY element). The only exception is the line-height property. (Line height is also known as interline spacing.) We discuss this property in depth in Chapter 6. We also give you an example there.

Keywords as values

Keywords are not units of measure, but some have connotations of being relative. In this case, they have the same advantage of relative units and percentages in that they can be scaled. For example the keywords "bolder" and "lighter," which are for the font-weight property, are clearly relative: they are relative to the font weight of the parent element. The same applies to "larger" and "smaller" for the font-size property. See also the next section, where we discuss relative values and inheritance.

Inheritance with relative values

When a relative value, including a percentage or keyword, is specified, a child element inherits the computed value of its parent, not the relative value.

For example, suppose you wrote this style sheet, which uses a relative unit, the em:

```
BODY {
    font-size: 12pt;
    text-indent: 3em;
    /* 3em is the equivalent of 36pt (3 x 12pt) */
}
H1 {
    font-size: 15pt
}
```

The text-indent property is an inherited property, that is, its children inherit its value. So the H1, as a child of BODY, will inherit BODY's indent. However, the value it inherits will be the actual computed value of BODY's indent, not the indent's relative value. In this example, BODY's indent is 36 pt, the same as for BODY, not 45 pt (3 x 15 pt).

Inheritance works similarly for percentages. When a value is specified as a percentage, a child element inherits the actual computed value, not the percentage of the parent. For example:

```
<STYLE>
    DIV { font-size: 10pt }
    P.intro { font-size: 120% }
</STYLE>
<DIV>
    <P CLASS="intro">He has a feeling of <EM>déja vu.</EM>
</DIV>
```

The font size of the DIV element is set to 10 pt, while that of P.intro, a child of DIV, is set to 120%. This percentage is a percentage of the value that the font-size property has in the parent element, DIV. Hence, P.intro's font size is 12 pt. The EM inside P.intro will inherit that 12 pt value of its parent, not the 120%. If EM were to inherit the 120%, it would have a font size of 14.4 pt instead, that is, 120% of 120% of 10 pt.

MAKING YOUR DOCUMENT SCALABLE

Making your document scalable is important to enabling users on the Web to display it. A document that is scalable can be *re*-scaled to fit different output media. This is particularly important for Web documents because users may want to make your document appear larger or smaller on their screens. If your document is not scalable, they won't be able to do this.

Scalability is achieved by using relative units rather than absolute units. An absolute unit is used usually because it looks good in combination with something else. If any part of the combination changes, the intended effect is lost. For example, suppose you use an absolute unit, the point, to set the font of a P element to 10 pt font and the indent of the first line of the paragraph also to 10 pt, as this style sheet shows:

```
P {
    font-size: 10pt;
    text-indent: 10pt;
}
```

This sets up a relationship between the size of the font and the size of the indent, expressed as a ratio of 1:1. But what if the user then decides to change the font to 14 pt because that size displays better on the user's screen? The indent cannot change to maintain the 1:1 ratio because it is set in an absolute unit. So it will shrink in proportion to the font size. Sometimes this shift in proportions isn't significant, but often it is.

Here's another example using the margin-left property, which we discuss in Chapter 6:

```
BODY { margin-left: 1in }
```

The style sheet sets the left margin of the document to the absolute value of 1 in. If the user later wants to widen your document, the margin will not rescale in proportion to the new, wider displayed document.

You make your document scalable by using relative units: em and ex, as well as percentages and keywords. In the first example, suppose your were to write this style sheet instead:

```
P {
    font-size: 10pt;
    text-indent: 1em
}
```

The font size stays the same, as an absolute unit, the point. But the indent is now a relative unit – 1 em – that is relative to the font's size. Recall that an em is the same size as the font size, so the indent will be 10 pt. If the user then were to increase the font size to 14 pt, the indent would stay 1 em, but increase to 14 pt, thus maintaining the original proportions.

Similarly in the second example, a margin of, say, 10% (meaning 10% of the parent element's width, see Chapter 6), would achieve the equivalent of your original 1-in. margin. But because a relative unit is used, that margin will be able to expand or shrink as the user increases or decreases the browser's window displaying your document.

Keywords also can work as relative "units." For example, consider this style sheet:

```
BODY { font-size: medium }
DIV.note { font-size: larger }
H1 { font-weight: larger; text-decoration: underline }
H2 { font-weight: large }
```

When it is applied to a document like this:

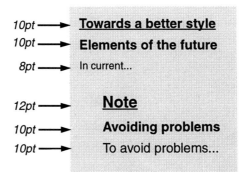

The H1 will always be larger than its surroundings, but the H2 will have the same size everywhere. So, while the H1 inside the DIV is larger than the H1 in the body, the H2 is the same in both cases.

CSS FONT PROPERTIES

CSS has five font properties that you can specify:

- font-family

- font-style

- font-variant

- <u>font-weight</u>

- <u>font-size</u>

A sixth property – <u>font</u> – lets you specify in one action the family, size, style, variant and line height. (We discuss line height in Chapter 6.)

We include two other property definitions that don't specify aspects fonts but that are closely related to fonts:

- <u>Text-decoration</u>: Adds embellishments such as underlining and strike through.

- <u>Text-transform</u>: Changes uppercase letters to lowercase letters and vice versa.

In the following sections, we discuss each property.

THE <u>font-family</u> PROPERTY

The <u>font-family</u> property lets you specify the font set used in your document.

Property name:	<u>font-family</u>
Allowed values:	[*<family-name>* ,]* [*<family-name>*	*<generic-family>*]
Initial value:	UA specific
Applies to:	all elements, except replaced elements
Inherited?:	yes
Percentages?:	N/A

This property accepts two kinds of values:

- family-name

- generic-name

The "family-name" value is the name of a type family. You may give any number of names, separated by commas. For example, a document that is to be displayed in Times might have a style sheet like this:

```
BODY { font-family: Times }
```

A document that is to be displayed in Garamond, if possible, and Times if Garamond is not available would have a style sheet like this:

```
BODY { font-family: Garamond, Times }
```

where Garamond and Times are both family names.

Most properties that have lists of values allow spaces to separate the values. However, a family name can contain spaces; for example, "New Century Schoolbook." To prevent confusion, commas are used to separate values. In addition, you may use quotation marks around family names, as in this example rule:

```
BODY { font-family: "new century schoolbook", serif}
```

The quotation marks are necessary if the name contains other things than just letters, digits, dashes and spaces. For example, if a font were named "Dollar$", the browser could otherwise get confused by the dollar-sign.

The value also can be a generic name – "generic-family" – instead of or in addition to the family name. Use of a generic name is another partial solution to the problem of dealing with unavailable fonts. A browser may not have any of the fonts listed in the value. To make sure that something will be displayed in the worst case of no match, you can add a generic name like "serif" to the list. In this case, if the browser does not have any of the given families, it will have to use any font it has that has serifs. Following are the generic names:

- Serif

- Sans-serif

- Monospace

- Cursive

- Fantasy

Look familiar? They correspond to the font categories we defined earlier in the chapter. Here's an example rule that includes a generic-family name:

```
BODY { font-family: Garamond, Times,
       "New Century Schoolbook", serif }
```

In this example, the browser will first check to see if it has Garamond. If it doesn't, it will check for Times. If it doesn't have Times, it will search all the fonts it has until it finds one in a serif style (if any) that it can use to display the document.

Don't put quotes around the generic name! The generic family is a special keyword for CSS, not a real font family. If you write `font-family: "serif"` the browser will think you really meant a font named "serif."

Design tips using type families

Good document design generally involves the use of just two or three different type families. When there are more, finding ones that look good together can soon become a problem. Unless you are a skilled graphics designer, restricting your creative urges to two or three families will give your document a more professional look. Unless you want a document that looks like a *RaNsom* letter. . .

A typical, time-proven scheme is to have all text in a serif font and the headings in a sans-serif font. Popular choices are Times Roman and Helvetica, respectively, and their clones such as Times New Roman and Arial. You may want to use a monospace font for some parts if you are writing about computer software. For example, code is often set in monospaced, as may be filenames, function names, method names, and the like. The rest of the variation in your document should be created by using different font styles, weights, and sizes within the same two or three families.

People writing multilingual documents, in which they may be using two or more alphabets, know that it is very hard to find two fonts that look well together, let alone three or more. Some alphabets such as Thai and Devanagari (a script from India) have very different ideas about a letter's baseline and therefore of its height and depth. For example, a 12 pt Devanagari font may look too big next to a 12 pt Latin font. But since there are only a very few multilingual fonts, there is often not much choice. Figure 4.10 shows a sample of Bitstream Cyberbit, a family with over 8000 characters. The normal style and weight is free; for italic and bold, you'll have to pay. See URL http://www.bitstream.com/

Figure 4.10 Sample of Bitstream Cyberbit family, which has over 8,000 characters.

abpmnABCD1234&!àá
âÈÉËþýßÆÞðÐşıŞğĞ ™
¾«""" •אתרשבבגנזזחטעŭαβ
πρςΓΔΘΙΛώύí Źήπ Παбв
ИЙЛюэЯЖЮpPŕČţĆŢđ
ąįāĖžżĘŽšŠ

Restraint is the key to good design. There are so many possibilities in CSS, it is easy to overdo the design.

THE <u>font-style</u> PROPERTY

The <u>font-style</u> property lets you specify an oblique or italic style within the current type family.

Property name:	<u>font-style</u>
Allowed values:	normal I italic I oblique
Initial value:	normal
Applies to:	all elements
Inherited?:	yes
Percentages?:	N/A

This property has three values:

- normal (aka roman, regular, or sometimes upright). This is the default.

- italic

- oblique

Italic and oblique styles are similar, but not the same. Sans-serif families usually consider the two to be the same. Both are a variant that looks slanted to the right. For some families, that is indeed how they are produced: by mechanically slanting the roman letters. For others, the italic and roman forms are designed separately.

Serif families usually distinguish between the two. The italic form looks very different from the oblique form. The two differ in the shape of their serifs and often look like completely different letter forms. Oblique refers to a version that looks like slanted roman. Figure 4.11 compares roman and italic/oblique styles.

	(a) Sans-serif (Helvetica)	(b) Serif (Times)
Roman	Aa	Aa
Oblique	*Aa*	*Aa*
Italic	*Aa*	*Aa*

Figure 4.11 (a) Sans-serif roman, oblique, and italic; (b) serif roman, oblique, and italic.

Font designers have used all kinds of names for their fonts without much consistency. Two other names that usually refer to what we described as oblique are *inclined* and *slanted*. Fonts with Oblique, Inclined, or Slanted in their names will usually be labeled "oblique" in a browser's font database and will be selected by the "oblique" value. Other names that usually refer to what we described as italic are *cursive* and *kursiv*. Fonts with Italic, Cursive, or Kursiv in their names will usually be labeled "italic" in a browser's font database and will be selected by the "italic" value.

If a type family has only an oblique style font, that font will be used as the italic as well. However, if you ask for oblique and the family has only an italic variant, you won't get the italic as a substitute for the oblique. Instead, the next family in the list will be tried to see if it has an oblique variant.

Here's are example rules using the font-style property:

```
H1, H2, H3 { font-style: italic }
P { font-style: oblique }
H1 EM { font-style: oblique }
```

THE font-variant PROPERTY

The font-variant property lets you specify a small-caps style within the current font family.

Property name:	font-variant
Allowed values:	normal	small-caps
Initial value:	normal
Applies to:	all elements
Inherited?:	yes
Percentages?:	N/A

This property has two values:

- normal

- small-caps

A small-caps font style, despite its name, does not really consist of small capital letters. It is a differently shaped letter entirely that resembles capital letters. They are a little smaller and have slightly different proportions. Figure 4.12 compares small-caps and regular capital letters. The first line of the figure shows a true small-caps font. The second line shows uppercase letters from a roman font that have been reduced by 80% to simulate small-caps.

AAa BBb CCc

(a) capital – lower case small-caps – lowercase

AAa BBb CCc

(b) capital – reduced capital – lowercase

Notice that the stems of the small caps are the same width as the stems of the lowercase letters around them while the reduced uppercase letters are too thin. The small caps are also wider than the reduced uppercase letters.

The value "normal" selects a font that is not a small-caps font, while "small-caps" selects a small-caps font. In the absence of a small-caps font, the browser may try to create one from an available normal font by scaling down and then stretching some uppercase letters. As a last resort, the browser may even use a normal font's uppercase letters, without reducing them. On the screen in low resolutions, as well as on low-grade printers, the difference between this adaptation and true small-caps will be hard to tell. On paper or a higher-quality output device, where the resolution is normally much higher, the difference will be noticeable.

If there is no small-caps style and the browser hasn't been configured to fake one, it will try the next family in the list of font families to see if it has a small-caps style. Following is an example rule that sets the font-variant property value:

```
H3 { font-variant: small-caps }
```

THE font-weight PROPERTY

The font-weight property specifies the weight of the desired font within the current family.

Property name:	font-weight
Allowed values:	normal	bold	bolder	lighter	100	200	300	400	500	600	700	800	900
Initial value:	normal
Applies to:	all elements
Inherited?:	yes
Percentages?:	N/A

This property has nine levels of weight:

- The nine values "100" to "900" form an ordered sequence, where each number indicates a weight that is at least as dark as it predecessor, 100 being the lightest.

- "normal" is the same as 400.

- "bold" is the same as 700.

- Two of the values – bolder and lighter – select a weight that is relative to the parent's weight. We discuss these more a little later.

The font-weight property is a superset of what is available for most families. Very few families have the equivalent of all nine different weights. Hence, many of the CSS weight values will result in the same font. On the other hand, some families, such as the Adobe's Multiple Master fonts, have an almost unlimited range. For those families, the browser will select nine of the possible weights and assign them to the nine values.

Numerical values are used because descriptive words, other than "normal" and "bold," could be potentially confusing. This is because there is no universal naming system for fonts. For example, a font that you might consider bold could be described, depending on the font, as Roman, Regular, Book, Medium, Semi-Bold, Demi-Bold, or a number of other names. These names are generally meaningful mainly within the family that uses them and are used to differentiate fonts within that family. Outside that family, a name may have a different meaning. So you can't tell the weight of a font from its name. In CSS1, the value "normal" (400) will have the weight that is normal *for the specified font*. What it means for another font may differ.

Figure 4.13 gives examples of the nine weights. These are only samples. Exactly what you will get if you select a value of, say, 300 will depend on the font you are using. But the figure should help you get some idea of how the weights vary.

Following are descriptions of the nine numerical values:

- 100 This is the lightest weight. Not many fonts have weights lighter than 400 ("normal"). Those that do for which the browser would select the 100 value will often have Thin, Light, or Extra-light in their names. But font names are very inconsistent in their descriptions, so we suggest you don't rely on them. Let the browser figure out which weight a font is.

- 200 This is usually not any different from 100. However, it is included because some fonts, such as the Multiple Master fonts, have very many weights.

- 300 This is a little heavier than the 100 and 200.

- 400 This is available for all fonts. It corresponds to the "normal" keyword that the property offers. You can choose either the number or keyword.

- 500 This a little bolder than 400, but not by much. Some fonts have a weight called Medium that is just a little bolder; 500 would result in that weight. If there is no such font, 500 will be the same as 400.

- 600 This is a little bolder than 500. A weight name of Demi-bold or Semi-bold would correspond to the 600 weight.

- 700 This is available for most fonts. It corresponds to the "bold" keyword that the property offers. You can choose either the number or keyword.

- 800 This is heavier than the usual bold. Fonts that have such a weight may have Extra-bold, Black, or Heavy in their names. Other possibilities are Poster and Ultra.

- 900 This is the very heaviest weight available in a font. Fonts with this weight often have rather strange names, such as Nord and Ultima. Or they may have cryptic numbers, often the case with Multiple Master fonts. Most fonts on the typical computer don't go beyond bold (700), so choosing either 800 or 900 will result in the same effect as choosing 700.

100 Font weight sample
200 Font weight sample
300 Font weight sample
400 Font weight sample
500 Font weight sample
600 Font weight sample
700 Font weight sample
800 Font weight sample
900 Font weight sample

Figure 4.13 Numerical values of the font-weight property.

"Bolder" and "lighter" select a weight that is relative to the parent's weight. For example, consider this style sheet:

```
P { font-weight: normal } /* same as 400 */
H1 { font-weight: 700 } /* same as "bold" */
STRONG ( font-weight: bolder }
```

In this example, a STRONG element that appears in either the P or H1 element will be bolder than its parent. However, the weight of STRONG when it appears in the P element may be less than its weight in the H1 element. This is because the parent elements' weights differ. We say "may" in this case because, as mentioned above, the font used also plays a role in how bold type looks.

For more information on how fonts are assigned to the numerical scale for each font, we recommend you check the CSS1 specification.

THE font-size PROPERTY

The font-size property specifies the size of the font.

Property name:	font-size
Allowed values:	*<absolute-size>*	*<relative-size>*	*<length>*	*<percentage>*
Initial value:	medium
Applies to:	all elements
Inherited?:	yes
Percentages?:	relative to parent's font size

This property has four possible types of values:

- absolute size

- relative size

- length

- percentage

The "absolute-size" value

The "absolute-size" value is an index to a table of font sizes that is computed and kept by the browser. These sizes are expressed as keywords, as follows:

- xx-small

- x-small

- small

- medium

- large

- x-large

- xx-large

These sizes form an increasing range. For computer screens, the CSS specification suggests that each of them is up to 1.5 times as large as the previous one. That is, if the "medium" version of a font is 10 pt, the "large" version would be 1.5 times that size, or 15 pt. Different media may use or need different scaling factors. When the browser is computing the table of size values, it takes into account the quality and availability of fonts. Figure 4.14 gives the table's keywords and a representative example of each. The actual size will vary some depending on the font.

xx-small	abcdefghijklmnopqrstuvwxyz
x-small	abcdefghijklmnopqrstuvwxyz
small	abcdefghijklmnopqrstuvwxyz
medium	abcdefghijklmnopqrstuvwxyz
large	abcdefghijklmnopqrstuvwxyz
x-large	abcdefghijklmnopqrstuvwxyz
xx-large	abcdefghijklmnopqrstuv...

Figure 4.14 Comparison of the values of the size table.

Here's an example usage of the "absolute" value of the <u>font-size</u> property:

```
H1 { font-size: xx-small }
```

The "relative-size" value

The "relative-size" value lets you specify the size in a context-dependent manner. Recall from earlier in the chapter that relative values usually are relative to the font size of the element itself. The only exception is the <u>font-size</u> property. For that property, the value scales in relation to the font size of the element's parent.

The value has two keywords: "larger" and "smaller." The keywords are interpreted relative to the table of font sizes mentioned in the previous section and the font size of the element's parent element. Specifying one of these keywords is a safe way to provide for context-dependent size changes. For example, suppose the parent element has a font size of "medium." If you then set the font-size property on the child element to "larger," that is, larger than "medium," the resultant size of the child will be "large," which is the next value in the table of size values. Here's the code for doing this:

```
BODY { font-size: medium }
H2 { font-size: larger }
P { font-size: smaller }
```

BODY has a font size of "medium." H2, as a child element of BODY, will be one size larger than BODY; that is, "large." P will be one size smaller than BODY; that is, "small."

See also Figure 4.14.

The "length" value

The "length" value lets you specify a font size as an absolute value in such units as points, millimeters, centimeters, inches, or other. Here is an example usage:

```
PRE.special { font-size: 14pt }
```

Traditional paper-based design specifies the size of a font in absolute units, most often points, but when working with Web pages, the use of absolute units for specifying sizes is not advised, since, for example, quality differences in screens will make some sizes hard to read and the font size you request may not be available on a particular browser. (Scaling may cause them not to align perfectly with the screen pixels.) It is better to use one of the other values for the property instead.

The "percentage" value

Another context-dependent method for specifying the size is a percentage. Like the relative value, the percentage is relative to the parent's font size, not the child (current) element's font size as in other properties. A percentage value gives an element the size of the parent's font times the percentage. Thus 120% gives a size that is 20% more than the size of the parent element, while 80% gives a size that is 80% of the parent element's size. For example, if the parent element size is 12 pt, a 120% value will result in a size of 14.4 pt, while an 80% value would result in a size of 9.6 pt. Here is an example usage:

```
EM.extra { font-size: 120% }
```

The use of percentages, however, suffers from much the same problem as the use of absolute lengths: You may end up with a size that is not available or that is hard to read on the screen.

Exactly equivalent to a percentage is the em unit. Since the em in this case is the font size of the parent element, a value of 120% is exactly the same as a value of 1.2 em. Using em therefore also suffers from the same problem as percentage.

THE font PROPERTY

The font property enables you to specify, in one action, all the other font properties plus the line height (which we discuss in Chapter 6).

Property name:	font
Value:	[<font-style> || <font-variant> || <font-weight>]?
	<font-size> [/ <line-height>]? <font-family>
Initial value:	see individual properties
Applies to:	all elements
Inherited?:	yes
Percentages?:	allowed on <font-size> and <line-height> only

This property has six parts that correspond to the previously discussed font properties:

- font-style

- font-variant

- font-weight

- font-size

- line-height

- font-family

The line height, also called leading or interline spacing, is the distance between the baseline of one line of type and the baseline of an adjacent line of type. We discuss it in detail in Chapter 6.

The acceptable values of each of these six are those given in the previous property definitions. All six values are set using the font property. The syntax resembles a shorthand common in traditional typography. That shorthand specifies in abbreviated form the size, line spacing, family, style, and weight of the type; for example, 12/14 Times bold italic. Following is an example of how to write a rule that reflects this shorthand:

```
P {
  font: italic bold normal 12pt/14pt bodoni, bembo, serif
}
```

This rule is the same as if you had written a rule for each property:

```
P {
  font-style: italic;
  font-weight: bold;
  font-variant: normal;
  font-size: 12pt;
  line-height: 14pt;
  font-family: bodoni, bembo, serif
}
```

For demonstration purposes, we set every property, including font-variant, which has its initial value of "normal." Specifying initial values is not necessary. The browser will automatically use the initial values for those properties not explicitly set. For example:

```
P { font: italic bold large palatino, serif }
```

sets all properties except font-variant and line-height, whose initial values will be used. In other words, the above is equivalent to:

```
P {
  font-style: italic;
  font-weight: bold;
  font-variant: normal; /* default */
  font-size: large;
  line-height: normal; /* default */
  font-family: palatino, serif
}
```

Here are some more examples:

```
P { font: italic 12pt/14pt bodoni, bembo, serif }
P { font: normal small-caps 120%/120% fantasy }
P { font: x-large/100% "new century schoolbook", serif }
```

In the second example, the font size is set to 120% of the size of the parent element's font and the line height is again 20% larger than that. In the last example all of font-style, font-weight and font-variant are implicitly set to "normal".

THE text-decoration PROPERTY

The text-decoration property does not specify a font property, but still it seems to fit best in this chapter because it affects type. The property is used to add underlining, overlining, strike-out or a blinking effect to the text.

Property name:	text-decoration
Allowed values:	none | [underline || overline || line-through || blink]
Initial value:	none
Applies to:	all elements
Inherited?:	no (but see below)
Percentages?:	N/A

The value is either "none", meaning no decoration, or any combination of these:

- underline – an underline is added below the text

- overline – an overline is added above the text

- line-through – a horizontal line is inserted through the text (aka strike-out)

- blink – the text is made to blink

In many browsers, underlining is used with the A element to mark the status of hyperlinks. The default style sheet for those browsers includes a rule like this:

```
A:link, A:visited, A:active {text-decoration: underline}
```

You cannot specify the exact position and thickness of the decorations. Many fonts come with indications of the preferred thicknesses of an over-line, underline, and line-through and their distances from the baseline, and the browser will try to use those thickness and distance values. Otherwise, it will compute appropriate values based on the size of the font. The color of the lines will be the same as the color of the text.

You have a similar lack of precise control over the blink decoration. The blinking text will be shown in its own colors about half of the time; how it looks the other half is not specified. It may be invisible, or it may show a different color so that the two colors alternate showing. Most browsers will blink at a rate of approximately half a second on and half a second off. Not all browsers can blink, and, of course, blink will have no effect when the document is printed.

The text-decoration property is not inherited. However, a decoration on a parent will *continue* in child elements. The effect of this continuation differs from the effect that would result if we were to give the child element its own decoration. For example, suppose you added this rule to your style sheet:

```
EM { text-decoration: underline }
```

In the following, the underline decoration will affect all of the EM element, even the child element, STRONG:

```
Some <EM>very, <STRONG>very</STRONG> important things</EM>
resulted from this effort.
```

The result would look like this:

Some <u>very, **very** important things</u> resulted from this effort.

The color of the decoration (if any) also will continue across child elements. Thus even if STRONG had had a different color value, its underline would still have been black.

The reason text-decoration is not inherited has to do with possible future additions to this property. For example, suppose the decoration were a fancy border (see Figure 4.15). The EM rule in the style sheet would change from "text-decoration: underline" to, say, "text-decoration: deco-border" (note, this value is not yet available in CSS). The child element is included as part of the decoration of its parent. Figure 4.15(b) shows the effect if the child element were to inherit the fancy box value of its parent. The child would have a fancy border of its own in addition to that of its parent.

Figure 4.15 (a) The decoration continues across the embedded element. (b) the embedded element has its own decoration.

(a)
Some (very, **very** important things) resulted from this effort.

(b)
Some (very, (**very**) important things) resulted from this effort.

THE <u>text-transform</u> PROPERTY

The <u>text-transform</u> property, like the <u>text-decoration</u> property, does not specify a font. However, it too seems to fit best in this chapter because it affects the case of text.

Property name:	<u>text-transform</u>
Allowed values:	capitalize I uppercase I lowercase I none
Initial value:	none
Applies to:	all elements
Inherited?:	yes
Percentages?:	N/A

This property has four values:

- capitalize

- uppercase

- lowercase

- none

"Capitalize" capitalizes The First Letter Of Each Word, To Give An Effect Like This. "Uppercase" converts everything to UPPERCASE LETTERS, LIKE THESE; "lowercase" does the opposite. "None" neutralizes an inherited value. These effects are often used in headings and titles but seldom in running text.

Here are some example usages:

```
H1 { text-transform: uppercase }
H1 { text-transform: capitalize }
```

The rules for converting from uppercase to lowercase and vice versa depend on the language used and on the browser. For example, the French typically remove accents when they write in uppercase so that, for example, téléphone becomes TELEPHONE. The Dutch have a special letter that is usually written "ij," although it is really a single letter. So a word like ijstijd would be capitalized as IJstijd.

The property also is useful for converting acronyms, like NATO, BASIC, PIN, and NASA to small-caps, as in NATO, BASIC, PIN, and NASA. Acronyms in standard uppercase letters look too large. Small-caps look better, so a rule like the following is applied. We use <u>font-variant</u> to change the font to small-caps. But we don't use the uppercase version of small-caps, since our intent is to make the acronym look smaller, as shown earlier in the paragraph. So we use the lowercase version of small-caps (text-transform: lowercase) to achieve the right effect, as shown in Figure 4.16.

```
.acronym {
   text-transform: lowercase;
   font-variant: small-caps }
```

Figure 4.16 Converting acronyms from standard uppercase letters into lower-case small-caps: (a) the acronym in standard upper-case letters; (b) the acronym in uppercase small-caps – this is not the effect we want; (c) the acronym in lowercase small-caps – this is the effect we want

(a)

Success for NASA

```
/* no rules */
```

(b)

Success for NASA

```
.acronym {
   font-variant:
   small-caps }
```

(c)

Success for NASA

```
.acronym {
   font-variant:
   small-caps;
   text-transform:
   lowercase }
```

```
Success for <SPAN CLASS="acronym">NASA</SPAN>
```

There often is confusion about the effects of text-transform's uppercase and font-variant's small-caps. However, as said earlier in the chapter, selecting a small-caps font doesn't change the characters. A text transform, on the other hand, does. font-variant selects a font, but text-transform doesn't. There is still a connection between them, though.

The fact that small-caps relies on the availability of a small-caps font also means that it can fail, if there is no such font available. For example, if the style sheet reads:

```
P {
   font-family: "Zapf Chancery", cursive;
   font-variant: small-caps
}
```

the small-caps will fail, since the Zapf Chancery family doesn't have a small-caps variant. The browser may be able to synthesize one by taking the capitals and reducing them in height, but if it is not able to do that, it will show the P in all capitals instead, exactly as if the rule had read text-transform: uppercase. In other words, uppercase is a fallback strategy for browsers that don't have access to small-caps fonts.

MORE INFORMATION ABOUT FONTS

The Internet offers a lot of information about fonts. A good place to start is the "Fonts FAQ" (Frequently Asked Questions), which is posted to the newsgroup *comp.fonts* regularly and is also available on the Web. The same person that compiled the FAQ, Norm Walsh, also maintains an overview of many fonts that you can get on the Internet or buy on CD. Most of them are accompanied by samples. For both documents, see URL

http://www.ora.com/homepages/comp.fonts/

Another resource is Yahoo's collection of typography links, at URL

http://www.yahoo.com/Arts/Design_Arts/Graphic_Design/Typography/

Chapter 5

Basic structures

When your document displays on the user's screen, what shows up is not your code, of course. Rather it is the browser's interpretation of that code. In the absence of any instructions from you, the browser will display the document using a set of default parameters. You can affect the shape of elements on the screen by using the <u>display</u> property. With this property, you can specify that each element be displayed on the screen as one of the following:

- a block of text – for example, paragraphs and headings are usually (but not always) displayed as a text block;
- as part of a line of text – for example, inline elements such EM and SPAN;
- a list item, a block with a label (number or bullet) on the side – for example, an LI.

In this chapter, we show you how to use the <u>display</u> property to influence the form of elements on the screen. You may be thinking that a heading will always be displayed in a block of its own or that a list item will always be part of a stepped-out list, with list item on top of list item, but this is not the case. By changing the <u>display</u> property, you can create entirely different effects. We give you some examples of how this is done.

We also discuss in this chapter two related properties:

- <u>List-style</u> property (actually a set of four properties), which enables you to create lists with different types of numbers or bullets;
- <u>White-space</u> property, which lets you control how tabs, newlines, and extra white spaces are handled.

THE BOX MODEL

Your HTML document consists of elements inside other elements. For example, an EM can be inside a P, which is inside BODY, which is inside HTML. In earlier chapters, we pictured this as a tree structure, a model that helps when we deal with inheritance. This arrangement also could be visualized as a box model, whereby smaller boxes fit inside increasingly larger boxes, as illustrated in Figure 5.1.

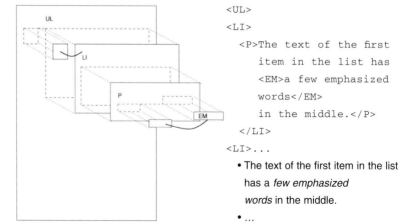

```
<UL>
<LI>
    <P>The text of the first
        item in the list has
        <EM>a few emphasized
        words</EM>
        in the middle.</P>
    </LI>
<LI>...
```

- The text of the first item in the list has a *few emphasized words* in the middle.

- ...

Figure 5.1 The box model.

The box model can be used to depict the structure of an HTML document. The outermost box is HTML. The last box contains either text, such as "a few emphasized words" in Figure 5.1, or nothing, such as an empty element like BR. In between is everything else – BODY, P, H1, DIV, IMG, and so on. A block-level element, like DIV and P, is normally shown as a box on its own. An inline element, like EM and SPAN, may be broken into several small boxes, if it is broken across lines. LI is commonly displayed as a box with a marker called a *label* – a bullet or number – on the side. The size and position of each element is relative to the enclosing box.

THE <u>display</u> PROPERTY

The <u>display</u> property determines whether an element is displayed as a block, inline or list item element.

Property name:	<u>display</u>
Allowed values:	block I inline I list-item I none
Initial value:	according to HTML
Applies to:	all elements
Inherited?:	no
Percentages?:	N/A

This property has four values:

- block

- inline

- list-item

- none

The block value

An element with a "block" value starts on a new line. For example, the start tag <H1> starts a box that contains the H1 element and the end tag </H1> ends the box. Here are some examples that you likely recognize by now:

```
P { display: block }
H1 { display: block }
```

The inline value

An element with an "inline" value does not start and end on a new line. It will be displayed in a box set on the same line as the previous content. The dimensions of the box will depend on the size of the content. If the content is text, it may span several lines and there will be a box of text on each line. Familiar examples are EM, STRONG, and SPAN:

```
EM { display: inline }
STRONG { display: inline }
SPAN { display: inline }
```

All elements have a value for the display property in the browser's default style sheet and that is usually the one you want, so you don't often have to use the display property yourself. But occasionally you may want to make an LI inline, or a SPAN block. Or you may want to set an element back to its normal display type if you cascade off a style sheet that changes the display of the element.

The list-item value

An element with a "list-item" value is displayed as a box with a label. This value usually applies to an LI. A series of LIs with this value forms either an OL or UL list.

The LI may or may not have a label: a bullet or number that appears to the left of the list item. Whether it has a label, and the properties of the label, are set with the list-style property, which we discuss in the following section, "More about lists."

The none value

To hide an element from view completely, you can set <u>display</u> to "none." The element will not be displayed at all. An example would be a document with questions and answers interleaved: first you display the document with the answers hidden and after you've tried to answer the questions you change to a different style sheet which shows the answers. The first style sheet could contain something like this:

```
.answer { display: none }
```

ACHIEVING DIFFERENT EFFECTS

An element needn't be displayed using the value you might assume. You can change the value depending on the effect you want to achieve. An inline element can be "block," a block-level element can be "inline," and a list item can be "inline."

For example, instead of placing LIs in separate blocks below each other with the "list-item" value, you could string them together in a running sentence and separate them by commas or semicolons. You would do this using the value "inline."

Figure 5.2(a) shows a typical UL list. The UL has its LIs set to "list-item." The labels, square bullets, were set via the <u>list-style</u> property discussed in the next section. Here are the rules:

```
LI {
    display: list-item;
    list-style: square
}
```

Figure 5.2 (a) Using "list-item" to format a list; (b) using "inline" to format a list.

```
<UL>
<LI><P>item one,
<LI><P>item two,
<LI><P>item three,
<LI><P>item four.
</UL>
```

- item one,
- item two,
- item three,
- item four.

item one, item two, item three, item four.

(a)   *(b)*

Figure 5.2(b) shows the same list, but now with all items following each other on the line (inline). In this case, the LIs have the value "inline" and there are no labels. Since LIs normally contain Ps, we've set the display for Ps inside LIs as well. Here are the rules:

```
LI { display: inline }
LI P { display: inline }
```

In another example, you can change an IMG that is inline to block. With this <u>display</u> property value:

```
IMG { display: inline }
```

and code like this example within the text:

```
<P>Text of a paragraph that is
interrupted <IMG SRC="http://www.image.file"> by this image.
```

you get the result shown in Figure 5.3(a).

To make the image block-level instead, write this rule:

```
IMG { display: block }
```

to get the effect shown in Figure 5.3(b).

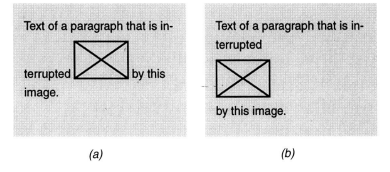

Figure 5.3 (a) An image with the value "inline: (b) an image with the value "block."

(a)　　　　　　　　　*(b)*

MORE ABOUT LISTS – THE LIST-STYLE PROPERTIES

List items may or may not have a label. If they do, the label will be usually a bullet, for example, ●○■, or a series of numbers, for example I, II, III or 1, 2, 3. Lists also may be nested, that is, there can be lists within lists, with each level of list having a different type of number or bullet. Labels may be displayed

- outside the box that encloses the LI, or

- to the left of the first line of the LI inside the box.

The list-style properties specify whether a list-item has a label, what kind of label (if the list item has one), and where it is placed. And, as mentioned earlier in the chapter, a list can be either stepped-out or run-in depending on the display property value you choose. The style and position of labels applies only to list items with the display property value of "list-item."

List-style is the most convenient property to use, since it sets all aspects of the label together, but you can also use list-style-type, list-style-image and list-style-position for setting individual aspects of the label.

THE list-style-type PROPERTY

The list-style-type property sets whether there is a label and, if so, its appearance.

Property name:	list-style-type
Allowed values:	disc I circle I square I decimal I lower-roman I
	upper-roman I lower-alpha I upper-alpha I none
Initial value:	disc
Applies to:	elements with display property value "list-item"
Inherited?:	yes
Percentages?:	N/A

You can set the style of the label by specifying either a keyword or a URL. The property has nine values that are keywords. They can be divided into groups as follows.

To set the label to a predefined symbol:

- disc (●) – this is the default

- circle (○)

- square (■)

To set the label to a number:

- decimal (1, 2, 3, …)

- lower-roman (i, ii, iii, …)

- upper-roman (I, II, III, …)

- lower-alpha (a, b, c, ...)

- upper-alpha (A, B, C, ...)

The ninth keyword, "none," suppresses the label.

However, "none" does not suppress the counting in a numbered list. If the next list item has a visible label, it will be two numbers higher than the item before the invisible label. For example, suppose you have a list of three list items and the value of the second item is set to "none." The first item will be numbered 1 and the last item will be numbered 3, even though there is no visible number 2 next to the second item. It will look like this:

1 Item with list-style-type: decimal

Item with list-style-type: none

3 Item with list-style-type: decimal

Following are several examples of rules that set labels:

```
OL { list-style-type: lower-alpha }
OL { list-style-type: lower-roman }
UL UL { list-style-type: square }
LI.nolabel { list-style-type: none }
UL UL.compact { list-style-type: circle }
```

THE list-style-image PROPERTY

Instead of a number or a predefined symbol, you can also use a (small) image as the label. That is done with the list-style-image property.

Property name:	list-style-image
Allowed values:	*<url>*	none
Initial value:	none
Applies to:	elements with display property value "list-item"
Inherited?:	yes
Percentages?:	N/A

For example:

```
UL { list-style-image:
  url(http://png.com/ellipse.png) }
```

Which might look like this:

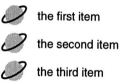 the first item

the second item

the third item

If there is a <u>list-style-image</u> other than none, it will be used as the label, instead of the <u>list-style-type</u>. However, if for some reason the browser is unable to download or display the image, it will use the <u>list-style-type</u> again.

THE <u>list-style-position</u> PROPERTY

The <u>list-style-position</u> property specifies the position of the list item label: inside or outside the list box.

Property name:	<u>list-style-position</u>
Allowed values:	inside	outside
Initial value:	outside
Applies to:	elements with <u>display</u> property value "list-item"
Inherited?:	yes
Percentages?:	N/A

This property has two values:

• inside

• outside – this is the default

"Outside" places the label outside the list-item box aligned with the first line of text. "Inside" places the label inside the list-item box aligned with the first line of the text. The latter value creates a more compact list. Figure 5.4 shows a comparison of the results of the two methods, along with the code that produced the results.

```
UL {
    list-style-position:
    outside }
            ↓
```

- First item of a list with labels on the outside. Note that the label is positioned at the same height as the first line of the text, outside the text block.
- The second item in this list. Notice also how the text aligns under the first word of the first line, not under the label.
- Third item of a list with labels on the outside.

(a)

```
UL {
    list-style-position:
    inside }
            ↓
```

- A list with labels on the inside. The text forms a box and encloses the label as well as the text. The label is the first thing inside that box.
- The second item in this list. Notice how the text aligns under the label, not under the first word of the first line, thus making the list look more compact.
- Third item of a list with labels on the inside.

(b)

Figure 5.4 (a) A list with labels outside the box; (b) a list with labels inside the box.

THE list-style PROPERTY

The list-style property is a shorthand means of setting both the label and its position at the same time. Its values are the legal values of the list-style-type, list-style-image and list-style-position properties. Following are examples:

```
UL { list-style: disc inside }
OL OL { list-style: circle outside }
```

When you set a URL, it's a good idea to also set a keyword so that if the image cannot be displayed, the browser can display the symbol indicated by the keyword; for example:

```
UL.files { list-style: url(images/file.png) square }
```

Using the list-style properties, you can create nested lists with a different numbering style at each level. Suppose you want to create a set of three nested lists. The labels of the first list are "decimal": 1, 2, 3, and so on. The labels of the first nested list are "upper-alpha": A, B, C, and so on. The labels of the second nested list are "upper-roman": I, II, III, and so on. You would write three rules, two of which use contextual selectors:

```
OL { list-style: decimal }
OL OL { list-style: upper-alpha }
OL OL OL { list-style: upper-roman }
```

Here is the resulting list:

1   First item of the first list
2   Second item of the first list
3   Third item of the first list; start of the first nested list
    A   First item of the first nested list
    B   Second item of the first nested list; start of the second nested list
        I   First item of the second nested list
        II   Second item of the second nested list
        III   Third item of the second nested list
    C   Return to the first nested list; back to uppercase letters
4   Back to the first list; back to decimal numbers
5   Fifth and last item of the first list

Note how the numbers align. You cannot change the alignment of the numbers. Nor can you specify the distance between the number and the text. (Perhaps in a future version of CSS you will.) However, you can control the distance of the text from the left margin by using the margin-left property, which we describe in Chapter 6.

THE white-space PROPERTY

The white-space property specifies how tabs, newlines (aka line breaks), and extra white space in an element's content are handled.

Property name:	white-space
Allowed values:	normal I pre I nowrap
Initial value:	normal
Applies to:	block elements
Inherited?:	yes
Percentages?:	N/A

This property has three values:

• normal

• pre

• nowrap

An HTML document may contain unwanted tabs, newlines, and additional spaces. These can be called collectively *white-space characters*. Usually, you'll want those extra white-space characters to be ignored. The browser will do this automatically for you and lay out the text in a way that fits the window. It will throw away any extra white spaces at the beginning and end of a paragraph and *collapse* (combine) all tabs, newlines, and extra white space between words into single white-space characters. In addition, as the window is resized larger or smaller by the user, the browser will reformat the text as needed to fit it in the new window size.

For some elements, you may have specifically formatted the text in such a way that it includes extra white-space characters. You don't want those characters thrown away or collapsed. One way to ensure preformatted text stays formatted is to use the PRE element, which we discussed in Chapter 1.

To ensure an extra white space stays where you put it, you also can use a nonbreaking space, written with the " " entity. For example:

```
<P>There will be   three spaces before the
word "three" no matter what the value of the display prop-
erty is. Also, there will never be a line break before
"three."
```

There will be   three spaces before the word "three" no matter what the value of the display property is. Also, there will never be a line break before "three."

The value "normal" of the <u>white-space</u> property causes all extra white-space characters in the element to be ignored or collapsed. The "pre" value causes all extra white space to be retained and newlines to cause line breaks. It also causes tabs to be converted into spaces according to a certain formula. The tab is replaced by 1–8 spaces so that the last one is at a column that is a multiple of 8. For example, suppose there are 52 characters to the left of the tab. The browser will insert 4 spaces to reach the nearest multiple of 8, that is, 56. So the next character after the tab will end up as the 57th character of the line. This effect is all right when you use a monospaced (fixed-width) type, but it looks strange when used with a proportional-spaced (variable-width) type. Here is how it looks with a monospaced font:

```
These words      have been aligned    with
tabs so that     the letters align    nicely?
```

And this is with a proportional font. The number of spaces inserted is the same, but that doesn't cause the words to be aligned:

If you wonder why tabs are interpreted in this strange way, it has to do with the traditional way tabs are displayed on computer terminals. Apart from word processors, most programs that manipulate text interpreted tabs this way (and many still do). Especially in the first pages on the Web, the PRE element was mostly used for displaying computer code; that's why it made sense to interpret a tab as a jump to the next higher multiple of eight. Real tabs – tabs that you can set to arbitrary positions and that will work with proportional fonts – will be added to CSS later (see Chapter 15).

```
These words    have been aligned    with
tabs so that    the letters align    nicely?
```

The "pre" value also suppresses justification. We discuss justification in Chapter 6.

Figure 5.5 compares the results of the "normal" and "pre" values on an example paragraph of text. Assume the HTML code looked like this:

```
<P>This is a paragraph
with some                random                tabs
            and     lots of        spaces. (It may
    have      been
the result of      some hasty copying and
            pasting.)
```

Figure 5.5 The result of formatting the example paragraph with two values for the white-space property. In (a) with value "normal"; in (b) with value "pre."

```
P { white-space: normal }                    P { white-space: pre }
              ↓                                        ↓
```

This is a paragraph with some random tabs and lots of spaces. (It may have been the result of some hasty copying and pasting.)

```
     This is a paragraph
with some        random  tabs
    and    lots of    spaces. (It may
    have     been
the result of    some hasty
    copying and          pasting.)
```

(a)   *(b)*

The "nowrap" value will collapse extra white space like "normal", but it will not automatically break lines that are too long. Line breaks only occur when there is a <BR> in the text. The example paragraph would be all on one line, too long to show on this page.

Although the value "pre" made the example above look strange, it can be a very useful value in other cases. Here is an example that uses the PRE element and a CLASS attribute to create an element that is specialized for simple poems.

```
<HEAD>
  <TITLE>A poem</TITLE>
  <STYLE TYPE="text/css">
    PRE.poem {
       white-space: pre;
       font-family: sans-serif
    }
  </STYLE>
```

```
</HEAD>
<BODY>
    <H1>A poem</H1>
    <PRE CLASS="poem">
In this little poem
all white space counts
    therefore this line
    and also this
were indented with four spaces
exactly as much
as between this word    and this.</PRE>
</BODY>
```

Here is the result:

A poem

```
In this little poem
all white space counts
    therefore this line
    and also this
were indented with four spaces
exactly as much
as between this word    and this.
```

Chapter 6

Space

Extra space around elements on a page can enhance your presentation and help get your message across to the reader. Along with influencing color (Chapter 8) and fonts (Chapter 4), influencing spacing has been high on the wishlists of Web page designers.

Before CSS, there were three ways to control space in HTML: with elements, images, and tables:

1 *Elements*. Recall that browsers normally throw away white-space characters – newlines, tabs, and extra white spaces (any more than the usual one space between words). However, inside the PRE element, these characters are preserved with their original meanings. (See Chapter 5, the section entitled "The white-space property.") By using PRE designers have used white-space characters to achieve, for example, a very crude, multicolumn layout. Other HTML tags also have been used in unexpected ways. For example, some designers rely on empty P elements to increase vertical spacing and on BLOCKQUOTE to indent paragraphs. Of course, the results are different in different browsers.

2 *Images*. Recall from Chapter 1 that we talked about the use of images as substitutes for text. Text has often been rendered as an image because in this way designers can control every pixel. Also, to make minor spacing adjustments, some designers insert transparent images into the text. For example, they indent a paragraph by placing five 1-pixel images at the beginning of each paragraph. However, using images has a downside: they are not scalable from one screen resolution to another.

3 *Tables*. The use of tables is the most recent and most "advanced" method for controlling space in HTML. Tables offer layout capabilities beyond CSS1. Unlike images, they are scalable from one screen resolution to another. The downside of tables is that the HTML markup is complicated. We talked about the use of tables also in Chapter 1.

Even with CSS1, all these methods have legitimate uses. However, they do not offer the depth of functionality for influencing space in your documents that CSS does. By using CSS, you can greatly expand your control of spacing in and around elements. In this chapter, we first show you how you can change the space *around* block-level elements. (We deal with images in Chapter 7.) For example, you will find out how to vary the margins and the vertical space between elements. Then we show you how to change the space *within* block-level elements, for example, by indenting the first line and by changing the spacing between lines (aka *interline spacing* or *leading*).

SPACE AROUND BLOCK-LEVEL ELEMENTS

In this section, we discuss properties that affect spacing around block-level elements. Recall from Chapter 5 that we talked about the box model. In accordance with that model, a block-level element – such as a paragraph or heading – is drawn inside an imaginary rectangular bounding box that fits tightly around the text, as illustrated in Figure 6.1. (The dashed line is for illustration purposes only and does not show up on the screen.)

A block of text – such as a paragraph – forms a "box", as shown by the dashed line you see around it.

Figure 6.1 A paragraph within a bounding box.

Outside the bounding box are three "belts" that can be manipulated in a style sheet:

- margin
- padding
- border

Figure 6.2 shows how these belts are layered around a paragraph.

In the next three sections, we discuss the properties that let you adjust the margins, padding, and borders of block elements. Then we discuss additional properties that let you fine-tune the spacing of elements:

- width
- height
- float
- clear

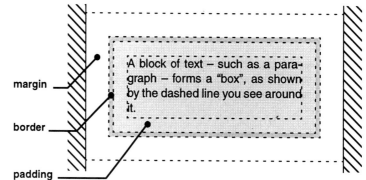

Figure 6.2 Example block-level element with bounding boxes shown by dashed lines (not shown on the screen) and with three belts around each.

MARGINS AND THE MARGIN PROPERTIES

One of the most common ways to specify spacing in your document is to adjust the margins. The margin is the space between the element's bounding box and the bounding box of any adjacent element. There are five margin properties. Four let you set the margins for the left, right, top, and bottom margins individually or in any combination: margin-left, margin-right, margin-top, and margin-bottom.

The fifth one – margin – is a shortcut by which you can set all four margins in one step.

All can be described by the following property definition, except that the "auto" value applies only to the margin-left and margin-right property.

Property name:	margin
Allowed values:	[*<length>*	*<percentage>*	auto] {1,4}
Initial value:	0
Applies to:	all elements
Inherited?:	no
Percentages?:	refer to parent element's width

(Only margin can have between one and four values; the other four can only have a single value.)

The properties have three possible types of value.

• A length – for example 10pt or 2em.

• A percentage – a percentage of the parent element's width; for example, 10% means indent the paragraph by 10 percent of the width of the parent element.

- *auto* – we discuss "auto" in more detail in "The whole story on width computation" later in this chapter.

These properties affect all the content of an element, for example all the lines of a paragraph. (To set the margin for only the first line of a paragraph, see "The text-indent property" later in this chapter.)

Following are example rules for using the margin-left, margin-right, margin-top, and margin-bottom properties. Figure 6.3 shows the results.

Figure 6.3 (a) Initial situation, all margins zero.

The artist is the creator of beautiful things. To reveal art and conceal the artist is art's aim. The critic is he who can translate into another manner or a new material his impression of beautiful things.

(b) Setting the left margin:
`margin-left: 3em`

     The highest as the lowest form of criticism is a mode of autobiography. Those who find ugly meanings in beautiful things are corrupt without being charming. This is a fault.

(c) Setting the right margin:
`margin-right: 25%`

There is no such thing as a moral or an immoral book. Books are well written, or badly written. That is all.

(d) Setting the top margin:
`margin-top: 5pt`

The nineteenth century dislike of realism is the rage of Caliban seeing his own face in a glass.

(e) Setting top and bottom:
`margin-top: 1.2em;`
`margin-bottom: 1.2em`

The nineteenth century dislike of romanticism is the rage of Caliban not seeing his own face in a glass. The moral life of man forms part of the subject-matter of the artist, but the morality of art consists in the perfect use of an imperfect medium.

(f) Setting left and right margins:
`margin-left: 5mm;`
`margin-right: 5mm`

No artist desires to prove anything. Even things that are true can be proved. No artist has ethical sympathies. An ethical sympathy in an artist is an unpardonable mannerism of style. No artist is ever morbid. The artist can express everything.

(g) Negative margins:
`margin-left: 1cm;`
`margin-right: -1cm`

Thought and language are to the artist instruments of an art. Vice and virtue are to the artist materials for an art. From the point of view of form, the type of all the arts is the art of the musician. From the point of view of feeling, the actor's craft is the type. All art is at once surface and symbol. Those who go beneath the surface do so at their peril.

Oscar Wilde

Using the <u>margin</u> property

Using the <u>margin</u> property, you can set all four margins at once. Here's how it works:

- If only one value is set on this property, then that value applies to all four sides.

- If two or three values are set, the missing value(s) are taken from the opposite side(s). For example, suppose the top is set to 3 ems and the right to 2 ems and no values are assigned to the bottom and left. The bottom is opposite the top, so it will take the value of the top: 3 ems. The left margin is opposite the right margin, so it will take the value of the right margin: 2 ems.

If four values are set on this property, the order they are applied is top/right/bottom/left.

Following are examples of rules for using the <u>margin</u> property in these various ways:

```
/* All margins will be 2 em */
BODY { margin: 2em }
/* The top and bottom margins will be 1 em, and the right
and left margins will be 2 em. */
BODY { margin: 1em 2em }
/* The top margin will be 1 em, the right and left margins
will be 2 em, and the bottom margin will be 3 em. */
BODY { margin: 1em 2em 3em }
/* All margins will be set, and values will be applied in
top/right/bottom/left order. */
BODY { margin: 1em 3em 5em 7em }
```

Common usages of the margin properties

One common usage of the margin properties is to indent a paragraph from the left and right margins to set it apart from the rest of the text. An example is a quotation. The following code example shows how you would do this:

```
BLOCKQUOTE { margin-left: 4em; margin-right: 4em }
```

This code would apply to all quotations in the entire document.

Another usage of the margin property is to provide space between paragraphs so as to visually distinguish them from each other. Here's the code for inserting space above and below paragraphs using the margin properties:

```
P { margin-top: 0.5em; margin-below: 0.5em }
```

A comparison of paragraphs before and after the extra space is added is shown in Figure 6.4.

Figure 6.4 Adding space above and below paragraphs to distinguish paragraphs from each other: (a) with zero margins; (b) with 0.5 em top and bottom margins.

The first of three paragraphs without any spacing in between. Both the top and bottom margins are zero.
The second paragraph is directly below the first one.
The third paragraph follows the second, again without any space above it to separate it from the second one.

(a)

The first of three paragraphs with some space in between them. The top and bottom margins are now 0.5em.

The second paragraph is now much better recognizable.

The third paragraph is again separated from the second one.

(b)

Another way to distinguish paragraphs visually is to indent the first line. We explain how to do this later in the chapter when we talk about the <u>text-indent</u> property. When <u>text-indent</u> is used, space above and below paragraphs is usually not necessary. Some people like to do it anyway, but it's a bit of an overkill.

You also can set negative margin values, although some browsers may not be able to handle them. You'll want to be careful when setting negative values; otherwise, unexpected effects may result. Figure 6.5(a) shows an example of a negative margin that is too large – part of the text ends up outside the window. This resulted from input like this, where the text indent was set to −4 em:

```
BODY { margin-left: 2em }
P { text-indent: -4em }
```

Figure 6.5 Using negative indents with the margin properties: (a) a too-large negative indent causes the text to move off the screen; (b) a negative indent used to achieve a specific design effect.

irst few letters of this paragraph end up outside the window, since the text-indent is set too far negative.

(a)

RARE FLOWERS

(b)

Figure 6.5(b) shows a potentially useful negative margin. In this case, we adjust the top margin by –50 px:

```
<STYLE TYPE="text/css">
   BODY { text-align: center }
   H1.overlap { margin-top: -50px }
</STYLE>
<P><IMG SRC="flower.png">
<H1 CLASS="overlap">RARE FLOWERS</H1>
```

We show many other examples of using negative margins in Chapter 9.

While the five margin properties allow flexible spatial control, there is no way to control the appearance of margins. Margins are transparent. This means that whatever is underneath will show through. Figure 6.6 shows a child element with a 3 em margin on all sides whose parent has a patterned background. Notice how the pattern shows through and seems to crowd the child element.

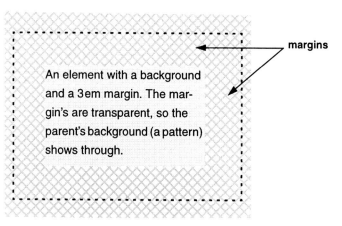

Figure 6.6 An element with a colored background and a 3 em margin. The margins are transparent, so the parent's background shows through.

To control the appearance of the area immediately around an element, you use the padding and border properties, which we discuss in the next two sections.

THE PADDING PROPERTIES

The padding properties describe how much space to insert between an element and its margin, or if there is a border, between an element and its border. (We discuss borders next.) You set the thickness of the padding with one of the padding properties. There are five padding properties. Four let you set the amount of padding to insert on the left, right, top, and bottom individually: padding-left, padding-right, padding-top, and padding-bottom.

The fifth one – <u>padding</u> – is a shortcut by which you can set all four padding values in one step.

All of these properties can be described by the following definition, except that only padding can have up to four values, the others can only have one.

Property name:	<u>padding</u>
Allowed values:	[*<length>* | *<percentage>*] {1,4}
Initial value:	0
Applies to:	all elements
Inherited?:	no
Percentages?:	refer to parent element's width

The properties can have one of two types of values. The default is 0, and the values cannot be negative.

- length

- percentage – a percentage of the parent element's width; for example, 10% means indent the paragraph by 10 percent of the width of the parent element

With these properties, you can add some breathing room around the element. For example, although you can place a border right up against the bounding box of the element, we recommend that you always put some padding between the element and the border; otherwise they will look like they're crowding each other.

The padding automatically takes on the same appearance as the element's background. (You set the background using the <u>background</u> property, which we discuss in Chapter 8.) That is, if the element has a yellow background, the padding will also be yellow.

Figure 6.7 shows an example of the use of padding to put space between an element and its margin.

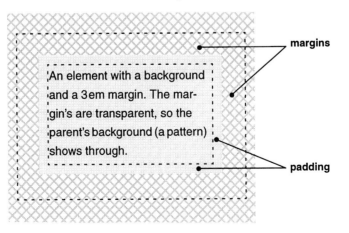

Figure 6.7 An element with padding around it: `padding: 1em.`

Using the <u>padding</u> property

Using the <u>padding</u> property, you can set all four padding lengths at once. Here's how it works:

- If only one value is set on this property, then that value applies to all four sides.

- If two or three values are set, the missing value(s) are taken from the opposite side(s). For example, suppose the top is set to 3 ems and the right to 2 ems and no values are assigned to the bottom and left. The bottom is opposite the top, so it will take the value of the top: 3 ems. The left padding is opposite the right padding, so it will take the value of the right padding: 2 ems.

- If four values are set on this property, the order they are applied is top/right/bottom/left.

Following are examples of code for using the <u>padding</u> property in these various ways:

```
/* All paddings will be 2em. */
BODY { padding: 2em }
/* The top and bottom paddings will be 1 em, and the right
and left margins will be 2 em. */
BODY { padding: 1em 2em }
/* The top padding will be 1 em, the right and left paddings
will be 2 em, and the bottom padding will be 3 em. */
BODY { padding: 1em 2em 3em }
/* All paddings will be set, and values will be applied in
top/right/bottom/left order. */
BODY { padding: 1em 3em 5em 7em }
```

THE BORDER PROPERTIES GROUP

A border is a way of highlighting an element. It is placed between the element's padding and the element's margin. Figure 6.8 shows an example of the use of a border around an element.

Figure 6.8 An element with padding and a border.

There are 12 border properties that form the border properties group and with which you can set the width, color, and style of the border in various combinations. Five properties let you set the width, color, and style at the same time on one or more of the four borders of an element:

- border-left
- border-right
- border-top
- border-bottom
- border

We recommend that generally you use these five. The remaining seven are useful if you need to set only one aspect of a border, that is, only the width, only the color, or only the style. You can set these on one or more borders in any combination of borders:

- border-color
- border-style
- border-left-width
- border-right-width
- border-top-width
- border-bottom-width
- border-width

A border can be applied to any element. When applied to an inline element that contains text that spans more than one line, the browser may render one border per line and possibly omit the edges. For example, this style sheet:

```
EM { border: solid }
```

applied to this text:

... This line contains an <EM>long piece of emphasized text, so long in fact that it is likely to be broken across lines</EM> somewhere in the middle...

will produce this result:

... This line contains a long piece of emphasized text, so long in fact that it is likely to be broken across lines somewhere in the middle...

The border is not closed at the end of the first line to indicate that the border continues on the next line and is not closed at the beginning of the second line to indicate the border is continuing from the previous line. Note that this behavior is browser-specific; that is, the browser doesn't have to do this. With some borders, especially the 3D borders groove, ridge, inset, and outset, closing the border may look better.

The border-color property

The border-color property sets the color of the border. The color may be specified using either one of 16 predefined and named colors or a numbered RGB color. See Chapter 8 for more information about specifying colors.

Property name:	border-color
Allowed values:	<color> {1,4}
Initial value:	taken from the color property of the element
Applies to:	all elements
Inherited?:	no
Percentages?:	N/A

With the border-color property, you set colors on all four borders at once, as follows:

- One value is set: that value applies to all four sides.

- Two values are set: the top and bottom borders are set to the first value, and the right and left borders are set to the second.

- Three values are set: the top border is set to the first value, the right and left borders are set to the second, and the bottom border is set to the third.

- Four values are set: the values are applied in top/right/bottom/left order.

Following are examples of code for using the border-color property in these various ways:

```
BODY { border-color: red }
  /* All borders will be red */
BODY { border-color: red black }
  /* The top and bottom borders will be red, and the left
  and right borders will be black */
BODY { border-color: red black yellow }
  /* The top border will be red, the left and right
  borders will be black, and the bottom border will be
  yellow */
BODY { border-color: red black yellow green }
  /* All colors will be set, and values will be applied in
  top/right/bottom/left order */
```

If no color is specified for the border, the border takes on the color of the element itself. For example, in this case:

```
P {
    color: black;
    background: white;
    border: solid
}
```

the border does not have a color specified, so it will be black, the same as the text of the P element.

The <u>border-style</u> property

The <u>border-style</u> property sets the appearance of the border.

Property name:	<u>border-style</u>
Allowed values:	*<border-style>* {1,4}
Initial value:	none
Applies to:	all elements
Inherited?:	no
Percentages?:	N/A

This property accepts one of nine keywords:

- *none* – no border is drawn, regardless of any border width (see later in this section) that may be set. This is the default.

- *dotted* – a dotted line

- *dashed* – a dashed line

- *solid* – a solid line

- *double* – a double line. The sum of the two lines and the space between them will equal the <u>border-width</u> value.

- *groove* – a 3D groove. The shadow effect is the result of using colors that are a bit darker and a bit lighter than that given by <u>border-color</u> or <u>color</u>.

- *ridge* – a 3D ridge

- *inset* – a 3D inset

- *outset* – a 3D outset

Figure 6.9 shows examples of each type of border style.

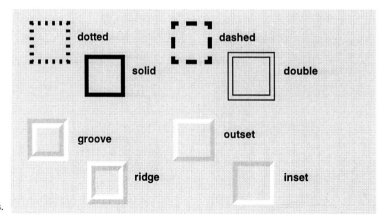

Figure 6.9 Border styles.

With the <u>border-style</u> property, you set the styles of all four borders at once, as follows:

- One value is set: that value applies to all four sides.

- Two values are set: the top and bottom borders are set to the first value, and the right and left borders are set to the second.

- Three values are set: the top border is set to the first value, the right and left borders are set to the second, and the bottom border is set to the third.

- Four values are set: the values are applied in top/right/bottom/left order.

Following are examples of code for using the <u>border-style</u> property in these various ways:

```
BODY { border-style: dotted }
  /* All borders will be dotted. */
BODY { border-style: dashed solid }
  /* The top and bottom borders will be dashed and the left
  and right borders will be solid. */
BODY { border-style: inset solid double }
  /* The top border will be a 3d inset, the left and right
  borders solid, and the bottom border will be a double
  line. */
BODY { border-style: ridge groove dashed dotted }
  /* Styles are applied in top/right/bottom/left order. */
```

The border-width properties

The border-width properties set the widths of the border individually or in any combination. There are five properties:

Four let you set the border width for the left, right, top, and bottom of the element individually: border-left-width, border-right-width, border-top-width, and border-bottom-width.

The fifth one – border-width – is a shortcut by which you can set all four border-widths at once.

All of these properties can be described by the following definition, except that four of the five properties only accept a single value, while border-width accepts up to four values.

Property name:	border-width
Allowed values:	[thin | medium | thick | *<length>* | *<percentage>* | none] {1,4}
Initial value:	medium
Applies to:	all elements
Inherited?:	no
Percentages?:	N/A

These properties have six types of values:

- *thin*

- *medium* – this is the default.

- *thick*

- a length value

- a percentage value

- *none*

When the keywords "thin," "medium" or "thick" are used, the actual width of the border depends on the browser. However, "medium" will be at least as thick as "thin" and "thick" will not be thinner than "medium." The thickness remains constant throughout a document. For example, a "thick" border will be the same thickness throughout the document regardless of any other properties you set. In the following code sample:

```
H1 {
   border-width: thick;
   font-size: 18pt
}
P {
   border-width: thick;
   font-size: 12pt
}
```

the borders will be the same width for both the H1 and the P elements even though the font sizes of the two differ.

Figure 6.10 shows examples of various border width values.

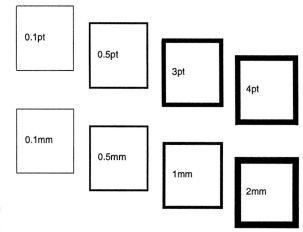

Figure 6.10 Examples of border-width values.

Using the <u>border-width</u> property

Using the <u>border-width</u> property, you can set all four borders at once, as follows:

- One value is set: that value applies to all four sides.

- Two values are set: the top and bottom borders are set to the first value, and the right and left borders are set to the second.

- Three values are set: the top border is set to the first value, the right and left borders are set to the second, and the bottom border is set to the third.

- Four values are set: the values are applied in top/right/bottom/left order.

Following are examples of code for using the <u>border-width</u> property in these various ways:

```
BODY { border-width: 2em }
/* All borders are set the same, to 2em. */
BODY { border-width: 1em 2em }
/* Top and bottom = 1em; right and left = 2em. */
BODY { border-width: 1em 2em 3em }
/* Top = 1em, right = 2em, bottom = 3em, left = 2em. */
BODY { border-width: 1em 3em 5em 7em }
/* All borders are set and are applied in top/right/bot-
tom/left order. */
```

The border properties

The border properties let you set the border width, color and style together on one or more borders. They build on the previously discussed properties and are the properties most commonly used to set border characteristics. Four of them let you set the border width, color, and style for each side of the element individually: border-left, border-right, border-top, and border-bottom. The fifth one – border – is a shortcut by which you can set all four border properties at once.

All of these properties can be described by the following definition:

Property name:	border
Allowed values:	*<border-width>* || *<border-style>* || *<border-color>*
Initial value:	see the individual properties above
Applies to:	all elements
Inherited?:	no
Percentages?:	N/A

These properties accept all the legal values of border-width, border-style and border-color. Omitted values are set to their initial values. For example, this rule

```
P { border: solid red }
```

sets all borders to be solid and red. Because "border-width" is not specified, its default – "medium" – is assumed. Also, the order in which you list the three values doesn't matter. All of the following will produce the same result:

```
border: thin solid red
border: red thin solid
border: solid red thin
```

Following are example rules for using the border-left, border-right, border-top, and border-bottom properties. Figure 6.11 shows the results.

Using the border property

Unlike the margin property and padding property, the border property cannot set different values on the four sides. With border, you can only set all four sides to the same style, color, and width. To set different values on the four sides, you must use one or more of the other border properties.

```
P {
  border-top: solid;
  border-right: solid;
  border-bottom: solid;
  border-left: solid
}
```

```
P {
  border-right: solid;
  border-left: solid
}
```

```
P {
  border-top: solid;
  border-right: solid thick;
  border-bottom: solid;
  border-left: solid thick
}
```

```
P {
  border-top: dashed;
  border-bottom: dashed;
}
```

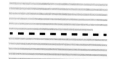

```
P {
  border-top: solid;
  border-right: solid thick;
  border-bottom: solid thick;
}
```

Figure 6.11 Example usages
of the border properties.

```
DIV.warning {
   border: solid red thick;
   padding: 0.5em 1em;
}
```

The style sheet above will put a thick red border around elements of type DIV with CLASS "warning." Between the text and the border there is half an em vertically and one em horizontally.

WORKING WITH THE BORDER PROPERTIES

The properties in the border properties group have overlapping functionality to some extent. Hence, the order in which the rules are specified is important. For example, in this example:

```
BLOCKQUOTE {
   border-color: red;
   border-left: double;
   color: black;
}
```

the border's color will be red, except for the left border ("border-left"), which will be black. This is because the border-left property sets the width, style, *and color* at one time on the left border. Because the color is not explicitly set in that property, the value of the color property is automatically picked up, in this case, black.

COLLAPSING MARGINS

The margins above and below elements are not simply added together to reach a total amount of space between the two elements. If they were, you'd often end up with quite a bit more space between elements than you want. Instead, the browser discards the smaller margin and uses the larger margin to space apart the two elements. This process is called *collapsing margins*. Collapsing margins affects only the top and bottom margins.

For example, suppose a P follows an H1 – a common situation – and that the P has less space above it than the H1 has below it – also common. To be more specific, assume the P has 1 pc (1 pica = 12 pt) space above it and the H1 has 2 pc space below it. The browser will discard the 1 pc space and put only 2 pc space between the two elements; it will not add the two and use the total, 3 pc space.

Collapsing margins ensures that space is consistent between any pair of elements. In another example, a list (UL or OL) normally has more space above it than a P does, but when either follows an H1, designers usually want the same amount of space above both. By the browser's going with the larger H1 margin, this can be accomplished.

The browser reacts similarly when two elements begin or end at the same time. For example, at the end of a list there are usually three elements that end at the same time: the last list item, the last paragraph within that item, and the list itself. There is one element, P, that begins at the same time as the other three are ending. Here is an example:

```
<UL>
   <LI><P>The first item in a list.
        <P>A paragraph below the first item of
        the list.
   <LI><P>The second, and last, item in the list.
        <P>The last paragraph of the last item of
        the list.
</UL>
<P>Start of next paragraph. This paragraph is not part of
a list.
```

The space between the *last line of the list* and the *first line of the paragraph that follows it* will be the maximum of four margins:

• The bottom margin of the last P in the LI

• The bottom margin of the last LI

• The bottom of the UL

• The top margin of the P that follows the list

Normally, the UL is the largest, so that is the amount of margin that will be placed between the end of the list and the beginning of the next paragraph. Figure 6.12 illustrates this situation using these rules:

```
P { margin-bottom: 0em }
LI { margin-bottom: 0.6em }
UL { margin-bottom: 1.2em }
P { margin-top: 0em }
```

However, there's a twist to this collapsing of margins: Margins collapse only if they touch each other. In the previous example, we assumed there was no padding or border. Hence, the margins touch. However, if either or both of

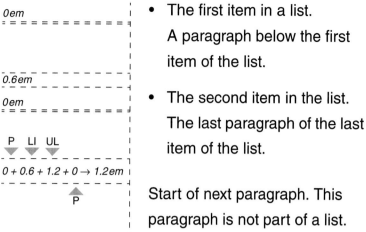

- The first item in a list.
  A paragraph below the first item of the list.

- The second item in the list.
  The last paragraph of the last item of the list.

Start of next paragraph. This paragraph is not part of a list.

Figure 6.12 A demonstration of collapsing margins.

the UL or the LI has a nonzero padding or a border, the margins will no longer touch. Hence, they no longer collapse, since there is something – padding or border – that separates them.

For example, a style sheet like this:

```
P { padding-top: 5px; padding-bottom: 5px }
```

will keep any two paragraphs 10 px apart (possibly more if there are other paddings and margins to consider).

THE <u>width</u> PROPERTY

The <u>width</u> property sets the width of the element. It is seldom used with block-level elements (but see the TSDesign case study in Chapter 10 for an example). In fact, its use with such elements poses some complications. This property is most useful with replaced elements, such as IMG (see Chapter 7).

Property name:	<u>width</u>
Allowed values:	*<length>*	*<percentage>*	auto
Initial value:	auto
Applies to:	block-level and replaced elements
Inherited?:	no
Percentages?:	refer to parent element's width

This property has three types of values:

- length

- percentage – a percentage of the width of the parent; for example, 80% means the element is 20% narrower than the parent element

- *auto* – this is the default

By default, width has the value "auto." Usually, you won't set the width of a block-level element explicitly; you'll set only the margins, padding, and border. Exceptions are possibly the HTML element and tables or table columns. The actual width of the element is what is left after subtracting the margin, padding, and border from the *parent's available width*, called the *inherited width*. We discuss in detail how to work with the width property in the next section, "The whole story about width computation."

THE height PROPERTY

The height property sets the height of the element. As with the width property, the height property is seldom used with block-level elements and its use in those cases poses some complications. This property is used most often with images (see Chapter 7).

Property name:	height
Allowed values:	*<length>*	auto
Initial value:	auto
Applies to:	block-level and replaced elements
Inherited?:	no
Percentages?:	N/A

This property has two values:

- a length

- *auto* – this is the default

Usually, you won't set the height of a block element explicitly; you'll set only the margins and padding. By default, the height has the value "auto." The height is determined simply by how much room is needed to display the number of lines in the element.

Explicitly setting the height is even rarer than specifying the width. If you do and the text needs more space to display than you have allotted, a scrollbar or similar device may be introduced into the element by the browser so that the user can get to the text that is out of sight. If the height is more than that needed by the text in the element, the extra space is treated as padding.

THE float PROPERTY

The float property allows you to place an element at the left or right edge of the parent element.

Property name:	float
Allowed values:	left | right | none
Initial value:	none
Applies to:	all
Inherited?:	no
Percentages?:	N/A

A value of "left" causes the element to be moved (to "float") to the left edge of its parent until it encounters any margin, padding, or border of another block-level element. "Right" causes the same action on the opposite side. "None" causes the element to be displayed where it appears in the text.

The "left" and "right" values of the property, in effect, take the element out of the normal flow of elements. The element is then treated as a block-level element regardless of what display property setting it has. The text that follows the element continues in the main flow and wraps around the floating element on the opposite side. If there is no room for the element to float at the specified edge, it will move down to the nearest spot in which it can fit.

This property is used most often for inline IMG elements, which are treated as block-level elements for purposes of this property. For example,

```
IMG.icon {
  float: left;
  margin-left: 0;
}
```

will place each IMG element of the class "icon" along the left side of the image's parent and flush against the parent's left edge.

With this rule:

```
IMG.icon {
  float: right;
  margin-right: 0;
}
```

those same IMG elements will be placed along the right of the parent, flush against the parent's right edge.

Typically, all of the floating element's margins, padding, and borders are honored; that is, margins are not collapsed with the margins of adjacent elements. There are 2 cases in which a floating element can overlap with the margin, border, and padding of another element:

- When the floating element has a negative margin. Negative margins are honored as they are on other block-level elements. See Figure 6.13(a).

- When the floating element is wider or higher than its parent. See Figure 6.13(b).

Figure 6.13 There are two cases when a floating element can overlap another element's margin, border, and padding: (a) the floating element has a negative margin; (b) the floating element is wider than its parent.

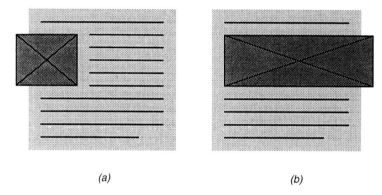

(a)   *(b)*

THE <u>clear</u> PROPERTY

The <u>clear</u> property works with the <u>float</u> property. It specifies whether an element allows floating elements at its side; that is, more specifically, it lists the sides on which floating elements are not accepted.

Property name:	<u>clear</u>
Allowed values:	none	left	right	both
Initial value:	none
Applies to:	all elements
Inherited?:	no
Percentages?:	N/A

This property has four values:

- *none* – this is the default

- *left*

- *right*

- *both*

"None" means the element allows floating elements on both of its sides. "Left" and "right" mean the element does not allow floating elements on its left side and right side, respectively. "Both" means the element doesn't want floating elements on either of its sides.

This property enables you to control text wrapping as a result of setting the <u>float</u> property. Commonly, you want text to wrap around a floating element. However, there likely are cases when you don't want this to happen. For example, if you are starting a new section, you may want to ensure that the heading of that section doesn't occur next to an image that belongs in the previous section. You can set the <u>clear</u> property on the heading so that it doesn't allow floating elements at its sides (value "both"). Instead, the heading will move down until it is free of the floating element of the previous section. Figure 6.14(a) shows what would happen if you did not set <u>clear</u>, while Figure 6.14(b) shows the result when you do. Here is the code that you would write to achieve the latter effect:

```
/* Make all images float left: */
IMG { float: left }
/* H2 headings must not be next to images: */
H2 { clear: both }
```

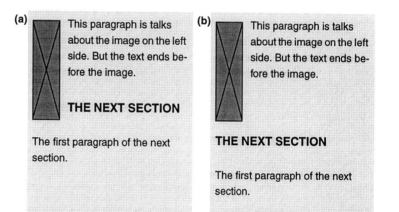

Figure 6.14 (a) With <u>clear</u> not set (the default "none" is assumed), the heading of one section is next to an image in the previous section; (b) with <u>clear</u> set to "both," the heading moves down until it is free of the image.

The <u>clear</u> property also can be used on floating elements. For example, this style sheet:

```
IMG {
  float: right;
  clear: right;
}
```

will ensure that an image floats to the right edge of its parent *and* that it won't be placed next to another floating element that may already be on the right edge. It will instead move down until it finds a clear spot in which it can fit. Figure 6.15 shows how this works.

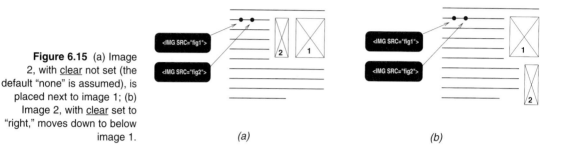

Figure 6.15 (a) Image 2, with <u>clear</u> not set (the default "none" is assumed), is placed next to image 1; (b) Image 2, with <u>clear</u> set to "right," moves down to below image 1.

For more examples of <u>float</u> and <u>clear</u>, see Chapter 7.

THE WHOLE STORY ON WIDTH COMPUTATION

Warning: This section is quite technical. It is not necessary reading to be able to use the <u>width</u> property.

We explained the normal uses of the various margin, padding, and border properties earlier in this chapter as they relate to block-level elements. In Chapter 7 we explain how they work with replaced elements such as IMG. In this section, we summarize all this information. We also explain some of the usual cases you may run into.

The horizontal position and width of a nonfloating, block-level element is determined by seven properties:

- <u>margin-left</u>
- <u>border-left</u>
- <u>padding-left</u>
- <u>width</u>
- <u>padding-right</u>
- <u>border-right</u>
- <u>margin-right</u>

For any child element, the values of these seven properties must always total the width of the parent element – the *inherited width*. This width is always known and cannot be changed from within. An element's width is computed according to this formula:

<u>margin-left</u> + <u>border-left</u> + <u>padding-left</u> + <u>width</u> + <u>padding-right</u> + <u>border-right</u> + <u>margin-right</u> = width of parent

Figure 6.16 shows a diagram of how the width is derived.

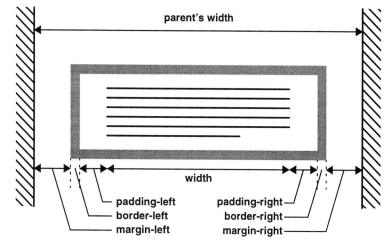

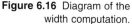

Figure 6.16 Diagram of the width computation.

When specific values are used, adjustments may need to be made to one or more values to ensure the total width does not exceed the inherited width. To simplify making these adjustments, CSS1 provides that the border and padding values are never adjusted. Only the <u>width</u>, <u>margin-left</u>, and <u>margin-right</u> values can be adjusted. That is, only they may be "auto." However, the meaning of "auto" as it relates to these properties depends on the type of element.

For replaced elements (images, objects), the <u>width</u> is automatically set to the *intrinsic width*. An image is assumed to have a preferred or built-in size as determined by its artist or designer. Although the image may be scaled larger or smaller, it still has this preferred size. This is its "intrinsic size." Any other value means the element is scaled. See Chapter 7.

For normal (non-replaced) elements, the meaning of "auto" depends on whether the element floats, and if not, on whether it is "block" or "inline": for floating elements, a width of "auto" always means 0, so it is not very useful; for inline elements the <u>width</u> property is ignored altogether; for block (and list-item) elements, the width will be as wide as the current margins allow.

For inline elements and for floating elements, a value of "auto" on <u>margin-left</u> or <u>margin-right</u> means that margin is 0.

A margin with value "auto" in a block element, on the other hand, means that margin should be as large as possible.

Table 6.1 summarizes the meaning of "auto" for <u>width</u>, <u>margin-left</u> and <u>margin-right</u>.

	inline elements		block elements		floating elements	
	replaced	**non-replaced**	**replaced**	**non-replaced**	**replaced**	**non-replaced**
<u>width</u>	intrinsic width	N/A	intrinsic width	maximize*	intrinsic width	0
margin-left, margin-right	0	0	maximize*	maximize*	0	0

* see explanation in text

Table 6.1 The meaning of "auto."

What gets changed when depends on the interaction of "auto" and specified values. These are the possibilities:

1 None of the three values is "auto."

2 Exactly one of the three values has the value "auto."

3 Two or three of the values have the value "auto."

Case 1 – no value is "auto"

When none of <u>width</u>, <u>margin-left</u> or <u>margin-right</u> is set to "auto," the right margin is ignored and treated as if it had been set to "auto," that is, it is the value calculated automatically, using the previous formula.

For example, if there is a P inside a BODY and the style sheet reads:

```
BODY {
    width: 30em }
P {
    width: 25em;
    margin-left: 3em;
    margin-right: 3em }
```

the P will be 25 em wide and have a 3 em margin on the left, but the right margin will be ignored and will be calculated as 30 – 25 – 3 = 2 em (assuming there are no paddings and borders set elsewhere).

Case 2 – one value is "auto"

When only one value is set to "auto," that value is the one calculated automatically, using the previous formula. That is, that value will be maximized – made as large as possible.

The previous example modified a little:

```
BODY {
  width: 30em }
P {
  width: 25em;
  margin-left: auto;
  margin-right: 3em }
```

Now the right margin will indeed be 3 em and the left margin will be calculated (2 em).

Case 3 – two or three of the three values are "auto"

There are two possible cases: one case is where width is "auto," and one where width has some other value. First, if width is "auto," the width value is the one that is calculated, using the formula given earlier. That is, the width will be maximized, after consideration of the size of the margins. Any margins set to "auto" will become 0. Here is an example:

```
<STYLE TYPE="text/css">
  DIV {
    width: 12cm }
  P {
    width: auto;
    margin-left: 5cm;
    margin-right: 2cm;
  }
</STYLE>

<DIV>
<P>This paragraph is inside a DIV that is exactly 12 cm
wide. The paragraph itself has a 5 cm margin on its left
and 2 cm margin on its right. No padding or border has
been specified, so we assume there aren't any.
</DIV>
```

In this example, the parent of the P element, DIV, has a width of 12 cm, so we use the previous formula as follows, filling in the blanks with the values of the various widths:

margin-left + border-left + padding-left + width + padding-right + border-right + margin-right = width of parent

5 cm + 0 cm + 0 cm + "auto" + 0 cm + 0 cm + 2 cm = 12 cm

Since 5 + 2 = 7 and 12 − 7 = 5, the numerical width of the P element is 5 cm.

The second possible case is if <u>width</u> is not "auto" but both <u>margin-left</u> and <u>margin-right</u> are. In this case, the two margins will each get half of the available space, thereby causing the element to be centered in its parent. Here is an example:

```
<STYLE>
  BODY {
    width: 10cm }
  P {
    width: 6cm;
    margin: auto; }
</STYLE>
<BODY>
<P>This paragraph is 6 cm wide and will be centered inside
its parent (BODY, in this case).
</BODY>
```

Completing the width formula:

<u>margin-left</u> + <u>border-left</u> + <u>padding-left</u> + <u>width</u> + <u>padding-right</u> + <u>border-right</u> + <u>margin-right</u> = width of parent

"auto" + 0 cm + 0 cm + 6 cm + 0 cm + 0 cm + "auto" = 10 cm

gives us 2 cm of space each for the left and right margins; that is, 10 − 6 = 4 cm total to be divided equally between the two margins.

SPACE INSIDE BLOCK-LEVEL ELEMENTS

You can affect the space inside a block-level element by changing the amount of space between letters, words, lines, and/or paragraphs as well as by varying the alignment of text. Six properties help you influence space inside paragraphs:

- <u>text-align</u>
- <u>text-indent</u>
- <u>line-height</u>
- <u>word-spacing</u>
- <u>letter-spacing</u>
- <u>vertical-align</u>

These plus the font properties discussed in Chapter 4 give you a significant amount of control over your document's appearance. Even then, future versions of CSS will likely include even more properties to allow you to fine-tune your documents.

Among these six properties, text-align, text-indent, and line-height are used most often because they are the primary means of expressing the character of the text and of safeguarding readability. The other three – word-spacing, letter-spacing and vertical-align – are usually used only to achieve special, localized effects. In the following sections, we discuss each of the six properties.

THE text-align PROPERTY

The text-align property sets the way the lines are adjusted horizontally between the left and right margins of the element.

Property name:	text-align
Allowed values:	left I right I center I justify
Initial value:	UA-specific
Applies to:	block-level elements
Inherited?:	yes
Percentages?:	N/A

This property has four values:

- *left* – lines are aligned at the left margin; the right margin is ragged (uneven). Sometimes called *left-justified*.

- *right* – lines are aligned at the right margin; the left margin is ragged. Sometimes called *right-justified*.

- *center* – lines are individually centered in the middle of the box; both the right and left margins are ragged.

- *justified* – lines are aligned on both the left and right margins; text is spread out between the margins as evenly as possible. Sometimes called *fully justified*.

Figure 6.17 shows examples of each type of alignment.

Figure 6.17 The four types of horizontal alignment: `text-align: ....`   left   center   right   justifed

Here's an example rule for changing the alignment of a P element from the default to "center":

```
P { text-align: center }
```

The text-align property is inherited, so you can set the alignment of the whole document by using the BODY element as follows, where we change the alignment from the default to "justify":

```
BODY { text-align: justify }
```

Note, alignment of text is relative to the width of the element, not the width of the canvas. For example, the text of an element with text-align set to "center" will be centered between the margins of the element, regardless of where the element is positioned on the canvas. Hence, the text may not appear centered on the canvas.

Right aligning text

The most common alignments are left, justified, and centered. Right-aligning text – placing it against the right margin – is seldom done in languages that are written and read from left to right, such as English – at least not for long stretches of text. It's too difficult to read in large amounts. Its use is usually reserved for titles, cells in a table, and special type design effects. Examples of these three are shown in Figure 6.18(a)–(c).

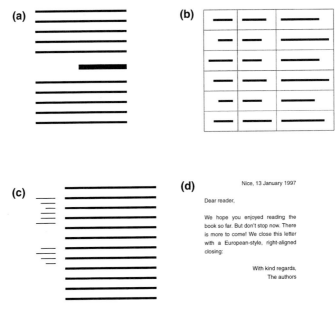

Figure 6.18 Examples of right-aligned text: (a) a right-aligned heading; (b) a table with right-aligned text in the first column; (c) right-aligned "side-heads"; (d) a letter with a right-aligned date and signature.

Another use for "right" is the signature below a letter. The traditional layout of letters in many languages is for a signature to be aligned against the right margin. Here's how you would code this. Figure 6.18(d) shows the result.

```
<STYLE TYPE="text/css">
   P.date, P.closing, P.signature {
     text-align: right }
   P.opening, P.closing { margin-top: 1.2em }
   P.opening { margin-bottom: 1.2em }
</STYLE>
<BODY>
<P CLASS="date">Nice, 13 January 1997
<P CLASS="opening">Dear reader,
<P>We hope you enjoyed reading the book so far. But don't
stop now. There is more to come! We close this letter with
a European-style, right-aligned closing:
<P CLASS="closing">With kind regards,<BR>
The authors.
</BODY>
```

Justifying text

Justified text is text that is spaced out from left to right margin so that the texts fills the space between the margins. For the value "justify," CSS1 does not specify how text is stretched, or spaced out, as part of distributing it between the margins. Some implementations will stretch only the spaces between the words. Others may stretch the spaces between the letters as well. Yet others may occasionally shrink spaces instead (and thus put more words on a line). Which method is used depends on the browser as well as on the language in which the text is displayed.

In languages with long words, you may want to avoid justifying lines, unless the lines are relatively long. Long words often will be stretched out to fill the line, sometimes resulting in too much space between the letters. You may have noticed this effect in newspapers, in which full justification can create rivers of white running downward through a column of type. One alternative is to use hyphens. CSS1 doesn't do anything with hyphenation – it doesn't turn it on or off. But then, most browsers don't do automatic hyphenation anyway. Future versions of CSS will allow you to control hyphenation. At that time, justifying such languages would be feasible, although perhaps at the trade-off of splitting words. In the meantime, you can manually insert hyphens in order to achieve a better-looking justified appearance.

Not all browsers support "justify." Those that don't will usually supply a replacement, typically "left" in Western languages.

HTML has a special entity for manually hyphenating words: ­ ("soft hyphen"). When you insert it in the middle of a word, like this: hy­phen­ate a browser may break the word at the position of the entity. A browser that cannot break words should ignore the entity. Unfortunately, at the time of this writing (January 1997), all the major browsers had a bug that caused them to insert a hyphen for every ­ without breaking the word.

THE text-indent PROPERTY

The text-indent property specifies the indentation of the first line of a paragraph. In a left-to-right language such as English or French, the indentation is added to the left of the first line. In a right-to-left language such as Arabic or Hebrew, it is added to the right of the first line. (CSS1 cannot deal with vertical languages, such as Chinese.)

Property name:	text-indent
Allowed values:	*<length>*	*<percentage>*
Initial value:	0
Applies to:	block-level elements
Inherited?:	yes
Percentages?:	refer to parent element's width

This property has two values:

- a length

- a percentage – a percentage of the width of the paragraph; for example, 10% means indent the first line by 10 percent of the width of the paragraph

Text-indent is an inherited property, but only the computed value is passed on. That is, the amount of indentation is computed once for the parent element and *the result* is inherited by all of its children. The value is not computed again in its child elements even if they have a different font size. For example, if the current font size of the parent element is 10 pt and the amount of indentation is set to 2 em, child elements will inherit an indent of 20 pt, no matter their own font size (10 pt × 2 em = 20 pt). Negative values are allowed, although some browsers may not be able to display them.

Using the text-indent property

Indenting first lines is more common in fiction than in technical texts. Some people consider it old-fashioned, although a very large indent may look quite modern again. At the same time, a too-large indent can hamper readability.

Perhaps the best and most common reason for choosing to indent the first line is that it is a good way to indicate the start of a paragraph. That's why we used it in this book. Also, when used in this way, you can save space within the document. Without the indent, paragraphs must have extra space between them so that one paragraph can be distinguished from another. This adds to the length of the document. See figure 6.19(b), which was achieved using this rule:

```
P { text-indent: 1em }
```

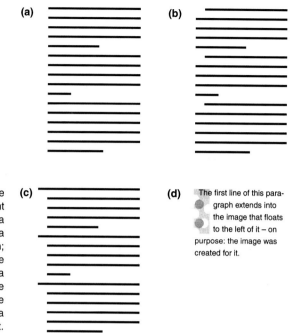

Figure 6.19 Using the text-indent property to indent paragraphs: (a) a nonindented paragraph; (b) a regular indented paragraph; (c) a well-done negative indented paragraph; (d) a negative indent with a large indent that was done intentionally to achieve a particular design effect.

Interesting effects can be achieved with *negative* indents. A negative indent causes the first line to stick out, outside the bounding box of the paragraph. Some newspapers use this effect to distinguish commentaries from news articles, or in order to differentiate themselves from the competition. Figure 6.19(c) shows a well-done negative indent, achieved using this rule:

```
P { text-indent: -1em }
```

However, you have to be careful when using negative indents; otherwise, unexpected effects may result. Figure 6.5 earlier in this chapter showed an example of a negative indent that is too large – the first words end up outside the window. This resulted from input like this:

```
BODY { margin-left: 2em }
P { text-indent: -4em }
```

Similarly, an effect that may actually be desirable from a design perspective is when the first word overlaps something that is to the left of the text, such as a floating image. Code like this could produce that result:

```
P { text-indent: -4em }
IMG { float: left; margin: 2em }
```

This effect is shown in Figure 6.19(d).

Text-indent indents only the first line of any element. However, some elements have a first line that is actually inside another element. In this case, text-indent may not be able to indent the first line. Here's an example of how this works. A style sheet with these specifications

```
DIV { text-indent: 2em }
P { text-indent: 0em }
```

and a document with this text:

```
<DIV><P>A nonindented paragraph...</DIV>
```

will result in the paragraph's not having any indentation. This is because the first line of DIV occurs inside another element, P, that has a text-indent of 0. The 0 em value of P overrides the 2 em value of DIV.

On the other hand, an element may appear to consist of several paragraphs, but it actually is a paragraph that is interrupted by another element. It will still have only one first line and hence only that first line will be indented by text-indent. For example, suppose you were to specify this style sheet:

```
P { text-indent: 2em }
```

and interrupt a paragraph element with a BR element written like this:

```
<P>This is a paragraph
broken by another
element.<BR><BR> This line
is not indented.
```

A paragraph broken by another element.

This line is not indented.

THE line-height PROPERTY

The line-height property specifies how far apart the lines in a paragraph are. Or more precisely, it specifies the *minimum* distance between the baselines of the adjacent lines.

Property name:	line-height
Allowed values:	*<number>*	*<length>*	*<percentage>*
Initial value:	UA-specific
Applies to:	all elements
Inherited?:	yes
Percentages?:	relative to the font size of the element itself

Figure 6.20 shows schematically what the line-height specifies.

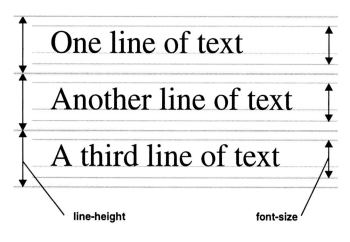

Figure 6.20 What the line-height property measures. The added space in addition to the font size is often called the *leading*. In CSS, half of the leading is inserted above the text and half of it below.

This property has three values:

- a number

- a length

- a percentage

The "length" value is an absolute, relative or device-dependent value; for example, 1 cm, 1.5 em and 16 px. A common absolute value for line height is 12 pt for a 10 pt font.

The "number" and "percentage" values, as well as a "length" value with an em unit, operate similarly to each other, with an important difference. All three are interpreted as relative to the font size; if we assume a font size of 10 pt, a line height of 1.2 means the line height is set to 12 pt (1.2 times the font size). A percentage value works similarly. That is, if the value is set to 120%, the resulting line height of a 10 pt font is 12 pt (120% × 10 pt). In the same manner, a value of 1.2 em means 1.2 × 10 = 12 pt. However, they differ in a very important way: how they handle inheritance. A line height specified as a number is computed for the parent *and also for each child*. The line height corresponding to the percentage and the em is computed once and *the result* is inherited by all children. (This is true for all properties that allow a percentage or em unit as the value.) Of the three methods for calculating the value, the number method is preferred.

Figure 6.21(a) shows the effect of using the "percentage" value. Figure 6.21(b) shows the effect on the same text using the "number" value. In (a), the paragraph has a line height of 120% times the font size of the body (10 pt), which computes to a line height of 12 pt. The quote is printed in a smaller font, but the line height is not changed. The value of 12 pt is inherited, which may be what the author wanted, but then again, it may not be. In (b), the paragraph has a line height of 1.2 times its own font size, which again computes to 12 pt. The quote is printed in a smaller font, but this time the line height is changed with it, since the line height is inherited as a factor, not as a fixed size. This looks better, doesn't it?

A rule of thumb in calculating line height is to start with a value that is 20% more than the font size, either a "number" value of 1.2 or a "percentage" value of 120%. You can adjust from there to achieve whatever effect you seek.

This paragraph has a line height of 120% times the font size of the body (10pt), which computes to a line height of 12pt.

> This quote is printed in a smaller font, but the line height is not changed. The value of 12pt is inherited, which may be what the designer wanted, but then again, it may not be.

This paragraph has a line height of 1.2 times its own font size, which again computes to 12pt.

> This quote is printed in a smaller font, but this time the line height is changed with it, since the line height is inherited as a factor, not as a fixed size. This looks better, doesn't it?

Figure 6.21 (a) The effect of setting the line-height of the body with a percentage; (b) setting the same line-height, but with a number.

```
<STYLE TYPE="text/css">
  BODY { font-size: 10pt; line-height: 120% }
  BLOCKQUOTE { font-size: 8pt }
</STYLE>
<BODY>
<P>This paragraph has a line height of 120% times the font
size of the body (10 pt), which computes to a line height
of 12 pt.
<BLOCKQUOTE>
<P>This quote is printed in a smaller font, but the line
height is not changed. The value of 12 pt is inherited,
which may be what the designer wanted, but then again, it
may not be.
```

```
</BLOCKQUOTE>
</BODY>
<STYLE>
  BODY { font-size: 10pt; line-height: 1.2 }
  BLOCKQUOTE { font-size: 8pt }
</STYLE>
<BODY>
<P>This paragraph has a line height of 1.2 times its own
font size, which again computes to 12pt.
<BLOCKQUOTE>
<P>This quote is printed in a smaller font, but this time
the line height is changed with it, since the line height
is inherited as a factor, not as a fixed size. This looks
better, doesn't it?
</BLOCKQUOTE>
</BODY>
```

Using the <u>line-height</u> property

The line height has a large effect on the character and the readability of text. Specifying a line height is often not just a matter of plugging in a standard value. Many factors go into deciding how large or small a line height should be for a given situation. These factors include the font's size, its appearance (for example, fancy versus plain), its x-height, the lengths of its ascenders and descenders, and the length of the line of text.

For example, large line heights are sometimes used in advertisements, where a profoundly modern look is called for, even if the result is reduced readability. In comparison, titles, which typically are of a larger font and usually short in length, often look better with a smaller line height. A font with relatively long ascenders and a small x-height introduce a lot of visual space between lines, so you can use a smaller line height. In contrast, relatively short ascenders and large x-height can seem to reduce the visual space between lines. Thus you can use a larger line height.

On the other hand, small line heights may force lines too close together, thereby interfering with readability. Longer lines often need extra space between them to guide the eyes on their way back from the end of one line to the start of the next. Shorter lines can often tolerate a smaller line height. An effect much like double spacing can be achieved by setting the line height to 2.0. This is too much for most cases, but it is sometimes required.

Because this property specifies the *minimum* distance between the baselines of the lines, an inline element with a larger font or an inline image may cause lines to be further apart than expected.

THE word-spacing PROPERTY

The word-spacing property enables you to adjust the amount of spacing between words. Each font has a normal word spacing – the amount of space that is put between words – that should be used in the "ideal" situation (ideal according to the font's designer). Browsers will try to use this value. However, you may sometimes want to achieve certain effects with your text by expanding or shrinking the word spacing.

Property name:	word-spacing
Allowed values:	normal	<*length*>
Initial value:	normal
Applies to:	all elements
Inherited?:	yes
Percentages?:	N/A

There are two values:

- *normal* – word spacing is left up to the browser. This is the default.

- a length

The given value is added to the normal word spacing, thus 0 and "normal" mean the same thing.

Word-spacing is an inherited property, but only the computed value is passed on. That is, the amount of word spacing is computed once for the parent element and the *result* is inherited by all of its children. The value is not computed again for its child elements even if they have a different font size. For example, if the current font size of the parent element is 10 pt and the word spacing is set to 1 em, its child elements will inherit a word spacing of 10 pt no matter their font size.

The value can be negative, provided the resulting amount of word spacing is not negative. What happens if the original word spacing minus the set value of word-spacing is less than 0 and is undefined. Some browsers will act as if the resulting space is 0; others may actually overlap the words.

Here are example rules of the use of the word-spacing property:

```
H1 { word-spacing: 15mm }
P { word-spacing: 0.4em }
```

In the first case, the space between words will be increased by 15 mm and in the second by 0.4 ems.

Using word spacing

To make the text appear a bit more open or dense, or to waste or gain some space, you use the word-spacing property to specify the amount of space to be added to or subtracted from the normal word spacing. Figure 6.22 shows an example of text with normal word spacing and the same text with extra word spacing and less word spacing. Increasing or decreasing the distance between words should be done with moderation. Generally, only small changes should be made if your intention is to improve readability.

(a) A text with some word spacing

(b) A text with some word spacing

(c) A text with some word spacing

Figure 6.22 Three different levels of word spacing: (a) normal; (b) more than normal word spacing; (c) less than normal word spacing.

Justifying a line with text-align set to "justify" often causes the word spacing to stretch or shrink. Text is justified starting from the adjusted word spacing. A browser may use any of many different algorithms to justify text, but the better algorithms will ensure that the average space in the paragraph is close to the adjusted word spacing. You may want to adjust the word spacing to improve the text's appearance.

THE letter-spacing PROPERTY

The letter-spacing property lets you adjust the amount of spacing that occurs between letters. Similarly to word spacing, each font has a normal *letter spacing* – the amount of space that is put between letters – that should be used in the "ideal" situation (as determined by the font's designer). Although browsers will try to use this value, you may sometimes want to achieve certain effects with your text by expanding or shrinking the letter spacing.

Property name:	letter-spacing
Allowed values	normal I *<length>*
Initial value:	normal
Applies to:	all elements
Inherited?:	yes
Percentage values:	N/A

This property has two values:

- *normal* – Letter spacing is left up to the browser. This is the default.

- length

Letter-spacing is an inherited property, but only the computed value is passed on. That is, the amount of letter spacing is computed once for the parent element and *the result* is inherited by all of its children. The value is not computed again for its child elements even if they have a different font size. For example, if the current font size of the parent element is 10 pt and the letter spacing is set to 0.5 em, its child elements will inherit a letter spacing of 5 pt no matter their font size (10 pt × 0.5 em = 5 pt).

The value can be negative, provided the resulting amount of letter spacing is not negative. What happens if the original letter spacing minus the set value of letter-spacing is less than 0 is undefined. Some browsers will act as if the resulting space is 0; others may actually overlap the letters.

Here are examples of the use of the letter-spacing property:

```
BLOCKQUOTE { letter-spacing: 0.04in }
P { letter-spacing: 0.1em }
```

In the first case, the space between letters will be increased by 0.04 in. and in the second, by 0.1 em.

Using the letter-spacing property

As with word spacing, increasing or decreasing the distance between the letters in a word should be done with moderation. Begin with small amounts if the intention is to improve readability.

Adjusting the letter spacing is seldom done in running text. When it is used, it is often because tradition calls for it. For example, a publisher producing a "critical edition" (a book comparing different versions of some other book) will often demand that letter spacing be used in certain types of footnotes. Professional designers often frown on the use of letter spacing for anything else than titles because it interferes with the spacing between the letters of a font. The font's designer usually has carefully determined the optimal distance between each pair of letters – ab, bo, bi, Bl, and so on – to achieve a uniform look for all pairs. Some pairs such as VA require less space between them; otherwise, they look too spaced out. Simply adding or subtracting a fixed amount is likely to give less than pleasing results. Increasing the spacing may cause nonuniform distribution of white space. Decreasing the spacing may cause some letters to touch each other while others don't. Also, if the shapes of certain combinations of letters don't match very well, the font designer may have provided ligatures to replace them. However, when a nonzero letter spacing value is requested, those ligatures must be abandoned and you end up with a displeasing match of characters.

Letter spacing may also be affected by justification. With the "normal" value, the browser is free to change the letter spacing in order to justify text. The results may not be very good, however. By setting letter spacing explicitly to 0 or another "length" value, you prevent the browser from doing this. A 0 value means the letter spacing will not be changed, while any other "length" value means the browser must change the letter spacing by that exact amount.

Figure 6.23 shows examples of two fonts, each with normal letter spacing, less than normal letter spacing, and more than normal letter spacing.

Figure 6.23 Examples of letter-spacing, using Helvetica and Times as examples: (a) normal text; (b) positive letter spacing; (c) negative letter spacing. As the examples show, letter spacing is useful for uppercase, but much less for lowercase text.

(a) A normal line of text – AND UPPERCASE
  A normal line of text – AND UPPERCASE

(b) A stretched line of text – AND UPPERCASE
  A stretched line of text – AND UPPERCASE

(c) A condensed line of text – AND UPPERCASE
  A condensed line of text – AND UPPERCASE

You may sometimes want to adjust the letter spacing to achieve a certain dramatic or other effect. For example, stretching a word is an alternative way of emphasizing it. This was done quite commonly in the nineteenth century, especially in German books, primarily because the font used in them didn't have an italic variant. (On the screen, there are many other ways to emphasize a text besides italicizing it; for example, by using color.) Figure 6.24 shows text in German Fraktur font with the word "emphasizing" stretched to draw attention to it.

Figure 6.24 Example of stretching a word for emphasis. This used to be quite common with the German Fraktur font, which is shown here.

Stretching a font can sometimes be used as an alternative way of emphasizing it. It used to be a quite common device in the nineteenth century, especially in German books. One of the reasons being that the font they used didn't have an italic variant.

Today explicit letter spacing is still used in titles; often extreme values are used to achieve extreme effects. Adjusting letter spacing is often used as well to achieve specific graphics effects. Figure 6.25 shows examples.

New! bubble-gum that lasts *l o n g e r . . .*

(a)

Figure 6.25 Examples of letter spacing: (a) 1 em; (b) 0.7 em; (c) −0.25 em for the word "NARROW" and 0.3 em for "WIDE."

T O O   L A T E

LONDON, yesterday. A truck driver that came to collect his truck, discovered that he had come too late. When he…

(b)

This new wall-to-wall carpet will fit in NARROW and also in W I D E rooms

(c)

THE vertical-align PROPERTY

The vertical-align property lets you raise or lower letters, as well as images, above or below the baseline of text.

Property name:	vertical-align
Allowed values:	baseline I sub I super I top I text-top I middle I bottom I text-bottom I <percentage>
Initial value:	baseline
Applies to:	inline elements
Inherited?:	no
Percentage values:	refer to the line height of the element itself

Text is normally aligned on an invisible baseline. The bottoms of the letters are on the baseline no matter what the style, weight, or even size of the letters. Sometimes a letter or a word has to be raised above the baseline or lowered below the baseline. This is the case with abbreviations that must be superscripted, such as N^o (numero), M^e (Madame), and Mlle (Mademoiselle) and for simple mathematics that must be superscripted or subscripted, such as y^2 or x_i.

Vertical-align applies to inline elements, including replaced elements (images) that are inline. These images can be put on the baseline, centered vertically between lines, aligned with the top of the letters, or any of several other possibilities.

This property has two types of values: a keyword and a percentage. Six of the eight available keywords are relative to the parent:

• *baseline* – aligns the baseline of the child element with the baseline of its parent. This is the default. An element without a baseline, such as an image or object, will have its bottom aligned with the parent's baseline.

- *sub* – subscripts the element, that is, aligns the baseline of the element with its parent's preferred position for subscripts. That position normally depends on the font of the parent. If the font does not explicitly define those positions, the browser chooses a "reasonable" (browser-specific) position.

- *super* – superscripts the element, that is, aligns the baseline of the element with its parent's preferred position for superscripts. That position normally depends on the font of the parent. If the font does not explicitly define those positions, the browser chooses a "reasonable" (browser-specific) position.

- *text-top* – aligns the top of the element with the top of its parent's tallest letters. Some people prefer this way of aligning, for example, N^o and Mlle, instead of using the value "super"

- *middle* – aligns the vertical midpoint of the element (typically an image) with the baseline plus half the x-height of its parent element, that is, the middle of the parent's lowercase letters. More precisely, the element is centered on a line 0.5 ex above the baseline.

- *text-bottom* – aligns the bottom of the element with the bottom of its parent's font.

Here are example rules using these six values of the <u>vertical-align</u> property:

```
SUP { vertical-align: super; font-size: 7pt }
SUB { vertical-align: sub; font-size: 7pt }
SPAN.index { vertical-align: sub }
IMG.initial { vertical-align: middle }
```

Figure 6.26 shows examples of the various alignments that can be obtained using these six values of the <u>vertical-align</u> property.

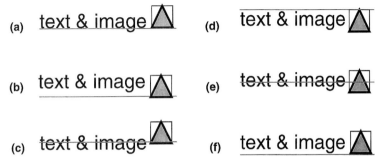

Figure 6.26 Different ways to vertically align. In this case the inline image is being aligned according to the keyword (a) baseline; (b) sub; (c) super; (d) text-top; (e) middle; (f) text-bottom.

The top and bottom keywords

The two keywords, "top" and "bottom," have definitions that look no more difficult than those of the six just described. The element with <u>vertical-align</u> set to "top" will have its top aligned with the top of the tallest thing on the line. The value "bottom" aligns the bottom of the element with the bottom of the lowest thing on the line. Sounds easy enough, doesn't it. Ah, but there's a snake in the grass.

The problem is, there may be two fairly tall elements on the line, one aligned to the top, the other to the bottom. If both elements are taller than the surrounding letters, the one aligned to the top will then also be the lowest thing on the line and the other one will be aligned to its bottom. But then that second element may be taller than the text and thereby cause the first element to move to align with the second element's top. But now the second element has to be aligned again….

Sound confusing? Not surprising. What you end up with is a loop. Implementations eventually will break out of this loop, but the vertical position that results cannot be determined clearly. Luckily, this situation is very rare.

Here's an example (Figure 6.27). Consider a line that has two images that are not the same height. The alignment of image 1 is set to "top" and Image 2 to "bottom."

Situation A: 2 is aligned to the bottom of the lowest thing on the line, which is 1, but 1 is not aligned with the top of the tallest thing (besides itself), which is 2.

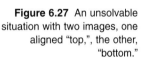

Figure 6.27 An unsolvable situation with two images, one aligned "top,", the other, "bottom."

Situation B: 1 is aligned to the top of the tallest thing on the line, which is 2, but 2 is not aligned with the bottom of the lowest thing, which is 1.

For Image 2 to align with the bottom of the lowest thing on the line, Image 1, it must move down. It is now base-aligned with Image 1. However, Image 1, set to "top," must be top-aligned with the highest part of the line, now Image 2, so it moves down. And we're right back where we started. We're in a loop.

You can handle this situation by ensuring at least one of the following exists:

1 Only one of the values is used, not both.

2 There is something else on the line that has a different vertical alignment than "top" or "bottom." Normal text – text aligned at the baseline – will work.

3 The item aligned at the top and the item aligned at the bottom do not occur on the same line.

4 The item aligned at the top and the item aligned at the bottom are of equal height.

However, in the last case the result is not always consistently determinable either. In the example above there was no solution, but in this case there are many solutions, which may be just as bad (Figure 6.28).

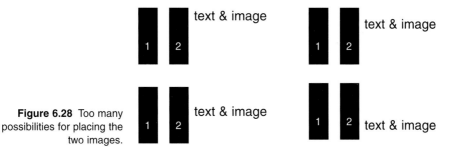

Figure 6.28 Too many possibilities for placing the two images.

In each of the four situations above, images 1 and 2 are now aligned to each other's top and bottom, but there is no way of knowing how high above the baseline they should be.

The value as a percentage

Apart from using the keywords, you also can specify a percentage as a value that indicates by how much the element is to be raised or lowered. A value of 50% means the element will be raised by half the element's line height. Negative values lower the element similarly. Here is an example:

```
He climbed higher,
<SPAN STYLE="vertical-align: 50%">
and higher,</SPAN>
<SPAN STYLE="vertical-align: 100%">
and higher still...</SPAN>
<SPAN STYLE="vertical-align: -100%">
until he fell</SPAN>
<SPAN STYLE="vertical-align: -200%">
down!</SPAN>
```

and here is the result:

He climbed higher, and higher, and higher still…

until he fell

down!

Chapter 7

Images

With CSS1, you can affect many characteristics of images. You can scale them, position them on the screen, add a border around them, and much more. To do all this, you use many of the same properties that apply to other elements: <u>margin</u>, <u>border</u>, <u>padding</u>, <u>width</u>, <u>height</u>, <u>float</u>, and <u>background</u>. We explain how to work with these in Chapters 6 and 8. When used with images, however, these properties sometimes behave a little differently.

In fact, these properties not only work for images, but for all multimedia objects that are embedded in an HTML document, including movies and buttons in a form.

REPLACED ELEMENTS

HTML has two elements for inserting images: IMG and OBJECT. As the names suggest, IMG is commonly used for inserting images, while OBJECT is normally reserved for more complex multimedia objects, such as animations, interactive programs, and sounds.

The OBJECT element was introduced in 1996 and may not yet be fully supported in all browsers.

Both IMG and OBJECT are replaced elements. Replaced elements are replaced by an image or an object such as a button. Other replaced elements are INPUT, SELECT, and TEXTAREA, all of which are used in forms and usually look like buttons. To CSS1, they are no different from images.

All replaced elements are handled similarly in CSS1. It assumes that each has a *natural*, or *intrinsic* size, which is the size the element will have if you (or a user) do not change its size in a style sheet. For CSS purposes, the content of replaced elements is irrelevant, since that content is coming from somewhere else replaced elements are considered to be just rectangular boxes in your HTML document. What the image or object looks like is determined by factors outside of your document. That is, images and objects are created in a different program and possibly by someone else. As such, you can influence in a style sheet only the size and the border area of images and objects.

As we discussed in Chapter 1, you should always try to include a textual description of the image or object as an alternative in those cases when the image or object cannot be displayed. When this happens, IMG and OBJECT are no longer replaced elements; they become like any other element that has textual content. As a result, all the usual properties that affect text apply to that text.

IMG is far simpler to work with than OBJECT. It has only two attributes (apart from the usual CLASS, ID and STYLE): SRC and ALT. We discussed IMG and its attributes in Chapter 1. The SRC attribute contains the address of the image file that is to be linked to the document. The ALT attribute contains a text description of the image for display by browsers that cannot display images. Here are two examples of the use of IMG:

```
<IMG SRC="http://www.image.org/logo.gif">

...as shown in this image: <IMG SRC="diagram"
ALT="Schematic view">...
```

OBJECT is quite a bit more complicated. It has about a dozen attributes. Also, you can insert more URLs in it as well as information about the type of object. Its DATA attribute is the equivalent of IMG's SRC. It has no equivalent ALT attribute, but you still can insert alternative text. You do this by placing the text between the element's start and end tags, <OBJECT> and </OBJECT>. This allows for the use of almost any HTML code, including other objects, as alternative text. This feature is in HTML because a browser will more likely have difficulty displaying an object than it will an image, so there needs to be more alternatives offered as replacements for the object. Here is some example code that has an OBJECT element:

```
... like in the following animation:
<OBJECT DATA="mov.mpg">
  If you see this text, your browser doesn't
  understand MPEG; here is an image instead:
  <IMG SRC="mov1.gif">
</OBJECT>
```

In this example, the alternative text provided by data is: "If you see this text, your browser doesn't understand mpeg; here is an image instead: <IMG SRC="mov1.gif">", where the last part is in turn replaced by an image.

We talk mostly about images in this chapter, but everything said here applies to all replaced elements, whether they are replaced by an image, some other multimedia object, or a button-like object. Here is some of what you can do to each of them:

- Put a background behind it that is a color or a pattern (or both). The background can be larger than the image. The background also will show through if the image has transparent parts.

- Place it either inline, as a floating image with text wrapping around it, or as a displayed image with text breaks before and after.

- Rescale it, either in both directions horizontally and vertically independently, or in one direction with the other direction following proportionally.

In the following sections, we give you examples of how to do these. Note, you need to have read and understood Chapter 6 before reading the rest of this chapter, as the material here builds on the properties and principles discussed in those chapters.

WORKING WITH TRANSPARENT IMAGES

Properties used: <u>background</u>. For more on the <u>background</u> property see Chapter 8.

Some types of images can have transparent parts. For example, images in the GIF or PNG format don't have to cover the entire rectangular area. They can have transparent spots through which will show the background of the parent element or of the canvas if the parent has a transparent background itself. In Figure 7.1, we put a partly transparent image against a background that is a repeating pattern. The pattern shows through where there is no image. Here's the code we used to set the background and padding of the top-most image:

```
IMG { background: url(hash.png); }
```

Figure 7.1 An image with transparent parts on top of a patterned or colored background lets the background show through the transparent parts.

FLOATING IMAGES AND WRAPPING TEXT

Properties used: <u>float</u>, <u>margin-right</u>, <u>margin-left</u>, <u>clear</u>

 Images can be shown inline – between the words of a line – if they are small enough. Usually, however, they are displayed either on a line of their own or to the side of the text, that is, floating. You can wrap text around a floating image by using the <u>float</u> property. This is what was done with the image at the start of this paragraph.

For example,

```
IMG.icon { float: left }
```

will place each IMG element of CLASS "icon" flush against its parent element's left edge. Figure 7.2(a) shows the result.

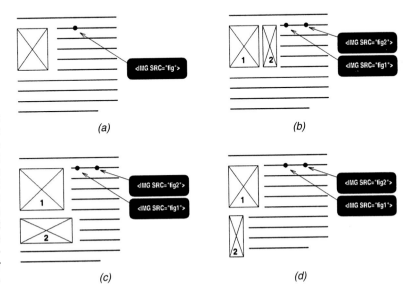

Figure 7.2 Floating an image: (a) the child element (IMG) floats to the left of the parent and text flows around the child; (b) the image floats next to an image already at the parent's edge; (c) the image floats to the parent's edge and moves down until it fits; (d) the image has the clear property set, so it cannot be put next to another floating image.

With this rule:

```
IMG.icon { float: right }
```

those same IMG elements will be placed flush against the parent's right edge.

An image that floats to the side will have its top aligned with the top of the text line. But if there is not enough room next to the text, the image will be put further down.

Sometimes a floating image will find another floating image already at the parent's edge. In this case, the images will be shown side by side, with their tops aligned, provided there is room. See Figure 7.2(b). If there is not enough room for the second IMG element to fit, it will move down to a spot in which it can fit. See Figure 7.2(c).

You can force a floating image never to be put next to another floating image, by using the clear property (see Chapter 6). For example, with a style sheet like this:

```
IMG.icon {
  float: left;
  clear: left;
}
```

the image will move down until it finds a clear spot along the parent's edge in which it can fit. See Figure 7.2(d).

An image that is so large that it won't fit on any line of the current paragraph will be put on a line of its own and stick out into the right margin (if it is floating left) or the left margin (if it is floating right).

POSITIONING IMAGES FROM THE MARGINS

Properties used: <u>margin</u>, <u>float</u>

The default value of the margin properties is zero, so normally, an image that floats abuts the margin, but you can specify its position by using the <u>margin</u> properties:

- A left-floating image will be positioned from the current left margin by the value of the image's <u>margin-left</u> property.

- A right-floating image will be positioned from the current right margin by the value of the image's <u>margin-right</u> property.

The image on the right has a 5 mm margin on all sides:

```
float: right;
margin: 5mm
```

(For clarity, an extra dotted line was added, to show where the margin goes.)

SCALING AN IMAGE

An image can be scaled – resized – by setting its <u>width</u> and <u>height</u> properties. If these are not set explicitly, the image's <u>width</u> and <u>height</u> properties will be set to the default "auto," which means the image will keep its natural width.

Actually, CSS doesn't guarantee that the image will be resized. The area that the image occupies gets a new size, but how the image fills that area depends on the type of image.

An image can be scaled in two ways. In the first, both the <u>width</u> and <u>height</u> properties are set. Doing this may cause the image to be distorted, as shown in Figure 7.3, which was produced using the following code:

```
<IMG SRC="pict.gif" STYLE="width:3cm;height:2cm">
```

original

3 cm × 2 cm

Figure 7.3 Resizing an image by setting both the <u>width</u> and <u>height</u> properties.

Distortion occurs when the *aspect-ratio* is not maintained, as occurred in this example. The aspect-ratio is the ratio of width to height. If you set the width and height of an image following its exact aspect-ratio, then distortion usually won't occur. However, determining the exact values to use can be a nuisance. It's much easier to follow the second method of resizing.

With the second method, you set only the width or the height value to a value other than "auto." You keep the other value at "auto." The image will be resized using the given value and the other dimension will be resized proportionally in accordance with the image's aspect-ratio. Figure 7.4 shows the same figure as in Figure 7.3 but with only the width set to an explicit value, as follows:

```
<IMG SRC="pict.gif" STYLE="width:3cm">
```

original

width: 3cm

Figure 7.4 Resizing an image by setting only one of the <u>width</u> and <u>height</u> properties.

The height value was determined automatically in order to retain the image's aspect-ratio.

DIFFERENCES BETWEEN REPLACED AND BLOCK ELEMENTS

For images and other replaced elements that are inline, interpreting width, height, padding, border, and margin properties is no problem. But when the image is made into a block-like element, by setting the display property to "block", the width and the margin are computed slightly differently than they are for normal block elements.

When the width property has an explicit value, images will be scaled as usual and the margins will be computed as for normal block-like elements. This means that if neither the margin-left nor the margin-right property has been set to "auto," the margin-right property will be ignored. However, when the width of the image has been set to "auto," things change some.

Recall that in Chapter 6, we explained that for normal block elements a width set to "auto" is computed by taking the width of the parent element and subtracting from it the values of the child element's left and right margins, left and right padding, and left and right borders. The result is the element's width.

For images and other replaced elements, a width set to "auto" means the image will get its natural width. In this case, the value "auto" is treated as if the width were set to the natural width of the image. But for block elements, including displayed images, the values of the margin, padding, border, and width still have to add up to the width of the parent element. That means that either margin-left or margin-right must be "auto." If neither of them has this value, the right margin will be forced to "auto."

Here's an example that illustrates how this works. We set the properties for three images: a default one without a class attribute, one with class "full," and one with class "center." The first one has its natural width and is left-aligned (Figure 7.5(a)). The right margin is implicitly changed to "auto" because no other property besides width has that value. "img.full" was scaled to the full width of the text because the width property is set to 100%. This image, too, is left-aligned (Figure 7.5(b)). "img.center" shows an image that has been centered. That is easily done by setting both left and right margins to "auto." The available space has been divided between the two margins (Figure 7.5(c)).

```
<STYLE>
  IMG { display: block }
  IMG.full { width: 100% }
  IMG.center { margin-left: auto;
    margin-right: auto }
</STYLE>
<BODY>
```

<P> This image has its natural width and is left-aligned. The right margin is implicitly changed to "auto" because no other property besides "width" had that value:

<IMG SRC="pict">

<P> The next image is scaled to the full width of this text because the width property is set to 100%. (This image, too, is left-aligned.)

<IMG CLASS="full" SRC="pict">

<P> The last example shows an image that has been centered. That is easily done by setting both the left and right margins to "auto." The available space will be divided between the two margins.

<IMG CLASS="center" SRC="pict">

Figure 7.5 (a) The image is
left-aligned; (b) the image is
scaled to the full width of the
text; (c) the image is
centered by setting both
margins to "auto."

This image has its natural width and is left-aligned. The right margin is implicitly changed to "auto" because no other property besides "width" had that value:

The next image is scaled to the full width of this text because the width property is set to 100%. (This image, too, is left-aligned.)

The last example shows an image that has been centered. That is easily done by setting both the left and right margins to "auto." The available space will be divided between the two margins.

Chapter 8

Colors

Printing color is expensive. Hence, in books color has always been used sparingly. On the Web, however, the use of color is virtually free. Most Web users have color monitors, so displaying color costs nothing, although printing it is still costly. So there is no reason for Web designers not to incorporate color into their designs.

Of course, color can be overdone. As with all aspects of print, and Web, design – whether fonts, space, images, or whatever – color should be used to achieve a purpose with the design. Color thrown in at random often doesn't work well. Remember, too much variety obscures, rather than clarifies.

Some combinations of colors are very hard to read, such as red type on a blue background. A background that differs from the foreground text only in color and not in brightness also strains the eyes. For some people, dark letters on a light background are easier to read, while for others, the opposite is true. People also may have associations with certain colors that may either help or hinder their understanding the text. For example, red seems to be almost universal in marking something that is important. But the interpretations of other colors often depend on culture and even on the user's personal experiences. Color and how we perceive it are both very technical and complex subjects, far beyond the scope of this book. We encourage interested readers to further explore the subject of color, particularly to learn how to combine colors effectively to achieve desired effects.

The range of colors that can be reproduced by a computer monitor is called its *gamut*. The gamut depends not only on the color and brightness that a computer monitor can produce but also on the brightness of the light that reflects off the screen. The effective gamut is reduced as the light in the room gets brighter; the largest gamut is available in a darkened room. Note that color printers work very differently from computers and their gamuts differ from those of computer monitors. Colors often appear one way on the monitor's screen and another when printed by a color printer or by a traditional printing process.

In this chapter, we show you how to use CSS to specify the color of text and the background color of text. You also can specify the color of borders, in addition to the ways we showed you in Chapter 6. This is done via the color property and the various background properties. (The background also can be an image, instead of or in addition to a color.)

RGB COLOR MODEL

Computer monitors commonly use the *RGB* – red, green, blue – *color model* to display color. It is one of several color models available. These include the HSB (hue-saturation-brightness) model, which is similar to how artists mix colors. Another is CMYK (cyan-magenta-yellow-black), a model commonly used by printers. We chose the RGB model because it represents how color is displayed on a color video monitor. Red, green, and blue light is mixed in specified proportions to represent colors on the monitor.

In the RGB color model, each of the three colors is represented by a value between 0 and 100%, where 100% represents the maximum brightness of a color. The values are arranged as a triplet, where the first number represents red, the second green, and the last blue. Black is represented as the triplet (0, 0, 0) – zero amounts of all three colors – and white by (100%, 100%, 100%) – 100% of all three colors. Every triplet with equal amounts of each color is a shade of gray. For example, (90%, 90%, 90%) is a light gray, while (40%, 40%, 40%) is a dark gray. When the values are not equal, it is often hard to predict what the color looks like. That (100%, 0, 0) is red is not too hard to see. But that a color with the values (65%, 16%, 16%) is a shade of brown is not so obvious.

Computers work best with bytes, as you likely know. A byte can contain a number from 0 to 255, so when working on-screen, it is usual to remap the RGB percentage values to values within the range of 0, inclusive, to 255, inclusive. Thus 100% remaps to 255. White, then, remaps as (255, 255, 255), red as (255, 0, 0), and the brown we mentioned in the previous paragraph as (165, 42, 42).

Because each color is represented by three bytes, each a value between 0 and 255, the number of potential available colors is 16 777 216, that is, 256 x 256 x 256. These are usually enough colors for most applications. Unfortunately, many monitors don't have enough memory to store three bytes for every pixel, particularly when it is not uncommon for a million pixels to be on a screen. So monitors play tricks (which we won't go into) in their efforts to display as many colors as possible. This usually means that although you potentially can use all 16 777 216 colors, you cannot use them all at the same time. Many monitors have a limit of 256 colors that can be displayed at any given time, although a 65 536-color limit is becoming more common.

This limit may not seem very important when you are working with a style sheet because usually you will specify only a handful of colors. However, a typical HTML document also contains images, which may use up colors quickly. There actually is very little you can do to ensure the desired color is available on the user's monitor. You can only hope that the browser will take care that if the exact color is not available (which it often isn't), then at least one that is close is available.

SPECIFYING COLORS

There are many ways in which color can be specified. You can use every-day names, such as "red", "blue," and "brown," but they are not very precise. Paint manufacturers often provide sets of numbered color swatches so that you can ask for paint that is "blue number 216," for example. Printing companies often have similar color-specification systems. Sometimes they require you to indicate the exact mixture of standard inks.

On computer screens, the most common way is to indicate an RGB value in the form of a triplet, as we described in the previous section. However, this, too, is an imprecise way of selecting colors because the result depends on the monitor on which the colors are displayed and on how much light is in the room in which the monitor is located.

With CSS, we elected to go with a compromise solution. For a few common names, you can specify the color by its common name, such as red and green. For all other colors, you specify an RGB value that will produce a certain color when displayed on some "ideal" monitor. We define this ideal monitor as having a well-defined relation between RGB values and screen brightness and it is assumed to be in a room with a certain kind of lighting. Many PC monitors (and UNIX workstations as well) in typical offices will be close to this ideal. If more precision is needed or if you must be certain that a certain monitor meets the ideal, measuring the actual monitor and environment is possible to find out how much adjustment to the RGB values is needed. In practice, of course, most browsers will just assume that the computer is close enough to the ideal.

See: M. Anderson, R. Motta. S. Chandrasekar, M. Stokes (1996). Proposal for a standard color space for the Internet – sRGB. URL: http://www.color.org/contrib/sRGB.html.

The RGB values of CSS1 are called "sRGB," for "standard-RGB." An article describes the technical details of the sRGB system.

CSS1 predefines 16 color names: aqua (a light greenish blue, sometimes called cyan), black, blue, fuchsia (light purple/pink), gray, green, lime (light green), maroon (dark red), navy (dark blue), olive, purple, red, silver (light gray), teal (blue-green), yellow, white.

Figure 8.1 shows samples of all of the predefined colors. They also are used in HTML version 3.2. Note that colors look different on screen than on paper. Keep this in mind when selecting your colors. If you plan to print your page on paper, some of the colors you choose for screen display may surprise you once printed. If this were a book about color, we would have tried for a better match (and the book would have been much more expensive ...).

Figure 8.1 Samples of the 16 predefined colors in CSS1.

All other colors must be specified as RGB triplets. That can be done by using any of three methods. The first two we've already discussed. Which you use is a matter of taste, since they all produce the same result.

1 *Percentages*: for example, a color specification like rgb(100%, 35.5%, 10%) specifies a maximum amount (100%) of red light, 35.5% of green light, and 10% of the blue light. The result is a deep orange red. ▬▬▬▬▬

2 *Numbers in the range of 0 to 255*: thus rgb(255, 91, 26) should be the same color as rgb(100%, 35.5%, 10%) in the percentage example.

3 *Hexadecimal numbers*: for example, #FF5B1A, which will produce the same shade of red as in (1) and (2).

In either of the first or second methods, if you enter a value that is outside the acceptable range, for example 125% in method one or 300 in method two, the value will be "clipped." That is, the errant value will be reduced to the maximum value allowed by the method – 100% in the first case and 255 in the second. In the process, the other two values may change slightly as well, but that depends on the browser.

Here are examples of how values might be clipped:

```
                   /* All values within the integer range 0-255 */
EM { color: rgb(255, 91, 26) }
                   /* 300 is clipped to 255 */
EM { color: rgb(300, 91, 26) }
                   /* 125% is clipped to 100%. */
EM { color: rgb(125%, 35.5%, 10%) }
```

Method 3, hexadecimal numbers, needs a bit more explanation. You use the same numbers as with the second method, 0 to 255, but you write them as a single hexadecimal number preceded by a hash mark (#); for example, #FF5B1A, which produces the same color red as rgb(100%, 35.5%, 10%) and rgb(255, 91, 26). This notation is not very intuitive, but it is included because it is still used a lot on the X Window System. The hexadecimal notation can be written in two variations that use either three or six hexadecimal digits. The three-digit form defines the same color as the six-digit form does but with all digits doubled; that is, #A84 is the same color as #AA8844.

Hexadecimal numbers The relation between hexadecimal and the normal decimal numbers is as follows: the digits 0 to 9 stand for themselves, the letters A to F mean A=10, B=11, C=12, D=13, E=14, and F=15. In a group of two hexadecimal digits, the first one is multiplied by 16 and added to the second. For example: 11 (= 1 × 16 + 1) = 17. Some more examples:

A7 = 10 × 16 + 7 = 167
FF = 15 × 16 + 15 = 255
22 = 2 × 16 + 2 = 34
5B = 5 × 16 + 11 = 91
1A = 1 × 16 + 10 = 26

We can apply this to color values:

#FF5B1A = rgb(255, 91, 26), since FF = 255, 5B = 91 and 1A = 26
#CEAA13 = rgb(206, 176, 19)

In the next two sections, we discuss the <u>color</u> property and the six background properties.

THE <u>color</u> PROPERTY

The <u>color</u> property sets the color of the text of an element. It is the foreground color. It also can set the color of text decorations, discussed in Chapter 4, such as underline, as well as borders that have been created with the border properties discussed in Chapter 6.

Property name:	color
Allowed values:	*<color>*
Initial value:	UA specific
Applies to:	all elements
Inherited?:	yes
Percentages?:	N/A

The property takes one value – a color – which is specified by one of the methods discussed in the previous section. Following are example rules to specify a color for text or a text decoration:

```
EM { color: red }
P { color: rgb(255, 0, 0) }      /* red */
H1 { color: #f00 }               /* also red */
H1 { color: #ff0000 }            /* same as above */
```

A color is inherited by child elements. The default color is set in the user's default style sheet, if one exists. Otherwise, the default color depends on the browser.

SETTING THE COLOR OF A BORDER

Setting the color of a border can be done in two ways. One is to set it directly by including the color via the border properties, as done here:

```
P { border: medium double red }
```

The result is shown in Figure 8.2(a). We discussed this method in Chapter 6.

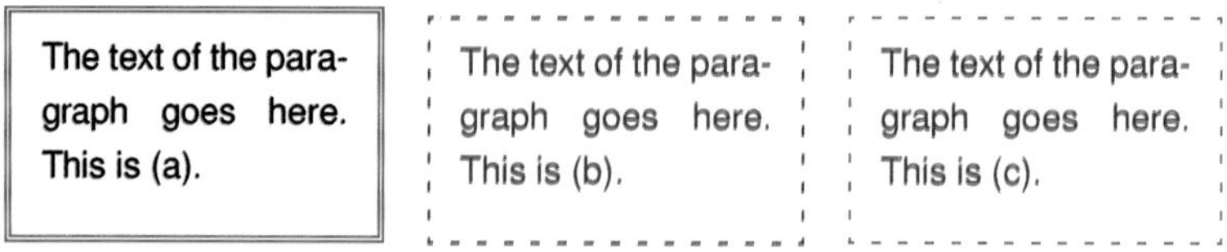

Figure 8.2 Different ways to set the color of a border using the color property: (a) setting the color using the border properties; (b) setting the border to the text color; (c) setting the border color independent of the text.

The text of the para-graph goes here. This is (a).

The text of the para-graph goes here. This is (b).

The text of the para-graph goes here. This is (c).

Another way is to set the color of the text that is the content of the element, as done here:

```
P {
  border: thin dotted;
  color: blue;
}
```

In this case, no color has been set on the border, so it will assume the color of the text, which is blue. This is shown in Figure 8.2(b).

If we set a color on the border itself, as done here:

```
P {
  border: thin dotted red;
  color: blue;
}
```

we end up with the result shown in Figure 8.2(c). (Some padding has been added between the text and the border, as described in Chapter 6.)

SETTING THE COLOR OF HYPERLINKS

Until CSS, the most common use of color in Web browsers (as opposed to the colors found in imported images) was to draw attention to hyperlinks. Some browsers use two colors: one for links to documents that the user has traversed before and another for links that he or she hasn't tried yet. Others use a third color for the "active" link, that is for the short duration while the user keeps the mouse button pressed over the text. In CSS1, rules for these can be written through a pseudo-class on an A element, as follows:

```
A:link { color: blue }        /* unvisited links */
A:visited { color: red }      /* visited links */
A:active { color: yellow }    /* active links */
```

See also the section on pseudo-classes in Chapter 3 for more information.

THE BACKGROUND PROPERTIES

The background properties set aspects of the background of an element, that is, the surface onto which text is displayed. That background can be either transparent, a color, or an image. You also can set the position of an image, if and how often the image should be repeated on the screen, and whether it should be fixed or scrolled relative to the canvas. Five of the properties set specific aspects of the background, while the sixth, the background property, is a shorthand method that lets you set all of the first five properties at one time. The properties do not inherit. Following are the background properties:

- background-color

- background-image

- background-repeat

- background-attachment

- background-position

- background

We discuss each of these in the following sections.

THE background-color PROPERTY

The background-color property sets the background color of an element.

Property name:	background-color
Allowed values:	[<*color*>	transparent]
Initial value:	transparent
Applies to:	all elements
Inherited?:	no
Percentages?:	N/A

This property has two values:

- a color

- the keyword "transparent" – this is the default.

When a "color" value is provided, the specified color will be visible behind the text of the element. How much of the surface will actually get that color depends on the type of element and on the amount of padding. We discussed the effect of padding on color in Chapter 6. It also depends on whether there is a background image in addition to the color, as specified with the background-image property below.

Background color in inline elements

For an inline element, the color will be visible only behind the text itself and behind the padding around the element. Hence, if the element is broken across lines, the background color will be visible behind the words and spaces at the end of the first line and also behind the words and spaces on the second line. For example, in Figure 8.3, the words in the middle of the sentence are displayed in white on black by putting them in an EM element with the <u>color</u> property "color" value of white and the <u>background-color</u> property "color" value of black. Here is the code to produce this result:

```
<STYLE TYPE="text/css">
  EM {
      background-color: black;
      color: white
  }
</STYLE>
<BODY>
  <P>This paragraph has <EM>a few emphasized words</EM>
in the middle.
</BODY>
```

Figure 8.3 Use of the <u>background-color</u> property with an inline element.

This paragraph has `a few emphasized words` in the middle.

Background color in block elements

For block-level elements, the color will occupy a rectangular region that includes the indent of the first line (if any) of the paragraph as well as any empty space at the end of each line. It will also occupy the padding around the block, if any. In such cases, it is a good idea to add a little padding to leave some room between the letters and the edge of the background, as has been done in the example shown in Figure 8.4. The figure was generated with the following style sheet set on the middle paragraph:

```
P.standout {
  padding: 0.2em;
  background: black;
  color: white
}
```

This is the first paragraph, it has no CLASS attribute.

`This is the second paragraph, it has CLASS="standout"`

Figure 8.4 Use of the "color" value in a colored block-level element.

This is the third paragraph, it has no CLASS attribute.

Background color in list items

For list item elements, the background is not applied to the label if the label is outside the text box. If the label is inside the text box, then the background will be behind the label as well.

The transparent value

If no color or image is specified, the background will be transparent. In this case, the background of the parent element is visible behind the text (or if that is transparent, the background of the parent's parent is visible, and so on). If all elements have a transparent background, the browser's default background is used; this is often light gray.

For example, the following code sets the background of certain paragraphs to red and the background of STRONG elements to yellow. Other elements keep their default transparent background. Figure 8.5 shows how a document with this style sheet may look.

```
P.special { background-color: red }
STRONG { background-color: yellow }
```

Figure 8.5 Examples using "transparent": the first and third paragraphs have a transparent background, as do the two emphasized elements. The middle paragraph and the two STRONG elements have a non-transparent background.

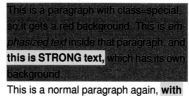

A background is not inherited; if it is not set explicitly, it will be transparent, so you often can omit this value. You'll only need to set it to "transparent" explicitly if you need to override an earlier rule – whether in your style sheet or another's – for the background-color or background properties.

THE background-image PROPERTY

The background-image property lets you set an image as the background for an element.

Property name:	background-image
Allowed values:	[<*url*>	none]
Initial value:	none
Applies to:	all elements
Inherited?:	no
Percentages?:	N/A

This property has two values:

- a URL

- the keyword "none" – this is the default.

To specify an image as a background, you enter the URL of the image as the "url" value. When specifying an image as the background, you should also specify a color (using the background-color property). When the document is displayed, the image will overlay the color. You would do this for several reasons:

- The color can be used to fill transparent regions of the image; otherwise, these areas will remain transparent.

- It can be used to fill in the screen while the image is loading, for example if loading takes too long.

- It can be used in place of the image if the image cannot be loaded, for example if the browser cannot locate it.

The following rule specifies both an image and a color for the background. The result is shown in Figure 8.6.

```
P {
    background-image: url(dot.gif);
    background-color: #FFAA00
}
```

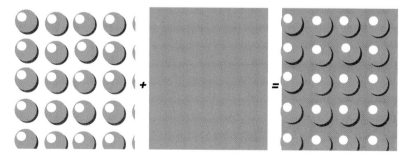

Figure 8.6 Setting both an image and a color as the background of an element.

THE background-repeat PROPERTY

The background-repeat property determines whether and how an image is repeated in the element.

Property name:	background-repeat
Allowed values:	[repeat I repeat-x I repeat-y I no-repeat]
Initial value:	repeat
Applies to:	all elements
Inherited?:	no
Percentages?:	N/A

This property has four possible values:

- *repeat* – the image is repeated both horizontally and vertically as often as needed to fill the whole element. This process is called *tiling*. This is the default.

- *repeat-x* – the image is repeated horizontally (along the *x*-axis) across the element in a single row, both left and right from the initial position.

- *repeat-y* – the image is repeated vertically (along the *y*-axis) down the element in a single column, above and below the initial position.

- *no-repeat* – the image is not repeated. It appears only once, in the upper left corner of the element, or wherever it is placed with the background-position property.

By default, an image is initially placed in the upper left corner of the element (or of the window if the image has the background-attachment value of "fixed"; we discuss this property shortly). Repetition of an element begins from either this default position or from a new position that you set with the background-position property, which we discuss shortly.

A repeated image is most often a picture of a repeat pattern, such as a dot or wave pattern. But you can repeat an image of anything you want. Note that repeating images may cause part of the image to be cut off at one or more edges of the screen, as Figures 8.7(a) and (c) show.

Following are example rules for each value of "repeat." Figures 8.7(a)–(d) show the result of each.

```
background-image: url(wave);                    /* (a) */
background-repeat: repeat

background-image: url(wave);                    /* (b) */
background-repeat: repeat-x;
background-position: center
```

```
background-image: url(wave);                    /* (c) */
background-repeat: repeat-y;
background-position: right

background-image: url(wave);                    /* (d) */
background-repeat: no-repeat;
```

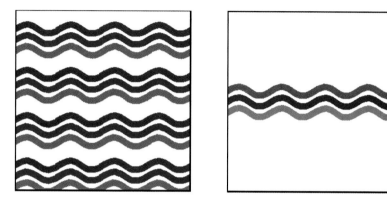

(a) repeat   (b) repeat-x

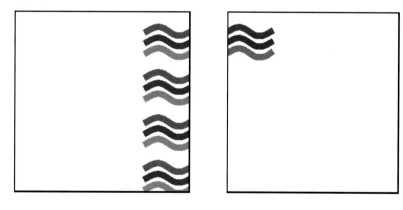

Figure 8.7 The four values of
"repeat" in action: (a) repeat;
(b) repeat-x; (c) repeat-y;
(d) no-repeat.

(c) repeat-y   (d) no-repeat

THE background-attachment PROPERTY

The background-attachment property determines whether the image should
be fixed or moveable on the canvas.

Property name:	background-attachment
Allowed values:	[scroll | fixed]
Initial value:	scroll
Applies to:	all elements
Inherited?:	no
Percentages?:	N/A

This property has two values:

- scroll – the image will scroll along with the content. This is the default.

- fixed – the image will be fixed with regard to the canvas.

A background image is visible only behind the element to which it belongs. When the element scrolls, you usually want its background to tag along. The "scroll" value causes the background to be attached to its element so that where the element goes, so goes its background. That is, as the user scrolls the document up or down or left or right, the background will stay behind its element. This is the default. "Fixed," however, means the background is not attached to the element. As the user scrolls the document, the element moves, but the background doesn't.

Unfortunately, we cannot show the effect in this book ….

The "fixed" value is most useful with BODY, where you would set BODY's background and you don't want it to move as the document is scrolled. Uses include the following.

You can use "fixed" to establish a "watermark" that will stay where you place it independent of the movement of any other element. A watermark is a translucent design that is impressed on paper during the (traditional) printing process and that can be seen faintly when the paper is held up to light. Watermarks are often corporate logos or other designs and are often used for stationery. Obviously, we can't produce a true watermark on a Web page. But it is possible to create the general idea: an image (usually faint so that text and images can be placed over it and still be read) that remains fixed on the window. A good place for a watermark would be the BODY element. Here's an example rule that establishes a watermark:

```
BODY { background: white url(watermark)
   no-repeat center fixed }
```

(It uses the compound background property, explained later in this chapter.) You also can use "fixed" to keep a background aligned with another background, such as when a parent element has a certain pattern and a child has a slightly different pattern, but the two fit together. The only way to ensure they stay aligned is to fix both of them to the same point of origin; the only fixed point of origin in CSS is the window. Hence, "fixed" set on both elements will fix both backgrounds to the window (see Figure 8.8):

```
BODY { background: url(orangetile.png) fixed }
H1 { background: url(redtile.png) fixed }
```

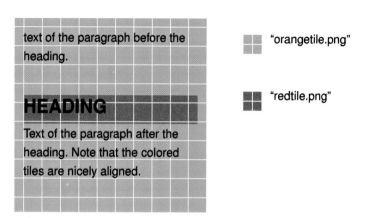

Figure 8.8 Using "fixed" to make sure the background pattern of the heading and the rest of the document are aligned.

You further can use "fixed" to form a horizontal or vertical band that will remain in place even as the document is scrolled over it. Following is example code that shows how you could do this. It specifies a wave pattern image (back/waves.png) across the top of the BODY element that will repeat in a horizontal band (using the "repeat-x" value). Figure 8.9 shows the result.

```
BODY ( background: url(backs/waves.png) repeat-x fixed }
```

Figure 8.9 Using "fixed" to place a permanent horizontal band across the top of the BODY element: when the scrollbar is scrolled up or down, the pattern across the top will stay where it is.

THE background-position PROPERTY

The background-position property lets you override the default position of an image and specify the image's *initial* position, whether a single image or an image that is repeated.

Property name: background-position
Allowed values: [<*percentage*> | <*length*>]{1,2}
                     | [top | center | bottom] || [left | center | right]
Initial value: 0 0
Applies to: all elements
Inherited?: no
Percentages?: refer to the size of the element itself

Essentially, you can set the position of a background image in one of three ways:

• Percentages

• Length values

• Keywords

Placing images using percentages

When you place an image using percentages, you tell the browser where the background image is relative to the size of the element.

Here's an example of how this works. Suppose you have an element and you want to place an image in that element. Assume the element is BODY and your percentage values are 20% and 60%, written as a rule like this:

```
BODY {
  background-position: 20% 60%;
  background-image: url(tile.png)
}
```

First, you locate the upper left corner of the element and the upper left corner of the image. Then from there, find the point in BODY that is 20% across and 60% down. Next, find the point in the image that is 20% across the image and 60% down the image. Finally, you put the image in the element and match the points. This is where the image will appear in BODY. Figure 8.10 shows how this works.

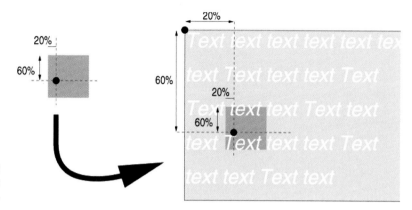

Figure 8.10 Using percentages to position images within an element.

You can enter either one or two percentage values:

- One value: that value will be used for the horizontal position, and the image will be centered vertically. For example, if you enter a single value of 20%, the image will be placed 20% across and 50% down the element. That is, "20%" equals "20% 50%."

- Two values: the first one is the horizontal (*x*-axis) point and the second is the vertical (*y*-axis) point.

Positioning images using percentages makes it easy to specify some very common positions. For example, to center an image in an element you would write simply 50% and to place an image against the right edge of the element requires simply 100%. See also Figure 8.11.

If the background image is "fixed" (see the <u>background-attachment</u> property), the position is not calculated relative to the element, but relative to the window.

Placing images using absolute positions

When you give two length values instead of two percentages, the upper left corner of the image will be that far away from the upper left corner of the element. For example:

```
BLOCKQUOTE {
  background-image: url(shape.png);
  background-position: 1cm 5mm
}
```

will put the background image "shape.png" at 1 cm from the left and 5 mm from the top of the element.

Like with percentages, if you only give one value, the image will be centered vertically. That is, a value of "1cm" is equivalent to "1cm 50%".

Negative values are possible, if you want to put the image partially outside the element. Only the part that is inside the element will be visible, though.

Placing images using keywords

When placing an image using keywords, you use any combination of two keywords. One of three keywords – top, center, bottom – represents the horizontal (*x*-axis) dimension. And one of three keywords – left, center and right – represents the vertical (*y*-axis) dimension.

You cannot combine keywords with percentage values or absolute values.

Figure 8.11 shows the nine positions you can indicate with the keywords, and in parentheses the equivalent percentage values. The order in which you list the keywords in your code doesn't matter. For example, "top left" produces the same result as "left top." This is not the case, however, when using percentages. The order in which you give the percentages makes a big difference in the result. For example, in the previous example in which we explained how to use percentages, we chose 20% and 60% as our values. Reversing the values – to 60% and 20% – in our code would produce a different effect than that shown in Figure 8.10.

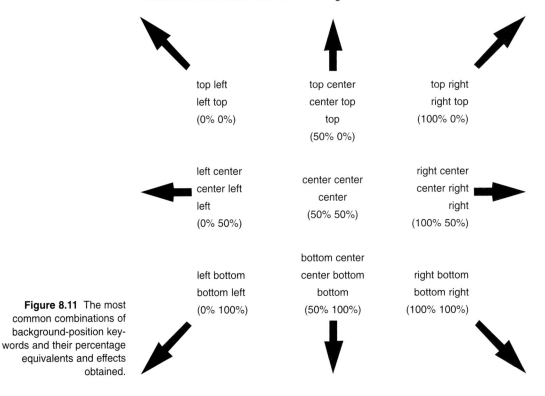

Figure 8.11 The most common combinations of background-position keywords and their percentage equivalents and effects obtained.

If you specify only one dimension, say "top," then the unspecified dimension is assumed to be "center." Hence, this rule:

```
BODY { background: url{banner.jpeg} top }
```

produces the same effect as

```
BODY { background: url{banner.jpeg} top center }
```

THE background PROPERTY

The background property is a shortcut means of setting all of the first five properties at the same time. Its values are all of the possible values of those five properties. You may set from one to five of the properties, in any order. However, this property will always set all five of the properties, regardless of whether you explicitly set values for all five. If you don't explicitly set a value for a specific property, the background property uses that property's initial value as the property's value. For example, here:

```
BODY { background: red }
```

only the value of the background-color property has been set. The background property will assume the initial values for all of the other properties. In contrast, here:

```
P { background: url(chess.png) gray 50% repeat }
```

sets values for four of the properties, but not that for the background-attachment property; hence, that property's value will be the initial value (which is scroll). In other words, the rule above is exactly equivalent to

```
P {
  background-image: url(chess.png);
  background-color: gray;
  background-position: 50%;          /* = 50% 50% */
  background-repeat: repeat;
  background-attachment: scroll      /* implicit */
}
```

You can set separately the five aspects of a background – color, image, repeat, scrolling and position – but we don't recommend this as a rule. The different aspects of a background are so tightly linked in how they work to produce effects that you could end up with some unexpected, even weird, results. For example, setting a <u>background-repeat</u> value without setting the image at the same time may produce a very strange-looking background. The same with specifying an image without also setting the color behind it. In both cases, problems could arise when style sheets are cascaded. Cascading involves using more than one style sheet for your document, for example yours (that is, the designer's), the browser's default style sheet, and possibly one attached by the user. If you were to specify an image without also setting a color behind it, the background might be composed of any combination of background from these three style sheets.

While the user might be able to adjust his or her style sheet to compensate for such an effect, you as the designer should be careful to set all pertinent aspects at the same time so that all aspects work together to produce pleasing results. The <u>background</u> property is the shortest way of setting all five aspects of the background and using it ensures that you don't forget one of them.

SETTING THE BACKGROUND OF THE CANVAS

Sometimes you need to specify the background color of the window; for example, if the document is so short that it doesn't fill the whole window.

The window (or *canvas*, as the CSS1 specification calls it, since it could also refer to paper if the document is printed) does not correspond to any element in the document. Hence, its color has to come from somewhere else. The background of the window will be the same as the background of the HTML element, unless that element is transparent. In this case, the background of the BODY element is used. If that is transparent as well, the result is undefined.

It is as if the background of the HTML element is stretched to the edges of the window. Even if there is a margin set on HTML, the background will stretch into the margin as well. Some people have described this rule as the canvas "stealing" the background of the HTML or BODY element.

Chapter 9

CSS arts and crafts

Welcome to the CSS arts and crafts gallery. On display, you will find some remarkable works of CSS-empowered artistic expressions as well as durable designs.

CSS was developed to be a robust little style sheet language for everyday document needs: a font here, a little white space there. Typographers, rather than graphic designers, were the group of people CSS started out to serve.

However, on the Web, anything that can be used to twiddle a few pixels on other people's screens will be used to do so. So, although graphic designers have not been the primary target for the CSS development, we certainly expect them to be among the users.

The pages on display in this chapter have been created by people eager to try out what CSS1 can offer. Not all examples are written with portability in mind, and some of them exploit bugs in early versions of CSS browsers. Therefore, the CSS code behind the curtain is not printed in this book (where we pride ourselves on very high standards), but you can get the sources behind the URLs listed below.

Two special effects are in much use in this chapter:

- To overlay text elements negative margins values are used. Negative margin values are allowed in CSS1, but as this is a quite complex feature some browsers may not support them.

- To display special symbols, the font family is changed to a "dingbat" font that contains only symbols and no normal letters. This practice is actually illegal according to the CSS1 specification. We are working on alternative methods to achieve the same effect.

Note that there is not a single image in this chapter. That is, the HTML source code of the documents on display contain no IMG elements; all effects produced with textual HTML elements are CSS.

As style sheets move towards artistry, they must be judged not only by their technical merits, but also by the scales of artistic professions. We have therefore invited an art critic who normally judges more traditional art to share with us his thoughts after seeing this chapter.

The Moment of Exterior

Jørgen Lund
Art Critic, Aftenposten, Oslo

It's often noted that western culture is based on the written word, but texts always face us as shapes and forms. Printed texts never escape imagery. The first letters were images and pictures, and writing repeatedly falls backwards into the image. In the largest newspaper headlines, text moves towards its old counterpart with affection. Not only towards the image in terms of a differentiated optical structure of forms and contours, but towards the image as appearance – that which actively overshadows and changes what was before. In traditional newspapers, extraordinary headlines signaling sensation or catastrophe transform a familiar front page into an instant figure, not unlike the way an empty window suddenly changes on the appearance of a human silhouette. The eye is instinctively drawn to the new, like it seeks out life. A text that surprises the viewer by transforming its externals turns into an image that in a second contains all possibilities, all hopes and fears. But if all texts woo the image, thanks to their vanity they become increasingly similar and soon resemble dour linguistic signs: the letters retaliate.

Meeting a text of some length, for example a novel, the eye confronts the gray anonymous rectangle of pages surrounded by white. The dull oblong hanging in a void is an image of the novel, or an image on it. For isn't the novel, or any text of some length, always tied to the magic of penetrating the gray carpet and experiencing the inside, and then again end up by a silent wall? The polarity between the internal and external, between fictive action and sequence of letters, transforms the anonymous page into the richest image: an image telling nothing but holding everything. This is similar to the relationship between the face and the personality, between the individual human being and the notion of him or her, where our opposite's humanity is precisely in the inconsistent and unexpected. Discrepancy between internal and external is a fundamental aspect of meaning. This is the original experience of writing, and typography's opportunity and curse.

Gazillion
Original: IBM advertisement in Wired

Verdana
Educator: Simon Daniels
http://www.microsoft.com/
truetype/css/gallery/spec1.htm

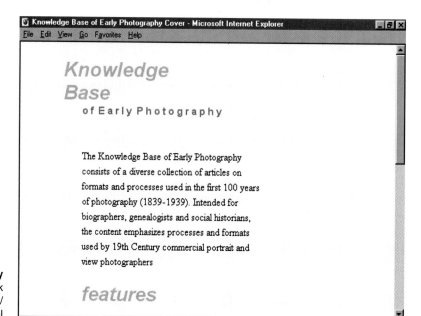

City Gallery
Designer: Steve Knoblock
http://www.webcom.com/cityg/
KnowledgeBase/Cover.html

Knowing When Enough is Enough

Part of authoring a good Web page is knowing what to leave out and when to stop. Adding one-browser-only and cutting-edge features often can create a one-browser-only Web page and, therefore, not a "world-wide" Web page. Currently "frames" are one of the features that fits into this category. For example, many browsers do not support frames. In addition, for some individuals frames can be annoying. One annoying feature (bug) is that they often force a browser to render images even if it is set with the images off. So just for starters, you may be harming low bandwidth users and/or forcing images upon those who prefer the efficiency of browsing with images off.

Java, to a large extent is still in *beta*. And most that I've seen nets little real benefit to viewers yet in relation to all the extra work and bandwidth an application may consume. In other words, currently in most cases, its marginal cost is not yet worth its marginal benefit. That will change when most have an ISDN, T1, or cable line; more powerful computers; 32 bit operating systems; and/or the language matures. But at the moment, the "sweet spot" for this language has not yet been reached.

Enough is Enough
Artisan: Stephen Traub
http://www1.shore.net/
~straub/wprmult6.htm

Grow Up
Designer: Simon Daniels
http://www.microsoft.com/
truetype/css/gallery/4e.htm

Notscape
Creator: John Holman
Based on: Original by
Netscape
http://www.eastax.com/
eastax/stylefun.html

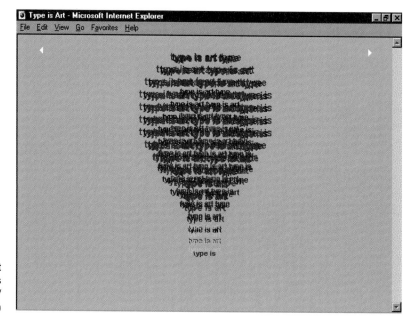

Type is Art
Designer: Simon Daniels
http://www.microsoft.com/
truetype/css/gallery/4c.htm

Surfers wanted
Anonymous contribution

Les Pages Jaunes
Original: France Telecom

Contrast
Designer: Simon Daniels

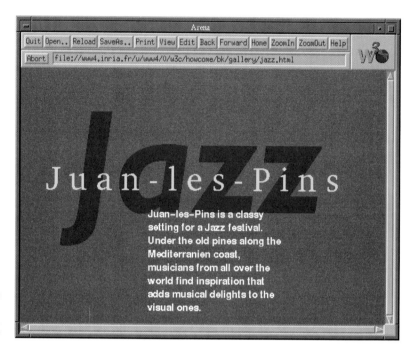

Jazz
Anonymous contribution, displayed in the Arena browser

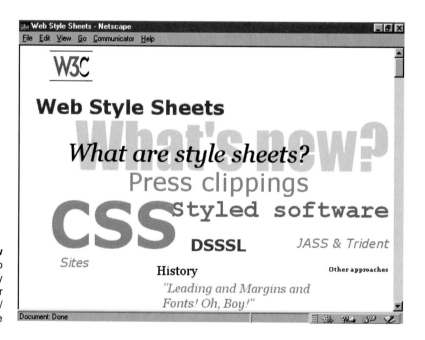

What's new
W3C resource page on Web Style Sheets, displayed by Netscape Navigator
http://www.w3.org/pub/WWW/Style

Chapter 10

CSS makeovers

If you author content for the Web, chances are you already use HTML extensions to achieve some of the stylistic effects that CSS offers. This chapter will present three case studies on how to convert current designs that use HTML extensions into a CSS-based design. Switching to CSS will result in a more compact document that will download faster and print better.

We have chosen the three case studies because we like their design. We do not try to improve the end result, but rather describe ways to enhance the underlying code. Since CSS has not been available until now, the designers of these pages have had no other options than using HTML extensions and images to convey their message.

The case studies in this chapter compare the CSS approach with that of HTML extensions. For more comparisons between CSS and alternative methods of conveying stylistic documents, see Chapter 14.

CASE 1: MAGNET

The original page design (see Figure 10.1) is done as one single image that contains all the text. Also the background color of the document has been set (through an attribute on the BODY tag) to be the same as the background color of the image. While the page looks good on the screen, the image has the undesirable effects of being slow to download and hard to print (although few users would want to print short pages like this – printing is more important for longer documents).

When converting an existing design into CSS, you should start by collecting design features that are used throughout the page. These design features will be turned into declarations on the BODY element and thereby effect all elements through inheritance. Let's start with the colors. The background color throughout the page is brownish (with an RGB value of #c96; see Chapter 8 for a description) and the dominating text color is very dark (#424). This is easily expressed in CSS:

Figure 10.1 Original design: Magnet Interactive Communications (http://www.magnet.com/) URL: http://www.magnet.com/mic/main/mic.html

```
BODY {
  background: #c96;   /* brownish */
  color: #424 }       /* very dark */
}
```

Not all the text on the page is dark and we will later express the exceptions. For now, we are still collecting declarations on the BODY element.

The dominant font family in the original design is a *serif* (see Chapter 4 for a description), but unless you are a typespotter, it's not immediately clear which one is being used. Studies reveal the font in use is "Bodoni."

Not all computers will have "Bodoni" installed, and – until we develop ways to download fonts over the Web – it's important to also specify a generic font family as a fallback option:

```
BODY { font-family: Bodoni, serif }
```

The dominant font size should also be set on the BODY element and the two declarations can easily be combined with the font family on one line by using the <u>font</u> property:

Typespotting is the fine art of detecting font families when seeing them. Becoming a true connoisseur in the field requires years of training and an appreciation of details.

Giambattista Bodoni: Italian printer and type engraver, 1740–1813. The Bodoni fonts are much used in advertising and newspaper headlines.

```
BODY { font: 30px Bodoni, serif }
```

By using the font property you also set the other font properties to their default values (see Chapter 4).

The last declaration to be added to the BODY element is a value on text-align to center the text:

```
BODY { text-align: center }
```

In the original design the lines are centered relative to each other, but are still on the left side of the window. With a "center" value on text-align, the lines will be centered in the window as well – arguably a better design.

The white text in the original design is clickable links, but since they are embedded in an image their appearance does not change when clicked. To set colors on links we use the anchor pseudo-classes described in Chapter 3. The following rules (there are three rules, although it may look like one since the selectors are grouped) express the same design in CSS by assigning the same color to all three pseudo-classes:

```
A:link, A:visited, A:active { color: #fff }   /* white */
```

The only stylistic aspect that has not been described yet is the signature at the bottom of the window. It shows the name of the company that produced the page, and is embedded in the same image as the main text. When converting the image to HTML and CSS, it's natural to place this text inside an ADDRESS element. This gives us a selector for the element, and we can easily set the color:

```
ADDRESS { color: #c11 }          /* reddish */
```

Also, we need to set the font for the ADDRESS element. The font family is clearly *sans serif*, but it's not the common "Helvetica" or "Arial." Rather, we're probably looking at a bold variant of "Eurostyle." The font size is roughly half that of the dominant text, and by using the font property we can set all the font values on one line:

```
ADDRESS {  font: bold 50% Eurostyle, sans-serif }
```

Often, companies feel strongly about the presentation of their name and logo, and since there is a chance the "Eurostyle" is not available, you may want to let the company name remain an image.

CASE 2: CYBERSPAZIO

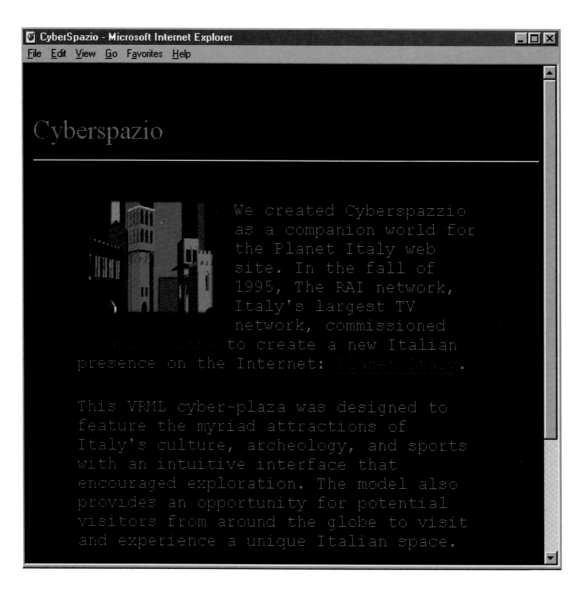

Figure 10.2 Original design: Construct Internet Design Co. http://www.construct.net/ projects/planetitaly/index.html

The original design (see Figure 10.2) uses some common HTML extensions to create this simple, balanced page. First, the background and text colors are set as attributes on the BODY tag. Second, the image (there is only one image on the page) has text wrapping around by way of an attribute on the IMG element. Third, to give the page more white space (actually, it's "black space" on this page), the whole page except the headline and horizontal rule has been put inside a table to set margins on the sides. Also, a chain of BR elements have been used to set more space around the headline. Fourth, TT elements have been used to set a monospace font.

Still, compared to most pages on the Web, this is a good page with a distinct design. No text has been put inside images, so the page will download quickly and print well. The main purpose of using CSS on a page like this is to simplify the HTML markup.

We follow the same strategy as in the first example: find design features that are used throughout the page and thereafter list the exceptions. Let's start with converting the attributes in the BODY element:

Colors

The body element of the Cyberspazio page looks like:

```
<BODY bgcolor="#000000" text="#999999" link="#006666"
vlink="#993300">
```

In Chapter 14 you will find the full set of guidelines on how to convert HTML attributes into CSS rules. Here is the resulting CSS style sheet:

```
BODY { background: #000000; color: #999999 }
A:link { color: #006666 }
A:visited { color: #993300 }
```

Since CSS allows color to be specified in only three digits, the above can be shortened into:

```
BODY { background: #000; color: #999 }
A:link { color: #066 }
A:visited { color: #930 }
```

Images

The only image on this page is found in the first paragraph. It has text floating around it due to the ALIGN attribute on the IMG element:

```
<IMG ALIGN=LEFT SRC="..">
```

It's easy to express the same in CSS:

```
IMG { float: left }
```

To set some space around the image, the original design uses the VSPACE and HSPACE attributes on IMG. In CSS, the margin property allows you to express the same:

```
IMG { margin: 5px 10px 10px 10px }
```

Fonts

The dominant font family on the page is monospace. In the original design this is expressed with a TT element (see Chapter 1 for a description), but since each element has a font family value in CSS there is no need for an extra element. By setting it on the BODY element, it will inherit to all other elements:

```
BODY { font-family: monospace }
```

The font size of the two paragraphs has been increased using the FONT element with a SIZE attribute. Chapter 14 describes in detail how attributes on the FONT element can be expressed in CSS. For example, to increase the document's default font size, you could say:

```
BODY { font-size: x-large }
```

If you hand-craft your style sheets (that is, write them in a text editor), you will appreciate the font property which allows you to combine the two declarations above into one:

```
BODY { font: x-large monospace }
```

The headline ("Cyberspazio") uses another font family. The original design does not specify a font family so the browser default will be used. This is fine, but most designers would probably set a font:

```
H1 { font: 20pt serif }
```

(The original design does not use the H1 element, but rather the presentational FONT element. Since the role of "Cyberspazio" is to be a headline, the use of H1 is recommended.)

White space

The original design uses empty columns in a table to create margins on either side of the text. In CSS, margins are more easily expressed:

```
BODY {
   margin-left: 10%;
   margin-right: 10%
}
```

Since the margin properties are set on the BODY element, they will establish document-wide margins that also apply to the H1 element. In the original design, the headline (and the horizontal rule) only has a very small left margin. You can accomplish the same by setting a negative margin on the headline:

```
H1, HR {
   margin-left: -8%;
   margin-right: -8%
}
```

Alternatively, we could have set only a small document-wide margin and then added extra margins on the P element:

```
BODY {
   margin-left: 2%;
   margin-right: 2%
}
```

```
P {
   margin-left: 8%;
   margin-right: 8%
}
```

This solution assumes that the paragraphs have been put inside P elements.

To set some extra white space around the headline, the original design uses chains of BR elements to add blank lines. CSS offers a better solution by allowing you to declare exactly how much white space you want above and below the element. To replicate the effect shown in Cyberspazio, you could write:

```
H1 {
   margin-top: 3em;
   margin-below: 0.5em
}
```

Recall from Chapter 4 that *em* units refer to the font size in use in the element itself. The above example will therefore give you three blank lines above the element and half a line below.

Similarly, you would want to set extra space below the horizontal rule:

```
HR { margin-below: 1em }
```

It may seem a little weird to refer to the font size of the HR element – whose purpose simply is to draw a horizontal line – but for CSS this comes naturally. All elements have a value for the font-size property even if the element never results in text being displayed.

CASE 3: TSDESIGN

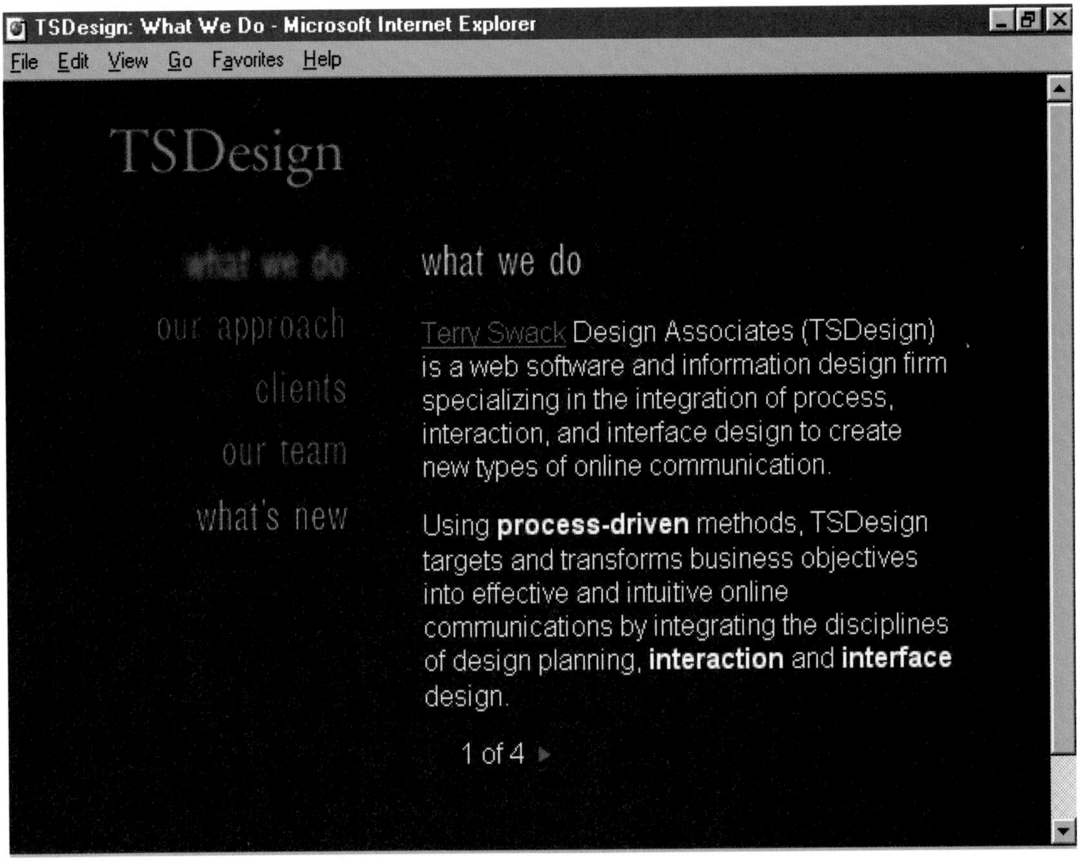

Figure 10.3 Original design: TSDesign http://www.tsdesign.com/ tsdesign/html/whatwedo.html

This elegant and seemingly simple page is the most complex among the three case studies. It includes one text effect not yet expressible in CSS, and the spatial layout poses some extra challenges. Still, the design is within the scope of CSS, and the rewritten code – when converted into CSS – is considerably simpler and more compact than the original design.

To follow the discussion in this case study, you will need an understanding of the concepts described in Chapter 6.

When converting a page like this into CSS, you should follow the same process as described in the two previous case studies. In order to not repeat ourselves unnecessarily we skip the full description of that process and concentrate on the design features which make this page more difficult than the others.

First, you will notice that one of the lines on the left is out of focus. Manipulating focus is a common cinematographic technique that is also much used in contemporary graphic design. Unfortunately, it was deemed a bit too advanced to be included in CSS1. If supported in the future, it will probably end up as a new value on the text-decoration property. But, for now we cannot express this effect and designers must continue to use images to achieve blurred text.

Second, the layout of the page is more complex than in the previous case studies. We can split the page into three distinct areas:

1 the top-level headline ("TSDesign")

2 the vertical menu on the left side, below the headline

3 the right side which includes a second-level headline and some paragraphs.

In the original design, a table has been used to place the various elements on the page. CSS can work alongside tables, but offers layout features of its own that have several advantages: the markup is simpler and the pages will work in browsers that do not support tables.

Another design feature you will notice on this page is that the text in area 2 is right-aligned (see Chapter 6 for a description of text alignment). Also, the headline in area 1 is right-aligned with area 2. Area 3 is more traditional; all text is left-aligned.

Figure 10.4 shows the three areas of the page.

In order to express this layout in CSS, we start by finding one HTML element that will correspond to each area. Area 1 is the simplest since it only contains one element:

```
<H1>TSDesign</H1>
```

We need to set two properties to make the H1 element correspond to area 1. First, the width of the element must be limited – by default an element will stretch out as wide as possible. Second, the text within the element must be set to be right-aligned. The style sheet becomes:

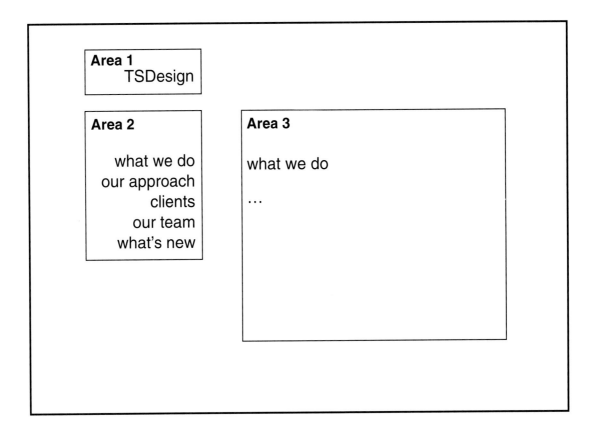

Figure 10.4 The three areas of the page.

```
H1 { width: 30%; text-align: right }
```

Area 2 is slightly more complex since it has multiple elements in it. The elements form a list, and it's therefore natural to put them inside a UL element – although the original design doesn't do this. The added benefit of using a UL is that we get an element that corresponds to area 2:

```
<UL CLASS=main-menu>
  <LI>what we do
  <LI>our approach
  <LI>clients
  <LI>our team
  <LI>what's new
</UL>
```

Since there may be other UL elements in the document, we added a CLASS attribute on UL.

Normally, LI elements within UL have a list marker. This is not the case in the original design, so we turn it off with:

```
UL.main-menu { list-style: none }
```

Also, we must set the width and the text alignment as we did for area 1:

```
UL.main-menu { width: 30%; text-align: right }
```

Area 3 is the last and the most complex among the three. It contains multiple elements of various types and the area has no natural enclosing element that corresponds to it. Thus we have to add one of our own, and the DIV element serves this purpose:

```
<DIV CLASS=main-text>
  <H2>what we do</H2>

  <P>...

</DIV>
```

Recall from Chapter 3 (Selectors) that DIV – in combination with a CLASS attribute – allows you to create your own elements. Now that we have an element we attach style sheet rules to it:

```
DIV.main-text { width: 60%; text-align: left }
```

Setting the text alignment is probably not necessary since this is how Western languages are normally presented. Setting the width, however, is very necessary unless you want the content of the area to use all the available space.

We have now found three elements that each represent an area as shown in Figure 10.4. Also, we have assigned values to the width and text-align properties so that they resemble the original design. What remains is to position the elements. The original design uses tables to accomplish the spatial layout, but we will – no surprise – use CSS.

The key property to archiving table-like behavior in CSS is the float property. Earlier in this chapter we used float to have text wrap around an image, thus placing the image and the text next to each other horizontally. When using HTML extensions you can only make images float, but CSS has no such restriction: any element can float.

By making area 2 (or, more correctly, the UL element that represents area 2) float we will allow area 3 to be placed next to it:

```
UL.main-menu { float: left }
```

If you have trouble understanding why this will work, think of area 2 as an image for a moment: surely images can have text floating around them. The only difference is that area 2 is not an image, but a textual element (namely UL).

Actually, there is one more difference. The text in area 3 is to the side of area 2, but it doesn't wrap around in the same way as text wraps around the image of case study 2. Instead it continues downwards along the same left margin. This is achieved by setting the left margin:

```
DIV.main-text { margin-left: 40% }
```

Recall from above that the width of the DIV element has been set to 60% of the available width. A left margin of 40% therefore makes sure the element moves over to the right.

Since not all aspects of re-creating this example in CSS were discussed, the complete style sheet is included as a reference:

```
<HTML>
<TITLE>TSDesign: What We do</TITLE>
<STYLE TYPE="text/css">
  BODY {
       background: #003;
       color: #fff;
       font: sans-serif;
       margin-left: 5%;
       margin-right: 5%;
  }
  A:link { color: #969 }
  A:visited { color: #666 }

  H1 {                          /* area 1 */
       font: 35px Garamond, serif;
       width: 30%;
       text-align: right;
  }

  UL {                          /* area 2 */
       width: 30%;
       float: left;
       text-align: right;
       font-size: 20px;
       list-style: none;
  }
```

```
    DIV.main-text {                    /* area 3 */
        width: 60%;
        margin-left: 40%;
    }

    H2 { font: 30px sans-serif }

</STYLE>

<BODY>
  <H1 STYLE="color: #999">TSDesign</H1>

  <DIV CLASS=main-menu>
      <UL>
          <LI STYLE="color: #668">what we do
          <LI STYLE="color: #b33">our approach
          <LI STYLE="color: #996">clients
          <LI STYLE="color: #695">our team
          <LI STYLE="color: #f93">what's new
      </UL>
  </DIV>

  <DIV CLASS=main-text>
      <H2 STYLE="color: #ff9">what we do</H2>

      <P>...

  </DIV>
</BODY>
</HTML>
```

Chapter 11

Cascading and inheritance

CSS is sometimes referred to as a style sheet *language* because the most visible part of CSS is the language in which one expresses style sheets. However, a major part of CSS is the mechanism that interprets style sheets and resolves conflicts between rules. All browsers that support CSS are required to use the same mechanism for this. This mechanism has two main parts: cascading and inheritance.

Inheritance was described in Chapter 2, where we also introduced cascading. However, we left out the technical details of how inheritance and cascading work. We present those in this chapter. You do not need to understand this chapter in detail to use CSS productively, but if you ever wonder why one rule wins over others, you will find the answer in this chapter.

"Cascading" refers to the cascade of style sheets from different sources that may influence the presentation of a document. Style sheets come from the browser and the designer, and may come from the user as well. The cascading *mechanism* is designed to resolve conflicts between these style sheets. Compared to other style sheet proposals, CSS is quite traditional in the stylistic properties it supports. However, as far as we know, cascading is unique to CSS.

The mechanism used now is not the first devised for CSS. The first published CSS proposal described a cascading mechanism that tried to combine conflicting rules to reach a median result in a process called *interpolation*. If the designer wanted, for example, headlines in sans-serif fonts while the user preferred serif fonts, the result would be something in between (fonts like this do exist). Interpolation didn't always work, however. For example, if the designer wanted fully justified text ("text-align: justify") while the user wanted left-aligned text ("text-align left"), there was no acceptable median alternative. So the interpolation of values was dropped at an early stage while the concept of cascading style sheets remained.

The current cascading mechanism always chooses only one value. That is, when there is more than one style sheet rule trying to set a certain property value on a certain element, the cascading mechanism will pick one of the rules. The selected rule will be given full control of the value in question. The challenge is to pick the right rule. This is not always easy, since conflicts can appear in several areas:

- *Designer style sheets versus user style sheets:* The most articulated conflict, and certainly the most political one, is the one between users and authors. Designers that come from a paper-based environment are used to having full control over the distribution and presentation of information. However, on the Web, users expect to have a say in how documents are presented. CSS supports the users' position by allowing user style sheets.

- *User style sheets versus browser style sheets:* Each browser has a built-in style sheet that also is part of the *cascade*. The default style sheet ensures that there always is a description of how documents are to be presented.

- *Conflicting rules set on the same element:* Different rules in the same style sheet may set conflicting values on the same element/property combination.

- *Added weight given to certain rules:* Designers and users can increase the weight of certain rules. These then escape the normal cascading order.

The inheritance mechanism is used only when *no* rules in any of the style sheets in the cascade try to set a certain property value. The property value then will be inherited from the parent element. If the property does not inherit, the initial value will be used instead. (Most properties do inherit. See the inside cover for a quick overview.)

The difference between cascading and inheritance can be illustrated graphically using a variation of the now-familiar tree structure. In the diagram below, inheritance works vertically. That is, values are inherited from parent elements to child elements as described in Chapter 2. Cascading, in contrast, works horizontally. All rules that apply to an element, no matter what style sheet they come from, are collected and subsequently sorted. In the cascading order, rules coming from the browser default style sheet have the lowest priority, followed by user style sheets and designer style sheets. See Figure 11.1.

Figure 11.1 Cascading is horizontal; inheritance is vertical. Inheritance moves values from parent elements to child elements. Cascading collects rules that apply to the same elements. The "cascade" moves from left to right: the rightmost style sheet has the highest weight.

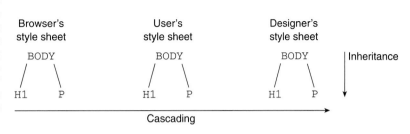

If you don't fully grasp the differences yet, don't worry. The following examples demonstrate how cascading and inheritance work.

EXAMPLE 1: THE BASICS

Here's a simple example of cascading and inheritance in action. We begin with a simple HTML document:

```
<HTML>
  <TITLE>A sample document</TITLE>
  <BODY>
    <H1>The headline</H1>
    <P>The text
  </BODY>
</HTML>
```

Then, we add two style sheets:

Browser's style sheet	Designer's style sheet
`BODY { font-family: sans-serif }`	`H1 { font-family: serif }`

Graphically, the document structure with style sheets attached looks like this:

CSS now must resolve differences between these style sheets. First, the cascading mechanism gets to work. For each element in the tree, rules are collected. In this example, no element has more than one rule for the same property, so there are no conflicts that need to be resolved. After cascading, the document structure looks like this:

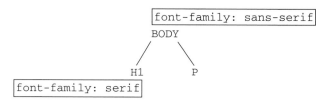

Next, the inheritance mechanism kicks in. The P element has no rule attached to it, so it inherits its parent's value. The document structure now looks like this:

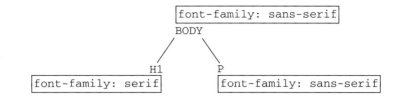

Since there were no conflicting rules in this example, combining the two style sheets only uses the inheritance mechanism. In the next example, conflicts are introduced.

EXAMPLE 2: CONFLICTS APPEAR

Most often, a user will accept the designer's style sheet. However, personal preferences or physical handicaps may prompt users to write their own style sheets. The following example demonstrates how CSS resolves conflicts between designers and users. We'll be using the same sample document:

```
<HTML>
   <TITLE>A sample document</TITLE>
   <BODY>
      <H1>The headline</H1>
      <P>The text</P>
   </BODY>
</HTML>
```

Two style sheets try to influence the presentation of the document:

User's style sheet

```
BODY {
   color: black;
   background: white;
}
```

Designer's style sheet

```
BODY {
   color: white;
   background: black;
}
```

(Although the browser's default style sheet always will be there as well, we have omitted it to simplify the example)

Graphically, the document structure with the style sheets attached looks like this:

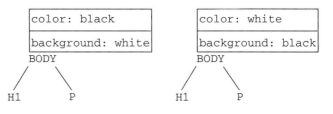

As you can see, both the user and the designer are trying to set the color and background for BODY, so the rules conflict. CSS first applies the cascading mechanism. The following principle resolves the conflict:

Designer style rules override user style rules.

(Some people think this rule is unfair. Read on. We offer two alternatives in the next example.)

Hence, after cascading the document structure looks like this:

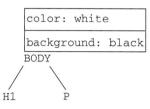

Next CSS applies the inheritance mechanism. The <u>color</u> property inherits, but the <u>background</u> property is among those that don't. So <u>background</u>'s *initial value* – "transparent" – will be used:

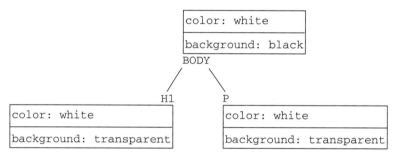

The background of the parent element will show through the transparent background, thereby producing, in effect, the same result as would inheritance. In this example, both the H1 and P elements will appear to have black backgrounds.

EXAMPLE 3: ACCOMMODATING USER STYLES

In the previous example, we showed how the cascading mechanism gives designer style sheets more weight than user style sheets. Some people consider this unfair, so we include in CSS two alternatives for letting the user's rules prevail:

1 The user can turn off style sheets. The CSS specification recommends that browsers allow the user to selectively turn style sheets on and off. Typically, the opportunity to do this would be offered via a pull-down menu that displays all available style sheets, thereby allowing the user to pick the one desired.

2 Users can mark rules in their style sheets as "important," thus overriding the designer's same rule for the same element.

In the previous Example 2, the designer's style rules were given more weight than the user's. To do the opposite, we change the user's style sheet as follows:

User's style sheet

```
BODY {
    color: black !important;
    background: white !important;
}
```

Designer's style sheet

```
BODY {
    color: white;
    background: black
}
```

Adding the keyword "!important" gives a rule added weight. That rule will thereafter override the designer's rule for the same property and element. After cascading, the document structure will be like this:

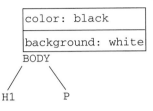

To keep CSS symmetric, we also allow the designer to mark rules as important. If the designer marks the same rules important that the user does, however, then the outcome will be like in Example 2.

A word of caution: overriding another style sheet often will be much harder than this example indicates. For example, if the designer's style sheet includes <u>color</u> and <u>background</u> rules for the H1 element, the user will have to override these rules as well. To fully override the effect of another style sheet, one must override each and every rule in it. This is hard to do if you don't know what the incoming style sheet contains.

Currently, it's hard to say how style sheets will develop on the Web. Will each and every document have its own style sheet, or will the whole Web converge around, say, 20 standard style sheets? The answer to these questions will to some extent determine the usefulness of the cascading mechanism.

EXAMPLE 4: A MORE COMPLEX EXAMPLE

In this example, we follow the steps a browser goes through to find the value of a certain property for a certain element. The numbered steps correspond to the definition of cascading in the CSS1 specification.

We will use a slightly more complicated sample HTML document:

```
<HTML>
  <TITLE>A sample document</TITLE>
  <BODY>
    <H1 CLASS=first ID=x45y>The headline</H1>
    <P>The text
  </BODY>
</HTML>
```

Also, the style sheets involved are more elaborate than earlier ones. They were written to demonstrate the specifics of the cascading and inheritance mechanisms.

Designer's style sheet

```
1  H1 { letter-spacing: 1em }
2  H1.initial { letter-spacing: 2em }
3  #x45y { letter-spacing: 3em }
4  #x45y { letter-spacing: 2em }
```

User's style sheet

```
5  BODY H1 { letter-spacing: 3em }
6  H1 { letter-spacing: 1em }
7  BODY { letter-spacing: 1em }
8  H1 { word-spacing: 1em }
```

The goal is to find the value of the <u>letter-spacing</u> property for the H1 element. This involves several steps. The search ends when the one specific rule is found that will set the value.

Step 1: Find all rules that apply

We begin by going through the rules in the style sheet examples and identifying the ones that apply:

- Rule 1 – A simple selector that match all H1 elements. We are looking for the value of <u>letter-spacing</u> on an H1 element, so the rule applies.

- Rule 2 – The selector is more complex. It matches H1 elements, but only those that are of class "initial." The element is question is of class "first," so the selector does not match and the rules does not apply. Note that class matching is based on a comparison of the class names. That "first" and "initial" are synonyms isn't important.

- Rule 3 – The selector looks for an element with a certain ID attribute. The element in question has an ID attribute with a matching value, so the rule applies.

- Rule 4 – Same as rule 3: the ID selector matches the element in question, so the rule applies.
- Rule 5 – The selector is contextual. It matches only if the element in question has a BODY element as an ancestor. This will always be the case in HTML, so the rule applies.
- Rule 6 – This rule is similar to rule one except it comes from the user's style sheet, not the designer's. The selector matches for the same reason rule one's selector matches.
- Rule 7 – This rule tries to influence the property in question, but the selector is BODY, so the rule does not apply.
- Rule 8 – This rule has the same selector as rules one and four, so it applies to the element in question. However, it sets a value for another property (word-spacing), so we ignore it.

Here's the situation after the first step. Grayed-out rules means they don't apply.

Designer's style sheet

```
1   H1 { letter-spacing: 1em }
/   H1.initial { letter-spacing: 2em } /
3   #x45y { letter-spacing: 3em }
4   #x45y { letter-spacing: 2em }
```

User's style sheet

```
5   BODY H1 { letter-spacing: 3em }
6   H1 { letter-spacing: 1em }
/   BODY { letter-spacing: 1em } /
/   H1 { word-spacing: 1em } /
```

If no rules had applied, the inherited value would have been used. That is, the inheritance mechanism will only be used if there is no applicable rule. This demonstrates that the cascading mechanism is stronger than inheritance.

Step 2: Sort the rules by explicit weight

Rules can be given extra importance by labeling them "! important." None of the remaining set of rules in the example are labeled, so this step has no effect on the cascading order. If a rule did have this label, it would have won the competition and the rule we seek would have been found.

Step 3: Sort by origin

Although CSS allows both designers and users to submit style sheets, users usually will be happy to accept the designer's style sheet. This assumption is reflected in this step: Designer style sheets are given a greater weight than user style sheets. (As described in Example 3, however, users have ways to circumvent this.) Accordingly, the remaining user's rules can be dismissed. Here is the result:

Designer's style sheet

```
1  H1 { letter-spacing: 1em }
/  H1.initial { letter-spacing: 2em } /
3  #x45y { letter-spacing: 3em }
4  #x45y { letter-spacing: 2em }
```

User's style sheet

```
/  BODY H1 { letter-spacing: 3em } /
/  H1 { letter-spacing: 1em } /
/  BODY { letter-spacing: 1em } /
/  H1 { word-spacing: 1em } /
```

Step 4: Sort by specificity

We now try to find the most *specific* rule among those remaining. The principle is that a very specific rule (for example, one that targets one specific element) should win over a more general rule that applies to a large number of elements.

CSS computes which is the *specific rule* based on the rules' selectors. A selector that addresses all elements of a certain type (for example, all H1 elements) is considered very general. This is the case with rule one. Rules three and four, however, apply only to one element (since the ID attribute is guaranteed to be unique across the document), so their specificity is higher.

(The exact formula for computing the specificity of a selector is perhaps the most complex part of CSS, so we have elected not to explain it here. Instead, we point interested readers to the CSS1 specification for more information.)

We now have two rules left:

Designer's style sheet

```
/  H1 { letter-spacing: 1em } /
/  H1.initial { letter-spacing: 2em } /
3  #x45y { letter-spacing: 3em }
4  #x45y { letter-spacing: 2em }
```

User's style sheet

```
/   BODY H1 { letter-spacing: 3em } /
/   H1 { letter-spacing: 1em } /
/   BODY { letter-spacing: 1em } /
/   H1 { word-spacing: 1em } /
```

Step 5: Sort by order specified

Finally, we sort rules by the order in which they are specified. The later a rule is specified, the more weight it is given. Rule four will therefore have a higher weight than rule three and can be declared the winner: the H1 element will have a letter-spacing of 2 em.

If you have followed us all the way through this chapter: congratulations, you know a lot about CSS1 selectors!

Chapter 12

Style sheets in organizations

CSS is designed to work equally well for large collections of pages as it does for individual documents. It's easy to maintain standard style sheets for use in any document while also providing the flexibility needed to make changes to individual documents to meet special needs. In this way, organizations such as companies, educational institutions, and nonprofit groups can establish organization-wide style sheets that apply to all documents. Doing this can help promote a unified public image as well as save resources, since people don't have to "reinvent the wheel" each time they create a document.

Three mechanisms are available to do this:

- The LINK element
- The @import declaration
- The CLASS attribute

We discuss each of these mechanisms in this chapter.

LINKING DOCUMENTS USING LINK

The easiest way to apply a standard, organizational style sheet to multiple documents is via the LINK element.

For LINK to work, the style sheet being linked to must exist as a separate file. Then the following line must be added at the head of each document that is to link to the style sheet:

```
<LINK REL=STYLESHEET HREF="mystyle">
```

"mystyle" is the URL of the requested style sheet. The attribute "rel=stylesheet" tells the browser that the link is to a style sheet and not to something else. Without this attribute, the browser will not attempt to load the indicated URL.

The linked style sheet becomes the default style sheet for the document, provided it is the only style sheet linked via LINK *and* there is no STYLE element in the document. If there is more than one linked style sheet, the first one is the default, while the others are alternatives from which the user may choose. If there is a STYLE element in the document, that element defines the default style sheet, while any linked style sheets are alternatives.

For example, suppose a document starts with the following:

```
<LINK REL=stylesheet HREF="blues"TITLE="Blues">
<LINK REL=stylesheet HREF="disco"TITLE="Disco">
<STYLE type="text/css">
  H1 { font-style: palatino, sans-serif }
  P {
    color: blue;
    background: white;
  }
</STYLE>
```

This mechanism is still under discussion. It may be that there will be a different method to indicate the default style sheet.

The style set out in the STYLE element will be the default. The "blues" and "disco" style sheets will be alternatives to the STYLE element. It depends on the browser how the user can select an alternative. Some browsers will have a menu for choosing styles.

ADDING SPECIAL STYLES WITH THE STYLE ELEMENT AND @IMPORT

If individual documents need special styles in addition to those in the organizational style sheet, the LINK element cannot be used to link to the organizational style sheet. Instead, you import that style sheet using the @import declaration in a STYLE element. In this way, *local rules* can override the organizational style sheet rules where necessary. A local rule is a rule that applies only to the document in which it appears. It does not affect the organizational style sheet or any other document (unless it is explicitly added there as well).

You always write the @import declaration as the first declaration in the STYLE element. The local rules follow, as the following example shows, and will override any conflicting rules in the imported style sheet:

```
<STYLE type="text/css">
  @import "mystyle";
  H1 { font-style: palatino, sans-serif }    ⎤ local
  P { color: blue; background: white }       ⎦ rules
</STYLE>
```

You can import any number of external style sheets using @import by inserting multiple @import declarations, each with the URL of a style sheet.

Importing multiple style sheets can result in a tier of style sheets. This is because an imported style can have its own @import declarations, which point to style sheets that may also have @import declarations, and so on. The order of the declarations is significant. Each additional level of @import has lower priority in case of conflicting rules, that is, style sheets that are imported later override those imported earlier. So you should place your basic style sheet(s) first and follow with supplementary style sheets included for specialized purposes.

You can use @import declarations in a modular fashion to customize your documents. For example, you may have as separate files style sheets that define different background images, default fonts, methods for handling tables, and special kinds of paragraphs and lists. Then in any particular document, you can use @import to pull in the appropriate style sheets to create the desired effect. For example:

```
<STYLE TYPE="text/css">
  @import "basics";
  @import "list-styles";
  @import "headings";
  @import "rules";
</STYLE>
```

Notice that we included the TYPE attribute in the STYLE element, for example, "type="text/css"." We talked about this attribute in Chapter 2. Its use is a convenient way to let the browser know which style sheet is being used. We recommend you include it to get in the habit. When other types of style languages become available (DSSSL, for example, see Chapter 14), you will need to use it so that the browser will know the type of style sheet being linked to.

CUSTOMIZING DOCUMENTS USING THE CLASS ATTRIBUTE

The CLASS attribute is ideal for defining new types of elements that can apply to all or most documents of a collection. In this way, HTML can be enriched with more elements for specific roles that can be used to customize documents.

HTML represents the greatest common denominator of a large class of documents. It has elements that specify titles, paragraphs, lists, and emphasis, as well as a few more specific ones such as BLOCKQUOTE. Many documents fit this structure, although the fit may be loose. Often documents, especially those in a business environment, have much stricter structures and require more refined formatting than can be achieved with just the HTML generic elements.

There are just so many HMTL elements, all but two of which are assigned specific meanings. The DIV and SPAN elements have no specific role.

With CLASS, you can create specialized versions of elements, called classed elements, to supplement the existing elements. We discussed the CLASS attribute in Chapter 3. For example, to create a specialized version of an H2 to act as a subtitle, you can do this:

```
<H2>Main title</H2>
<H2 CLASS="subtitle">A subtitle</H2>
```

In many cases, CLASS is used to indicate a semantic category; that is, the name of the class is meaningful. Even though the name you choose is not important for HTML or CSS (you could name all your classes C1, C2, C3, and so on), it is customary to use a descriptive term, like "subtitle," "first-par," "person." The term could even have a specific meaning in a different application.

For example, when the HTML is generated from a database, classed elements can indicate the database field from which the information is extracted. In this way, it is not only possible to give different styles to different types of information, but also to store enough information in the HTML to make a reverse translation possible, or at least a search for specific types of information. See Figure 12.1.

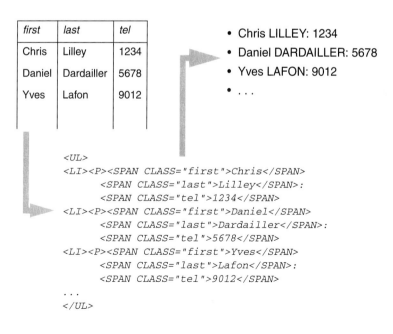

first	last	tel
Chris	Lilley	1234
Daniel	Dardailler	5678
Yves	Lafon	9012

- Chris LILLEY: 1234
- Daniel DARDAILLER: 5678
- Yves LAFON: 9012
- . . .

```
<UL>
<LI><P><SPAN CLASS="first">Chris</SPAN>
        <SPAN CLASS="last">Lilley</SPAN>:
        <SPAN CLASS="tel">1234</SPAN>
<LI><P><SPAN CLASS="first">Daniel</SPAN>
        <SPAN CLASS="last">Dardailler</SPAN>:
        <SPAN CLASS="tel">5678</SPAN>
<LI><P><SPAN CLASS="first">Yves</SPAN>
        <SPAN CLASS="last">Lafon</SPAN>:
        <SPAN CLASS="tel">9012</SPAN>
. . .
</UL>
```

Figure 12.1 Example of HTML that is generated from a database with a report generator. Although the format is different, it has much the same information, and could, in principle, be translated back.

CREATING A CUSTOM MEMO FORM

One type of a fairly specialized document that can benefit from classed elements is a memo. A memo usually consists of elements that contain information about the subject, date, sender's name, and addressee. In HTML, all of these would have to be either paragraphs or titles. Thus they would lose their specific roles. You could correct this by using the CLASS attribute to create additional elements.

For example, you could create variants of a heading element, such as `<H2 class="subject">`, `<H2 class="date">`, `<H2 class="sender">`, and `<H2 class="addressee">`. By default, all will have the same style as the H2 element itself; however, you can write style rules to override that.

It is not possible, however, to specify either in HTML or in CSS that the text must start with certain elements in a prescribed order, such as first `<H2 class=addressee>`, then `<H2 class=sender>`, then `<H2 class=subject>`, and then `<H2 class=date>`. For files that play a certain role in a company, such a fixed structure is often necessary. (If the text is generated by a program from some other source, the generating software will ensure the correct structure. But if the HTML is typed directly, either the author has to have some self-discipline or somebody has to provide him or her with a tool that checks the text against the company rules.)

Following is the code for an example memo form. The resulting memo form should look like Figure 12.2.

```
<HTML>
<TITLE>memo: Book writing</TITLE>
<LINK REL=STYLESHEET HREF="/styles/memo">
<BODY>
   <H1><IMG HREF="/logos/strict"> Strict
        Manufacturing Inc.</H1>
   <DIV CLASS=head>
        <H2 CLASS=to>To: everybody</H2>
        <H2 CLASS=subject>Subject: Book writing</H2>
        <H2 CLASS=from>From: John</H2>
        <H2 CLASS=date>Date: 29 Nov 1996</H2>
        <H2 CLASS=confidentiality>Confidentiality:
             no restriction</H2>
   </DIV>
   <DIV CLASS=body>
        <P>Everybody should write a book!
   </DIV>
</BODY>
</HTML>
```

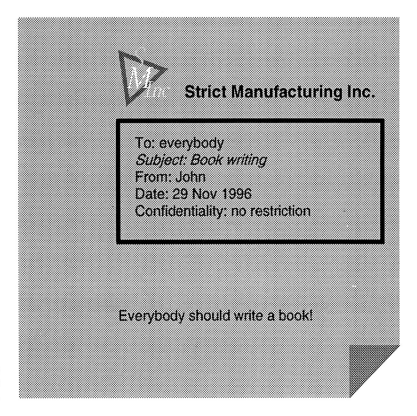

Figure 12.2 A possible rendering of the memo example.

The style sheet is included via a LINK to the relative URL "/styles/memo". It looks like this:

```
body {
    background: rgb(100%,70%,70%);
    font: 12pt/14pt helvetica;
}
div.head { border: thick; padding: 5mm; }
div.body { margin-top: 2cm; margin-left: 3cm; }
h2.to, h2.from, h2.date, h2.confidentiality {
    font-style: normal; font-weight: medium; }
h2.subject { font-style: italic; font-weight: medium; }
```

Note that in this type of document, there is no stylistic difference between four of the five H2 elements. In the memo, they are recognizable by their order, which CSS can't enforce. They are still labeled with different CLASS attributes, so that a search tool can find them. The labeling also allows the memos to be stored in a database.

OTHER WAYS OF LINKING STYLE SHEETS TO DOCUMENTS

The two ways of associating a style sheet with a document, the LINK element and the STYLE element, are currently the only two. In both cases, the HTML document needs to be modified to add a style sheet: you'll need to add either a LINK or a STYLE near the top of the document. However, a system is under development to allow a document and a style sheet to be linked together without touching either of them at all. The idea is to associate a style sheet with the hyperlink to the document, instead of with the document itself. Chapter 15 contains more information.

Chapter 13

Style sheets with style

CSS is a powerful mechanism for describing the presentation of HTML documents. Used with care, it can enhance the esthetics and readability of your document. But, like any other powerful mechanism, it can be abused.

In this chapter, we give you guidelines for ensuring your style sheets are flexible and your documents are as attractive and useful as possible. We emphasize that these are guidelines, not laws. They sometimes need to be disregarded. As you work with CSS, you will likely develop an understanding of when to do this in order to achieve your intended effect.

Following is a summary of the guidelines that you can use for quick reference:

- Design for reusability
- Design for scalability
- Design to accommodate cascading
- Test your style sheets on more than one browser
- Work with the document structure, not against it
- Make your documents legible
- Provide generic font families
- Don't depend on a specific font to achieve a design effect
- Use negative margins carefully
- Use numbers, not names, for colors
- Know when to stop

Design for reusability

Write your style sheet so that more than one document can use it. Try to distinguish between general rules and document-specific overrides. The general rules should go into a style sheet that is referred to through a LINK element. The document-specific overrides should go into a STYLE element or STYLE attributes in the document.

Design for scalability

Ensure your documents are scalable, since they will be displayed in dynamic environments and need to adjust to many sorts of devices. This is most easily done by choosing the right units of measure; choosing the right unit is one of the most important design decisions you will make when using CSS. Although all types of units discussed in this book have valid use in CSS, you should choose relative units and keyword values over absolute units whenever possible, particularly for the various margin, width, and font properties.

Design to accommodate cascading

Realize that some users will have personal style preferences when reading your documents. Write your style sheets so that a user's personal sheet will cascade gracefully with yours. You can help with this by setting properties in recommended places. Style rules that apply to the whole document should, for example, be set on the BODY element – and only there. In this way, the user can easily modify document-wide style settings.

Test your style sheets on more than one browser

Test your style sheets on more than one browser to ensure users will not be surprised. In this book, you learned about the wonderful world of style sheets. However, your documents will enter a Web in which not all browsers are CSS-enhanced. Even though browser vendors have quick release cycles for their browser software, it still takes time to deploy new versions. So, always include a non-CSS browser in your test suite to ensure your documents display well on them as well as on CSS browsers. If you do use features that not every browser supports, make sure they degrade gracefully. That is, your document should look great in some browsers and at least reasonable in others.

Work with the document structure, not against it

Take advantage of document structure; don't ignore it. For example, using STYLE and ID attributes, it's possible to write style sheets that use, say, only P elements. However, doing this is against the principles of the use of style sheets. Style sheets should augment the document structure, not replace it.

Make your documents legible

Ensure the text color contrasts sufficiently with the background. When using an image as a background, also specify a background color that contrasts with the text color. Also, use font sizes that are easily read – not too small, not too big.

Provide generic font families

Realize that your document will end up on systems that have different fonts. Always specify a generic font family as part of the font list that the browser can use if it doesn't have the specific font families.

Don't depend on a specific font to achieve a design effect

Avoid using a specific font, such as Wingdings, to achieve a design effect. The effort will fail miserably on browsers that do not have that font. Actually, according to the CSS1 specification, browsers should not support these sorts of effects since they inevitably will lead to documents looking very differently depending on the font resources available. W3C and others are working on finding reliable solutions to this problem.

Use negative margins carefully

Use negative margins with discretion. Although they can greatly enhance your document (for some stunning examples, see Chapter 9), their internal construction may not be supported by all browsers. Be sure to test your designs that use negative margins on several different browsers.

Use numbers, not names, for colors

Use numbers for colors if your choice of color is not on the list of 16 specifically supported in CSS1 (see Chapter 8). Color names may seem friendlier that the somewhat cryptic RGB notation described in that chapter, but the Web has yet to see the ultimate list of color names that work on all platforms. Color numbers, on the other hand, can easily be interpreted by any browser.

Know when to stop

Be critical when designing your style sheet. Just because you can use 10 different fonts and 30 different colors on the same page doesn't mean you have to – or should. Simple style sheets often will convey your message better than overloaded ones.

Chapter 14

Other approaches

One of the main goals of CSS is to provide an attractive presentation of electronic documents. But CSS also has other aims, such as to separate the structure and content of documents (which makes them accessible on a wide range of devices) and to simplify the creation and maintenance of documents.

There are other approaches to the problem of creating attractive presentations. This chapter describes some of them. They have different goals from CSS, or they give different priorities to their goals. Broadly speaking, they fall into three categories:

- other style sheet languages

- HTML without style sheets

- other formats than HTML

This chapter assumes a little more knowledge of Web-related technology than the preceding chapters. It is included for those who want to compare CSS to other systems. You can skip it, if you only want to know how to use CSS.

USING OTHER STYLE SHEET LANGUAGES

SGML (Standard Generalized Markup Language) is an ISO (International Standards Organization) standard for storing text documents (ISO 8879:1986). It defines general rules, not a single format. HTML conforms to those rules and is thus an example of an SGML format. An SGML viewer is a program that can display documents in many SGML formats. Typically, an SGML viewer can also display HTML, but an HTML viewer (such as a browser) cannot display other SGML formats.

Some SGML viewers have their own style languages. Some of these languages, such as the one used by SoftQuad's Panorama (and Panorama Pro), can even be used over the Web.

Panorama

To use Panorama, you need Panorama, either Netscape or Mosaic, and, for the moment, a PC running Windows (3.1, 95 or NT). Panorama's style sheets are similar in scope to those of CSS1, but they are richer in some areas and weaker in others. They are written in a language based on SGML, which makes them hard to write by hand. But they are intended to be created with the style editor of Panorama Pro, so designers never need to see them.

To use Panorama's style sheets over the Web, a Web server needs to send HTML documents labeled as SGML (official name on the Internet: "text/sgml") rather than the normal HTML ("text/html"). Panorama also has its own way of linking style sheets to documents. It doesn't use the LINK tag. Its approach is cleaner than LINK in many ways in that it works for all SGML documents.

Panorama's style language doesn't seem to be developed any further, and it likely will be replaced by either DSSSL (see the next section) or CSS in the future. SoftQuad can be found at http://www.softquad.com/.

Document Style Semantics and Specification Language (DSSSL)

Document Style Semantics and Specification Language (DSSSL) is an ISO standard (ISO/IEC 10179:1996) for describing the formatting of SGML documents and their transformation from one SGML format to another. It was created by the same ISO working group that created SGML. It is not meant to be written by the average Web designer. Its style sheet must either be created by a programmer or generated by a tool, such as a word processor with an appropriate "save-as" command.

DSSSL is actually two languages: transformation language and style language. The former describes how to transform documents from one SGML format to another. The latter describes how to transform an SGML document into a formatting tree – a detailed arrangement of nested boxes called *flow objects*. The tree of flow objects is then used to create the actual output, usually on paper. The style language of DSSSL has its roots in the printing industry. It is rich in features for creating, for example, columns, footnotes, and hyphenation. However, online displays and multimedia capabilities were added as an afterthought and hence remain weak. DSSSL is extensible, however, and applications can add nonstandard flow objects.

The flow objects are similar to CSS1's boxes (see Chapter 5). But where CSS1 only has three – inline, block, and list-item – DSSSL has a few dozen, including many for math. DSSSL creates flow objects not only for every element, but also for each letter that is to appear in the output.

The flow objects have properties similar to CSS's boxes; in DSSSL they are called "characteristics." Inheritance of characteristics within the tree of flow objects is supported, but cascading of style sheets is not. The flow objects and characteristics allow complicated multicolumn page layouts but omit some common features such as large initial letters and text-wrapping. Such features can be added only by creating application-specific flow objects.

The syntax of DSSSL is based on Scheme, a programming language similar to Lisp. DSSSL allows the usual arithmetic operations and has an extensive query language that can be used to inspect and copy unrelated parts of an SGML document. DSSSL also uses the query language to express its selectors, which are more powerful than CSS1's. For example, you could make a style for a list item dependent on whether the item is the second, fourth, sixth, etc. in the list.

More information about DSSSL can be found on the Web. The main site is http://www.jclark.com/dsssl/ which has a copy of the official definition and also has examples of DSSSL style sheets as well as a free program that implements it.

CREATING A DOCUMENT WITHOUT USING A STYLE SHEET

HTML 3.2 has some attributes and elements – commonly called "extensions" – that allow you to specify the layout to some degree. However, this is done at the cost of making the document less portable and harder to maintain. These extensions were added by various browser software vendors before it was clear that style sheets would provide a better alternative. Most of these stem from the Netscape browser.

Using elements for layout

There are some elements that have little or no meaning apart from indicating a certain style, while some others are structural elements that have often been misused for the effect they usually have on the layout.

The first category contains these elements:

- B
- HR
- BASEFONT
- I
- BLINK (in Netscape Navigator)
- MARQUEE (in Microsoft Internet Explorer)
- BIG
- SMALL
- BR
- SPACER (in Netscape Navigator)
- CENTER
- SUB

- FONT

- SUP

- FRAME

- TT

The second category consists of structural elements that often are abused for their visual effect: BLOCKQUOTE, DL (to indent paragraphs), and the heading elements H1 to H6 (to enlarge the text).

SUB and SUP are borderline cases: it is arguable whether they carry semantics or not. Their role is to indicate subscripts and superscripts, but they don't tell anything beyond that. They don't tell how the subscript or superscript is used (for example, as an index item, an exponent, an atom number, or other). However, inventing more meaningful names than SUB and SUP would be almost impossible because there are so many different functions. In mathematics, many of the roles subscripts and superscripts play don't even have agreed-upon names.

Also borderline is BR. Recall that it is an empty element that represents a hard line break; a line break will be placed where it is used no matter how the text of the paragraph around it is aligned or justified. Like SUB and SUP, BR doesn't tell why there is a line break at that point: is it because a line in a poem ended? Does it separate lines of an address? It really should have been a character instead of an element, but the intended character is not part of the Latin-1 character set. This character set contains only about 200 characters and was the only one allowed in early versions of HTML. With the advent of support for the Unicode character set of more than 30 000 characters, BR could have been replaced by, for example, the line separator character. But people were used to BR, so it stuck.

Here is an example that uses the extension elements exclusively:

```
<font size="+2"><b>How to write HTML</b></font><br><br>
For headings, the FONT element is ideal, since it can
enlarge the font. The BR breaks lines, so two BR's in a
row make for a perfect paragraph separator. When a word
needs emphasis, the I tag will <i>italicize</i> it. For
even more emphasis, the B element puts the text in
<b>bold</b>...
```

Because extensions are inserted purely to force a particular style, their meanings can be expressed completely in CSS, as given in Table 14.1.

MARQUEE is not translatable to CSS1. Its effect is to make the text scroll horizontally. It would be a text decoration, much like BLINK.

FRAME divides the window into a number of rectangles, each containing a different document. CSS1 deals only with text formatting within a single document, not with window layout, but its successors will support a layout model for multiple windows (see Chapter 15).

`<tt>`	`<span style="font-family: monospace">`
`<b>`	`<span style="font-weight: bold">`
`<u>`	`<span style="text-decoration: underline">`
`<big>`	`<span style="font-size: bigger">`
`<small>`	`<span style="font-size: smaller">`
`<sub>`	`<span style="vertical-align: sub">`
`<sup>`	`<span style="vertical-align: sup">`
`<hr>`	`<p style="border-top: solid">` On some browsers, the border style is groove rather than solid.
`<center>`	`<div="text-align: center">`
`<font-size=??>`	`<span style="font-size: ??>`, where ?? depends on the value of the SIZE attribute: `<FONT SIZE=1>` corresponds to "xx-small," SIZE=7 to "xx-large"
`<font-color=??>`	`<span style="color: ??">`
`<basefont size=??>`	`<html style="font-size: ??">`, where ?? is determined as for FONT above
`<spacer>`	A shortcut for the "single-pixel GIF trick," see the next section
`<blink>`	`<span style="text-decoration: blink">`

Table 14.1 CSS translations of HTML elements used for layout.

Using attributes for layout

You also can use these extension attributes on a number of elements to set layout:

- ALIGN (various elements)

- LINK (on BODY)

- ALINK (on BODY)

- BACKGROUND (on BODY)

- TEXT (on BODY)

- VLINK (on BODY)

- BGCOLOR (on BODY)

- VSPACE (on IMG)

- HEIGHT (on IMG)

- WIDTH (on IMG, TABLE)

- HSPACE (on IMG)

- BORDER (on IMG)

ALIGN combines a number of functions, depending on the element to which it is attached and on the value. On headings and paragraphs, it sets the alignment of the text. For example, to center a title, you would write

```
<H1 ALIGN=CENTER>Centered title</H1>
```

On IMG, it makes the image float to the left or right or align vertically with the text around it. For example, the following two lines have the same effect:

```
<IMG SRC="image" ALIGN=left>
<IMG SRC="image" STYLE="float: left">
```

as have these:

```
<IMG SRC="image" ALIGN=top>
<IMG SRC="image" STYLE="vertical-align: top">
```

WIDTH and HEIGHT on IMG allow an image to be scaled. HSPACE and VSPACE add padding around an image. BORDER sets the thickness of a border around an image, in case it is part of a hyperlink. All these attributes accept only numbers as values, which are interpreted as lengths in pixels.

WIDTH on table cells allow the cells to be rendered with a fixed size in pixels or as a percentage of the screen width. A fixed-size table often is (mis)used to add fixed margins to a text or to align the text to a background image.

ALINK, BACKGROUND, BGCOLOR, LINK, TEXT, and VLINK, set on BODY, add a background image and color to the document and set colors for link anchors.

The single-pixel GIF trick for controlling space

One trick to control the spacing outside of a style sheet comes from David Siegel, author of *Creating Killer Web Sites*. He calls it the "single-pixel GIF trick." The trick is to create a transparent GIF image consisting of a 1×1 pixel. Although the image is essentially invisible, it still takes up space. Everywhere you need to add some space, you insert such an image. For example, here's how to indent paragraphs using this trick:

Siegel D. (1996) Creating Killer Web Sites, 1st edition, Hayden Books

```
<P><IMG SRC="1pixel.gif" WIDTH=20 HEIGHT=1> text text text...
```

Don't look at a document like this with image loading turned off!

You can even use this trick to affect line spacing. Here's how you would insert a few extra pixels between lines:

```
... some text<IMG SRC="1pixel.gif" WIDTH=1 HEIGHT=20
ALIGN=MIDDLE> with a narrow, tall<IMG SRC="1pixel.gif"
WIDTH=1 HEIGHT=20 ALIGN=MIDDLE> image every four
words<IMG SRC="1pixel.gif" WIDTH=1 HEIGHT=20
ALIGN=MIDDLE> or so...
```

Doing this is a bit of a gamble, since you don't know the size of the user's font. Assuming that in many cases the font will be around 14 pixels high, creating a 20-pixel image should therefore ensure about 6 pixels between lines.

The single-pixel GIF trick also can do word spacing and letter spacing. The nice part of doing this is that it doesn't add to the download time. The downside is that pages containing these images are a nightmare to maintain: You have to make sure that there is an image between every two words or every two letters, and that they are all the same. If you change one, you'll have to change all of them. Also, robots will have a hard time finding the keywords among the images.

The definitive book on layout without style sheets is David's *Creating Killer Web Sites* (Hayden Books, 1996).

USING A FORMAT OTHER THAN HTML

You can avoid using HTML altogether by using a different format than HTML, such as the Portable Document Format or an image.

The Portable Document Format (PDF)

The Portable Document Format (PDF), often called the "Acrobat" format after the program most commonly used to display it, is a format for storing formatted documents in a device-independent manner. Created by Adobe Systems Inc., it inherits much from PostScript, an earlier and still much used page description language also by Adobe.

PDF is like "digital paper." It can store one or more pages of text and images, ready to be printed or viewed on screen. Compared to image formats such as PNG, GIF, and JPEG, it has a number of advantages. First, it can contain actual text, not just images of text (bitmaps). As a result, it can scale the pages and print at any resolution: the text looks as good as the printer allows. Second, it can replace fonts by generated approximations

("Multiple Master fonts") in case the document uses uncommon fonts and the document's creator didn't embed the font, either for copyright reasons or just to save space. Third, since the text in the document is stored as text and not as bitmaps, you can search the document for keywords. Fourth, PDF can even contain hyperlinks, not only within the document but also as URLs that point to documents on the Web.

The disadvantage is that the text is already formatted as you get it. Resizing the window won't change the number of words per line, as it normally does in HTML. The structure of the text is also lost: you cannot save the document and edit it. Even if you manage to save the text and load it into some other program, there are no tags anymore that tell you that a certain piece of text is a heading or a list item.

PDF is a good solution for old documents that cannot be converted to HTML, or would need a lot of work to allow conversion. Usually, when you can print a document, you can also convert it to PDF. Many documents created with old word processors were never meant to be used on the Web and printing them is pretty much the only thing you can do with them.

Images

You also can use images that are stored in PNG, GIF or JPEG format. We briefly discussed using images in place of text in Chapter 1. A Web page consisting of just an image gives the page's designer control over every pixel, especially when the PNG format is used. PNG is the most accurate when it comes to defining the color of pixels. But that level of control comes at a price.

First, robots cannot read the page. Second, the page is much larger in terms of bytes than a page that consists of text with a style sheet and thus takes longer to download.

Third, the page has a fixed size. As a result, users may have trouble reading the image, for several reasons. On large screens, the image may be too small. On small screens, the image may be too large. On noncolor screens, too many colors may be shown as almost the same shade of gray. And on text-only browsers, users won't see anything.

Fourth, printing the page also will give less than satisfactory results. Not many printers can print in color, so the result in black and white may either be very small or look grainy (see Figure 14.1).

Fifth, as with any format that doesn't rely on style sheets for the layout, it will not be readable by somebody who is blind (images can be converted neither to speech nor to Braille) and will be hard to read for somebody with limited eyesight (although the images can be enlarged, it is hard to change the colors, like you can do with the text).

Figure 14.1 (a) Normal text, (b) an image. On the screen, the two looked the same, but on paper, the text was printed with all the quality the printer could offer, while the image was just copied pixel for pixel.

The Quick Brown Fox Jumped Over The Lazy Dog

(a)

The Quick Brown Fox Jumped Over The Lazy Dog

(b)

And finally, when you want to modify the document, it is harder to change an image than a text or a style sheet.

For the above reasons, it is advisable to use images only for effects that cannot be achieved with a style sheet. And then only if the look is so important that it outweighs the disadvantages. Of course, you should also include the text in the ALT attribute of the IMG element, for people that cannot see the image.

Chapter 15

Looking ahead

CSS1 is the first of a family of layout languages, all based on CSS. In this chapter, we take a look ahead at what we see happening with CSS. We describe some of the expected new features, along with the processes that will eventually lead to the definition of each of them.

New capabilities can be added, because CSS has been designed with extensibility in mind. We expect to see advancements in the following areas:

- Style sheets that enable a computer to speak HTML
- Layout capabilities
- Capabilities of hyperlinks
- High-quality printing
- Fonts and special characters
- Selectors
- Use of gradients, color, and image operations
- Tabs and leaders
- Tables
- Hooks to external layout methods
- Computed values
- Generated text

FORWARD COMPATIBILITY

Usually, software vendors are concerned with providing *backward compatibility*, the ability of a newer version of software to read files created by earlier versions. However, we wanted CSS to offer more than backward compatibility. We wanted it to provide *forward compatibility*, the ability of older (or current) versions to read files created for newer versions.

Of course, predicting what later CSS versions will contain is impossible. If we could do that, then we would have written the whole of CSS now. So, a browser for CSS1 will not understand features added later. However, we can make sure that such a browser doesn't crash and that it will be able to find what it does understand amid the new features.

To that end, CSS1 is defined with the help of a special *grammar*, a formal definition of the syntactic structure of the language. (See the CSS1 specification for more details.) All future versions of CSS will adhere to this grammar. Using a metaphor from human languages, we can say that a CSS1 browser will always be able to tell where a sentence ends and what the subject and the verb in a sentence are, even if it doesn't know what the words mean. Implementers of CSS will have to look carefully at that grammar and at the explanation that accompanies it, but most users won't. To demonstrate how it works, following are two examples of style sheets that use (hypothetical) new features.

The first example shows how a new keyword may be added to an existing property. In this case, we're adding the keyword "stretch" to the background property. A CSS1 browser won't understand the keyword, so it will ignore the whole declaration for the background. You can use that fact by providing two rules, one for CSS1 browsers and one for (hypothetical) newer browsers that understand "stretch":

```
TABLE {
  background: white url(logo2) repeat;
  background: white url(logo) stretch
}
```

According to the rules of cascading, the second declaration will override the first one. However, the second one is unintelligible to the CSS1 browser, so that browser will use the last one it understood. The result is that the browser will display a different, but still reasonable background.

In a second example, say we want to add page numbers to printed output. A future version of CSS may add a definition for page layout like this:

```
@page {
  pageno-position: top left;
  pageno-start: 5;
  pageno-style: upper-roman;
  background: yellow
}
```

This is an example of an at-rule, a rule that starts with an @-sign. (CSS1 has only one type of at-rule: @import.) A CSS1 browser skips at-rules it doesn't understand. Note that the @page rule contains something that looks like a background property; however, by placing it inside the @page rule, a CSS1 browser will not be confused by it.

AURAL CASCADING STYLE SHEETS

See
http://www.w3.org/pub/WWW/
TR/NOTE_ACSS

The initial research for spoken HTML has been done and there is a proposal for a specification. Much of the work has been done by T. V. Raman of Adobe Systems.

Style sheets for generating speech will have properties that control the volume, speed, pitch, balance, and other voice characteristics of the speech synthesizer that reads out the HTML. The volume property works similarly to font-size: it can be set to an absolute value, a symbolic value, or a relative value that is relative to the inherited volume. The azimuth property lets you set the sound for stereo. Cue-before, cue-after, and play-during allow the synthesizer to insert "audible icons" into the text, such as a beep before a hyperlink or some noise during a quote. Other, special properties help with speaking elements that contain numbers, dates, acronyms, and other things that are not normal words.

LAYOUT CAPABILITIES

CSS1 has only one layout model: boxes that are either nested or laid out one below the other. The boxes can't be placed next to each other or on top of each other. And you can't put multiple columns of text in a box. The layout extension to CSS is designed to correct these deficiencies.

The syntax and the names of the new properties for doing complex layout are not known yet. However, we expect there will be two, somewhat independent parts to the layout extensions. The simplest would be a property that changes how an element formats its child elements. Currently, a block-level element puts its child elements below each other. A new property, perhaps called layout, would change the layout method. Values would include "fixed," "row," and "stack." "Fixed" means all nested elements would be expected to provide their own x- and y-coordinates. "Row" means all child elements would be put in a single row. "Stack" means the child elements would be put on top of each other like a stack of cards.

The second part of the layout extensions would allow a fixed page design, containing several documents; somewhat like the "frames" seen on some browsers, but with more possibilities.

Another property, columns, would set the number of columns or the column width for elements to be laid out in a multicolumn style. If the column width, rather than the number of columns, is given, the number of columns will be computed based on the available screen space. In this way, columns would appear when the window was made larger, but the column width would stay more or less the same.

New types for the <u>display</u> property also are possible, including values that make the element "collapsible," that is, it would collapse to a button and expand to the full text when clicked, or "pop up," that is, it would collapse to a button that pops up a dialog box when clicked.

CAPABILITIES OF HYPERLINKS

The default behavior of a hyperlink is to replace the current page with a new one. But when multiple regions and pop-up windows become available for displaying parts of documents, you can also display two documents at the same time.

One attractive scheme calls for a hyperlink to point to a short page that is shown in a pop-up box, which contains a link to a long page. This would allow a summary or a menu to be shown before the whole text is loaded.

HIGH-QUALITY PRINTING

Style sheets can improve the way HTML documents are printed. However, CSS1 doesn't provide any properties specific to printing, such as properties that let you control page numbers, running headers and footers, and widows/orphans, among others. (A widow is a short last line of a paragraph that falls at the top of a page; an orphan is a first line of a paragraph that falls at the bottom of a page. A good page design will avoid both.) High-quality printing extensions to CSS would provide properties for these features, as well as for controlling, for example, where page breaks may fall, how much hyphenation to use, and whether to print double-sided (with different margins on left and right pages).

You will be able to print a book from a collection of linked pages. This feature will rely heavily on the REL attribute that HTML defines for the LINK and A elements. That attribute indicates the relationship of HTML documents to each other. It can, for example, indicate that two documents are chapters of the same book, or that one document is the table of contents of another. Conventions for using the REL attribute are currently being defined by a working group within the World Wide Web Consortium.

FONTS AND SPECIAL CHARACTERS

CSS1 offers some control over font selection, but for fonts with many variants or with nonstandard variants the mapping of the properties to actual fonts is not specified. In many cases, this is an advantage, since it gives the browser the freedom to apply its knowledge of the local system, knowledge that the designer likely doesn't have. For example, it allows the browser to use an oblique font if the italic variant is not available on this particular computer. But in some cases, the designer may want to have more control over the selected font.

The font extensions under development will provide several extra features. One is a new at-rule in the style sheet, provisionally called @font-face, that contains rules for how a particular combination of family, weight, and style maps to a specific font. @font-face also will be able to optionally contain a URL that points to a font on a remote server. It also can offer detailed information about the intended font, such as visual characteristics (boldness, x-height, and the like), so that the browser can if necessary generate a font that looks just like it.

Here is one suggested extension to CSS, to tell a browser that the font "clown italic" can be found at the given URL, in case it is not already present on the computer:

```
@font-face {
   family-name: clown;
   font-style: italic;
   font-weight: all;
   source: url(http://font.com/clown)
}
```

@font-face will be powerful enough to completely disable any automatic font selection; for example, it could disable the keyword "bolder." Designers must balance the importance of an exact reproduction against the accessibility of the document to people with less powerful browsers and to people with visual handicaps.

SWASH LETTERS AND OTHER ALTERNATIVE GLYPHS

Many fonts offer several choices for each letter. Sometimes there is a normal letter plus one or two others with a slightly different shape or with an extra long tail or a flourish. The latter are called *swash characters* and are designed to be used in titles, usually at the start or end of a word. Figure 15.1 shows examples of swash characters.

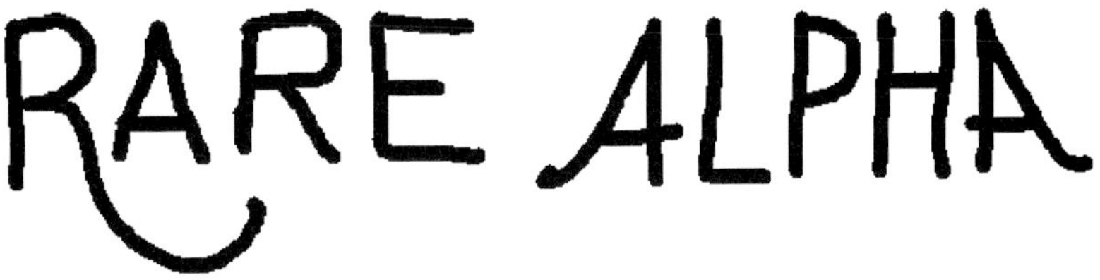

Figure 15.1 Swash characters.

Although swash letters are different shapes, they represent the same letter, so there is no way in HTML to differentiate between them. Technically speaking, these shapes are different *glyphs* (letter shapes) of the same character. As a rule of thumb, the difference between a character and a glyph is that replacing a character in a word will change the word's meaning, while replacing a glyph just changes the way it looks. For example, replacing a normal letter with an italic one is a change of glyph.

Since HTML can only contain characters, CSS will need extra properties to associate other glyphs than the default with each character. These extra properties can probably be combined with the @font-face rule described in the previous section. Part of the extra information about a font that @font-face could provide may be a table that shows which alternative glyphs may be used for each character.

SELECTORS

In CSS1, elements may be selected based only on their name, class, or ID and on those names, classes, or IDs of their ancestors in the document tree. In creating selectors under later CSS versions, you will be able to distinguish between ancestors and direct parents and to pick elements based on what elements they follow. A special case of the latter would be a child element that doesn't follow any other child element, that is, it is the first child of its parent. A selector based on such an element would, for example, allow the first paragraph to be given a different look from all other paragraphs.

Selecting elements based on the attributes they have and on the values of those attributes also will be possible. This will allow, for example, an anchor to be colored differently based on the value of its REL attribute. It also will allow the style sheet to pick up the value of an element's ALIGN attribute (see Chapter 14) and override that value if needed.

The selectors won't become much more complex than this, however. A browser still must be able to determine whether a selector applies based only on the text that precedes an element. For reasons of speed, it cannot afford to wait for the element that follows it. That excludes a selector that matches only the last element, since the browser won't know whether an element is the last one until it has read past the element.

GRADIENTS, COLOR, AND IMAGE OPERATIONS

CSS is not intended to become an image manipulation language, but certain modifications may be needed to make an image fit into the design (Figure 15.2)

Abc defg hi jklm nop qrst uvwxy za bcdef ghi jkl mn opq rst uvw xyza bcde fghij k lmno pqrs tuvwx yz. Abc defghi jklm nop qrst uvwxy za bcdef ghi jkl mn opq rst uvw xyz a bcde fghij kl mno pqrs tuvwx yz. Abc defg hi jklm nop qrst uvwxy za bcdef ghi jkl mn opq rst uvw xyz a bcde fghij k lmno pqrs tuvwx yz.

Figure 15.2 A non-rectangular image, with the text wrapping around it. Not yet possible in CSS.

You can already use CSS1 to scale foreground, but not background, images. Future possible features may correct this, as well as add the ability to crop images to a possibly nonrectangular outline. Then it would be possible to wrap the text around the real contour, instead of only round the bounding box. Another feature may be the ability to blend an image into the background by specifying how transparent the image is. All operations, including scaling, would also be applied to background images.

Because only a limited number of colors are available on a computer screen, future CSS versions may include some way of making the color requirements of a certain style sheet explicit, with hints as to which colors are most important and which may be replaced if needed.

Another extension being considered is the ability to define simple images in CSS itself. Some simple line art may be possible, as well as some two-color gradients. For example, a linear gradient between two colors could be very useful as the background for slides (Figure 15.3).

Figure 15.3 Two-gradient backgrounds.

TABS AND LEADERS

Although HTML lets you build tables, in some cases they don't have the right formatting. You also can't specify leaders between columns. A layout based on tabulators (tab stops) may be better for some types of tabular material.

For simple columnar material, such as a list of expenses or a table of contents, a property such as tab-position could be enough to make the contents of the element start at a certain distance from the margin, if necessary after skipping to the next line. It also could insert the proper *leaders*. A leader is a dotted or solid line that connects the entry in one column to the entry in the next; for example, connecting a chapter heading to its starting page number in a table of contents. Leaders are most often either a solid line or dots. The dots would come in two varieties: those that line up vertically throughout the document and those that are centered in the available space. In a table of contents, for example, the dots are normally aligned (if you look closely, you can see that the dots are exactly below each other):

> 1. *Favorite pets* *3*
> 1.1. *Dogs* *3*
> 1.2. *Cats* *12*

It also should be possible to set the tab position symbolically by referring to a position defined earlier. In other words, you would set tab stops and refer to tab positions by number. The still hypothetical tab-position property might accept either a length to indicate a specific position, or a number to refer to a previously defined tab stop.

Note that using a tab to indent the first line of a paragraph, as you would typically do in a word processor, does not translate to a tab-position in CSS. In most cases, you would express the tab using a margin property or the text-indent property. Even the layout of computer programs, which require many different indents at the start of a line, can better be expressed as a set of nested lists (*sans* bullets).

TABLES

CSS1 has no properties for tables and the method by which HTML tables are laid out is undefined. New properties would exactly define table cell elements and table row elements and refine the setting of borders on table cells.

New properties for the borders of table cells are needed because the existing border properties work only if each element has its own border, and this isn't the case for tables. In a table, the border between cells cannot be said to belong to one cell or the other. You can get around this by assuming the cells share the border and define a method for resolving possible conflicts when the two cells have different border properties. This is probably the method that table extensions for CSS will follow. That is, if one cell has border type A and the next cell border type B, a set of rules would be checked in succession to determine which of them is used. For example, if A is thicker than B, the border will be of type A.

HOOKS TO EXTERNAL LAYOUT METHODS

HTML has the possibility to link in an external object, such as a Java applet, to access information that cannot be expressed in HTML itself. There is no reason why CSS could not do the same.

Properties could be made to refer to procedures in some programming language for computing the representation of a part of the document. Such a procedure could be used, for example, to make a word blink in the rhythm of its Morse code equivalent, to make a text cycle through a rainbow of colors, or to display some words upside down.

COMPUTED VALUES

All property values in CSS1 are either simple values or lists of simple values. In CSS1, you can make some values depend on the font size, but there is no general way to compute values relative to other values. Extended expressions could allow common arithmetic operators, parentheses, and references on the right-hand side of a declaration.

Such expressions would make it possible, for example, to express a font size as a percentage of the parent's width. Special operators might allow values to be specified with a minimum, a maximum, and a linear range in between the two.

It should be possible to refer not only to all the properties of the parent element, but also to information from outside the style sheet, such as the screen resolution, the color depth of the screen, and the current date and time. Another possibility is using the values of HTML attributes inside such expressions.

Even before CSS acquires an expression syntax, one special value may be added to almost all properties: "inherit." The "inherit" value would dictate that the property should use the value inherited from its parent. This explicit inheritance would differ from the automatic inheritance that most properties already exhibit because it would be done *after* cascading. Specifying "inherit" for a property would enable a designer to give the property the same value as in the parent element, even if that value is unknown.

GENERATED TEXT

Usually a style sheet only tells how existing text is formatted; it doesn't contain the text itself. But in some cases, the text can be thought of as decoration or as part of the style. This is called *generated text*.

An example of generated text is list numbers and bullets for items in a list. Another is the title of a section or chapter, where the word "Chapter" followed by a number would be generated automatically. Also, you should be able to set properties to generate text in several styles. For example, the word "Chapter" might be on a separate line and in a different font than the number. (CSS1 currently assumes that list numbers are in the same font as the list item itself.)

Counters are probably the most common type of generated text. A counter is a variable that is used to keep track of anything that must be counted. Counters come in many types. Some are global throughout a document, such as sequential equation numbers in mathematical textbooks. Others are subcounters of other counters, for example, illustrations within a chapter. These usually have a fixed part and a variable part. For example, if the generated text is "Figure 6.1", the fixed parts are "Figure" and ".", the variable parts are "6" and "1".

SPECIAL EFFECTS

It is not possible in CSS1 to modify a font, for example by stretching it, adding a shadow behind it, bending it around a curve, or rotating and mirroring it. Some of these effects are invented for a specific purpose, such as the brand image of some product. It is not useful to add these effects to CSS; for such rare cases, an image will do just fine. But some effects are quite common. A few simple ones will likely be added to CSS in the future.

One such effect is rotated text (text written sideways or diagonally). Another is the drop shadow (Figure 15.4). In the latter case, a single property, text-shadow, could be enough, but further research may show a need for more properties.

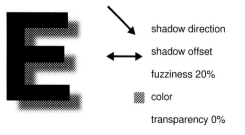

shadow direction

shadow offset

fuzziness 20%

color

transparency 0%

Figure 15.4 Example of a letter with a drop-shadow, and the parameters that govern the look of the shadow.

OTHER WAYS TO LINK STYLE SHEETS

As mentioned in Chapter 12, the two ways to associate a style sheet with a document both involve modifying the document: you can either put a LINK element in the document with a URL pointing to the style sheet, or you can embed the style sheet itself with the help of a STYLE element.

However, an extension to HTML is under development that will make it possible to put the LINK element in a different document. A browser that sees that LINK element will remember it and apply it when it comes to the target document.

The HTML extension is variously called "resource" or "about." It will work approximately like this: Assume you have written a document A that contains a link to document B, written by somebody else; that is, A will contain something like:

```
<A HREF="B">
```

Now assume you want document B to be displayed with a certain style sheet. That is currently not possible without editing the document, which you can't do, since it is owned by somebody else. The new extension will allow you to create a new document C that contains two links, one to the style sheet and one to document B. Instead of linking directly to B, you now link to C:

```
<A HREF="C">
```

and C will contain something similar to this:

```
<RESOURCE>                        <!-- or <ABOUT> -->
  <BASE HREF="B">
  <LINK REL="stylesheet" HREF="style.css">
</RESOURCE>
```

Since C is clearly not a normal HTML document, but something that gives information about a document, the browser will immediately continue to document B, but taking the link along.

HOW EXTENSIONS COME ABOUT

The CSS language is a product of the World Wide Web Consortium (W3C). It is developed by W3C staff, with help from Consortium members and other people. The members decide whether a proposed specification becomes a Consortium Recommendation. Members then agree to follow the Recommendation in their products.

Consortium members usually get to see a new specification some time before it is made public. In that time, they can discuss it, suggest changes, and, most importantly, start implementing it before nonmembers see it. Most discussions about what it should contain take place on a public mailing list, *www-style@w3.org*.

Note, the mailing list is meant only for discussions about developing style sheet solutions for the Web, in particular CSS. Both the features of CSS and the way to implement them are discussed. It is not for questions about how to use CSS. To subscribe to the mailing list, send a one-line mail message to the address *www-style-request@w3.org*. The message should contain one word: subscribe. You also can send the command HELP to get some information about how the mailing lists works.

HTML quick reference

This appendix gives an overview of the successor to HTML 3.2. (Note: At the time of this writing, it was not finalized yet. However, we believe that everything described in this appendix will work.) This version of HTML is the first to contain the elements and attributes necessary for effective use of style sheets, in particular STYLE and CLASS, but it also still contains all the elements of earlier versions, including several of the extensions introduced by Netscape.

The text below focuses on the elements that are most useful in combination with a style sheet. Other elements are also mentioned, but with less explanation. For the same reason, not all of the possible attributes are described. The rules for how elements can be nested have been stratified, by leaving out some cases that are allowed in HTML. The result is much simpler to explain than the full rules, but a little more restrictive.

The text is not a tutorial on HTML. It assumes you've read at least Chapter 1. The purpose of this appendix is merely to list all elements of HTML and the rules for combining them.

DOCUMENT STRUCTURE

An HTML document consists of elements nested inside other elements. Each element starts with a start-tag <XXX> and ends with an end-tag </XXX>. In some cases one or both of the tags may be omitted. In general, it is safest to always include both of them. When a document is created with the help of a dedicated HTML editor, the tags will be inserted automatically by the editor. At the highest level, a document consists of one element, called HTML. Inside that are two elements, HEAD and BODY.

```
<HTML>
<HEAD>...</HEAD>
<BODY>...</BODY>
</HEAD>
```

Elements can have attributes, which have a name and a value, separated by an equals sign (=). The value is enclosed in quotes (" ... " or ' ... '). Attributes are listed only in the start-tag, never in the end-tag:

```
<EM CLASS="surname">
<A REL='copyright' HREF='copy.html'>
```

Element names and attribute names can be spelled with capitals or small letters, and even mixtures of the two. The example above can also be written as:

```
<em class="surname">
<a rel='copyright' href='copy.html'>
```

THE HEAD ELEMENT

The HEAD contains information about the document. It is normally not displayed. The elements that can occur in the HEAD are: BASE, ISINDEX, MAP, META, LINK, STYLE, SCRIPT.

TITLE

There must be exactly one TITLE element. It can contain only text, no other elements. The title is often used in the title bar of a window.

LINK

Specifies a relationship between the document and some other document. The relationship is a keyword that is put in the REL attribute. The URL of the other document is put in the HREF attribute. There may be zero or more LINK elements. The element has no content and the end-tag must be omitted. The relation "stylesheet" is used to associate a style sheet with a document:

```
<LINK REL="stylesheet" HREF="http://place.com/sty/rf.css">
```

STYLE

The STYLE element can contain a style sheet, as described in Chapter 12. An attribute TYPE must be added that declares the type of style language, for example `<STYLE TYPE="text/css">` or `<STYLE TYPE="application/dsssl">`.

META

The META element is used for attaching various kinds of meta-information about the document. The element has no content and the end-tag must be omitted.

BASE

Can contain the URL of the document itself or the URL that serves as the base for relative URLs in the document. The URL is included as the value of the HREF attribute. The element has no content and the end-tag must be omitted. Here is an example of a typical HEAD:

```
<HEAD>
<TITLE>The oak tree</TITLE>
<LINK REL="author" HREF="../people/Jones">
<STYLE TYPE="text/css">
H1 {font-family: Helvetica, sans-serif}
BODY {font-family: Bodoni, serif}
</STYLE>
</HEAD>
```

THE BODY ELEMENT

The BODY can contain three types of elements: container elements, bridge elements, and special elements. Container elements are elements that can themselves contain exactly the same elements as the BODY. These elements are used to create divisions, interactive forms, long quotations, and other high-level structures. Bridge elements contain text and text-level elements. Paragraphs and headings are bridge elements. Special elements include lists, tables, and certain elements for interactive forms.

All the elements that can appear in the BODY can appear any number of times. All of them accept these five attributes: CLASS, STYLE, ID, LANG (to indicate the language in which the element is written), and DIR (to indicate the writing direction if it is not clear from the language: ltr is left-to-right, rtl is right-to-left).

Container elements

The container elements are: DIV, BLOCKQUOTE, ADDRESS, FORM, FIELDSET. DIV is a general division, such as a chapter, section, abstract or note. It is customary to indicate the type of division in the CLASS attribute, for example:

```
<DIV CLASS="verse">
```

BLOCKQUOTE is a quotation consisting of one or more paragraphs. ADDRESS is a name and/or address, usually after a heading or a block-quote, or at the end of the document, to indicate the author of something. FORM is a container for an interactive form. The ACTION attribute contains the URL of the server that will process the form. The METHOD attribute contains the method used to send the form data to the server, either "get," "post," or "put."

The FIELDSET element is used to group a part of a form. In addition to all other elements that can occur in BODY, it can also have one CAPTION element in its content, which, if present, must be the first element in the FIELDSET. Browsers can use the FIELDSET to activate a set of form elements together. The CAPTION acts like a container element.

Bridge elements

The bridge elements are: P, H1, H2, H3, H4, H5, H6, and PRE. P is a normal paragraph. H1 to H6 are headings of different levels. H1 is the most important. PRE means preformatted. Typically the white-space property for this element is set to "pre" (Chapter 5).

Special elements

The special elements are: OL, UL, DL, HR, TABLE.

OL and UL are simple lists. They contain only LI (list item) elements (one or more). The LI element itself acts like a container element: it accepts the same content as the BODY element. UL is typically shown with a bullet as a label, OL typically uses numbered labels.

```
<UL>
<LI><P>First item</P></LI>        • First item
<LI><P>Second item</P></LI>
</UL>                             • Second item
<OL>
<LI><P>First item</P></LI>        1. First item
<LI><P>Second item</P></LI>
</OL>                             2. Second item
```

DL is a "definition list". It contains one or more definitions, where each definition consists of one or more DT (term) elements, followed by one or more DD (definition) elements. The DT element is like a bridge element: it contains text and text-level elements. The DD is a container: it contains the same elements as BODY.

```
<DL>                                 term A
<DT>term A</DT>
<DD><P>Definition for term A</P></DD>  Definition for term A
<DT>term B1</DT>
<DT>term B2</DT>                      term B1
<DD><P>Definition for terms         term B2
B1 and B2</P></DD>
</DL>                                Definition for terms B1
                                     and B2
```

HR is an element without content and without an end-tag. Its purpose is to separate paragraphs, without grouping them. It is usually rendered as a horizontal rule (hence its name) or simply as white space.

The TABLE element creates a table. A table has a complex structure, but the main part consists of rows of cells. The content of the table starts with three optional parts: a CAPTION, a THEAD and a TFOOT (in that order), after that are one or more TBODYs, which contain the actual table. The TABLE element has an optional attribute BORDER, which contains a number. The higher the number the thicker the border around the cells. Default is 0, which means no border.

The CAPTION has the same content as a container. It defines a caption that can be displayed above or below the table.

The THEAD contains the first few rows of the table, those that contain the headings of the columns. Putting those headings in the THEAD allows certain browsers to treat them specially, but they can also be put in the table's body. TFOOT also contains column headings, possibly the same, but meant to be put at the bottom of the columns. For small tables, it is OK to omit the TFOOT and put any headings directly in the table's body.

The table's body is contained in one or more TBODY elements. In large tables, rows can be grouped together into multiple TBODY's. For small tables a single TBODY suffices.

THEAD, TFOOT and TBODY all have the same structure: they contain one or more TR elements (Table Row). Each TR contains zero or more table cells.

There are two types of table cells: TH and TD. The former is for table headings, the latter for table data. TH and TD act like containers: they can contain the same elements as the BODY element. TH and TD can have two attributes: COLSPAN and ROWSPAN. They indicate, respectively, how many columns and how many rows the cell spans. Default is 1.

Here is an example of a simple table (to make it easier to read, all end-tags are omitted; this is allowed according to HTML):

```
<TABLE BORDER=1>
  <TBODY>
  <TR><TH ROWSPAN=2>
    <TH COLSPAN=4><P>year 1996
  <TR><TH><P>Q1
    <TH><P>Q2
    <TH><P>Q3
    <TH><P>Q4
  <TR><TH><P>cars
    <TD><P>365
    <TD><P>320
    <TD><P>258
    <TD><P>191
  <TR><TH><P>bicycles
    <TD><P>165
    <TD><P>208
    <TD><P>358
    <TD><P>391
  <TR><TH><P>trains
    <TD><P>35
    <TD><P>45
    <TD><P>53
    <TD><P>72
  </TBODY>
</TABLE>
```

	year 1996			
	Q1	Q2	Q3	Q4
cars	365	320	258	191
bicycles	165	208	358	391
trains	35	45	53	72

TEXT-LEVEL ELEMENTS

Text-level elements are mixed with text inside the bridge elements and inside the element DT. Text-level elements indicate the function of a certain word or a phrase. Here is an example of a paragraph with text and several text-level elements. Note that text-level elements can be nested inside each other.

```
<P>A <DFN>square</DFN> is a rectangle
of which all sides are of equal
length. <EM CLASS="instruction">Squares
should <STRONG>not</STRONG> be used for
solving problem A.</P>
```

A **square** is a rectangle of which all sides are of equal length. *Squares should **not** be used for solving problem A.*

All text-level elements accept the attributes CLASS, LANG, DIR and STYLE.

Most text-level elements can be nested inside each other arbitrarily, but a few have restrictions. The unrestricted ones are: B, BDO, CITE, CODE, DFN, EM, I, KBD, LABEL, Q, SPAN, STRONG, SUB, SUP, VAR. The ones with restrictions are: A, BR, IMG, INPUT, SELECT, TEXTAREA.

Normal text-level elements

EM and STRONG mark words or phrases that need emphasis or strong emphasis.

DFN contains a word or term that is being defined. The first occurrence of a new term in a technical document is often marked this way.

CODE and KBD are mostly used when talking about computer-related topics. They indicate literal code (such as a word from a program or a command) and literal text to type on the keyboard. VAR indicates a variable, either in a computer program or in a formula.

SUB and SUP are for subscripts (like the 2 in H_2O) and superscripts (like the 2 in $E=mc^2$). Although HTML doesn't yet have support for mathematical formulas, these elements can help create the most simple one.

B and I are used to indicate that words were bold or italic in the text from which the current words are derived. They are useful when the text is converted from a document format that doesn't allow the role of the words to be encoded. For text entered directly in HTML, EM and STRONG are usually better choices.

CITE encloses a bibliographic reference (a type of "link" that is not a *hyperlink...*), such as (*Raggett 1996*).

Q encloses a short quotation or a word that is used metaphorically. The appropriate quote marks are inserted by the HTML program. For example, the sentence: He said: <Q>Hi!</Q>

A LABEL is used in conjunction with a form element (SELECT, TEXTAREA, INPUT, FIELDSET) or with an OBJECT element, to provide a description for it. Usually it occurs quite near that other element. It has an extra attribute, FOR, that is required and that contains the ID of the element that it is associated with. Typically, in a browser, clicking on a label will activate the element to which it is joined and put the cursor on it.

The BDO element is needed for certain rare cases that can occur in documents that contain both left-to-right text (such as English) and right-to-left text (such as Hebrew). It stands for Bi-Directional Override. It has a required attribute DIR that is either "ltr" or "rtl." Depending on this attribute, it tells the HTML program that the content is left-to-right or right-to-left, even if the characters inside the element would normally be used in the opposite direction. (Note that this is different from the DIR attribute that all elements have, and that only indicates the default direction, for those characters that don't have a definite direction.)

For more information on this, see Yergeau *et al.* Internationalization of the Hypertext Markup Language at http://ds.internic.net/rfc/ rfc2070.txt

SPAN is a general purpose element that can be used when none of the other text-level elements is suitable. It must have either a CLASS attribute to indicate the role of the element, or a STYLE attribute to set a style directly.

For example, to mark people's names, you could do: <SPAN CLASS="person"> Berners-Lee</SPAN>.

Restricted text-level elements

Restricted text-level elements differ from normal text-level elements in what can be nested inside them. Apart from A, they don't allow other text-level elements in their content.

A is perhaps the most important element of HTML: it is the source anchor of a hyperlink. Besides the normal attributes (CLASS, ID, STYLE, LANG, DIR) it has a required attribute HREF that contains the URL of the target anchor. It accepts all text-level elements in its content, except other A elements.

The BR indicates a forced line break, without starting a new paragraph. It has no content and no end-tag.

The IMG element inserts images and other simple objects. It has a required attribute SRC, that holds the URL of the image. It also has a recommended attribute ALT, that can hold a short text that describes the image for the benefit of browsers that can't display images. For example: <IMG SRC= "w3c_48x48" ALT="W3C logo">. The element has no content and no end-tag.

INPUT is an element that is used in interactive forms. It creates a button or a short text field, depending on the value of the (required) TYPE attribute: "text," "password," "checkbox," "radio," "submit," "reset," "file," "hidden" or "image." It has a required NAME attribute and a VALUE attribute that is required for some values of the TYPE attribute. INPUT has no content and no end-tag. Here are some examples of INPUT elements.

```
<FORM ACTION="xx">
<INPUT TYPE="text" NAME="fld9" VALUE="Type here">
<INPUT TYPE="radio" NAME="r7" VALUE="a" CHECKED>
<INPUT TYPE="radio" NAME="r7" VALUE="b">
<INPUT TYPE="radio" NAME="r7" VALUE="c">
<INPUT TYPE="checkbox" NAME="pu8">
<INPUT TYPE="submit" VALUE="Send!" NAME="sub-a">
</FORM>
```

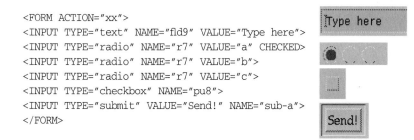

SELECT is a list or menu for use in an interactive form. It can only contain one or more OPTION elements. An OPTION element contains only text, no other elements. The SELECT element has a required NAME attribute, with an arbitrary text as its value. For other attributes, please refer to a full HTML specification.

```
<FORM ACTION="xx">
<SELECT NAME="hh44" SIZE="3">
<OPTION SELECTED>option 1</OPTION>
<OPTION>option 2</OPTION>
<OPTION>option 3</OPTION>
<OPTION>option 4</OPTION>
</SELECT></FORM ACTION="xx">
```

TEXTAREA is another element for interactive forms. It represents a fill-in field of more than one line. It can contain text, but no other elements. It has three attributes: a required attribute NAME, which contains an arbitrary text; ROWS, which contains a number indicating the height of the field; and COLS, which contains the width of the field. Other attributes are optional.

```
<FORM ACTION="xx">
<TEXTAREA NAME="kk12"
ROWS=3 COLS=15>
Type here
</TEXTAREA>
</FORM>
```

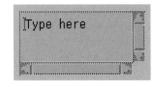

OBJECT is a very sophisticated element. It can be used to insert images into the text, to include applets (small programs that run inside a document), and in general to put arbitrary multimedia objects inside the text, including other HTML documents. In principle, it obsoletes IMG, but IMG is retained for simple cases. The most important attribute of OBJECT is DATA, which contains a URL that points to an external object. It has several other attributes that are used for some types of objects. This is only a quick reference, so we can't list all the different multimedia objects and their attributes here.

Although OBJECT is itself a text-level element, its content is the same as that of BODY. However, in the ideal case that content is not displayed. The intention is that the content is displayed only when the OBJECT itself could not be displayed, for whatever reason. The content constitutes an alternative, in the same way that the ALT attribute of IMG is an alternative. But the alternative of OBJECT is much richer, it can be almost a complete HTML document. Here is a simple example:

```
<OBJECT DATA="nonexistent.ngf">
<P>Your browser failed to load
the NGF image. If it had worked,
you would have seen a gold
edged mirror that reflected
your face.</P>
</OBJECT>
```

Your browser failed to load the NGF image. If it had worked, you would have seen a gold edged mirror that reflected your face.

SPECIAL CHARACTERS

A few characters can be entered by name. This may be useful when the HTML file is to be sent over old mail systems, or when your keyboard doesn't allow you to enter those characters in an easier way. For example, instead of 'é' you can enter 'é' (including the & and the ;). Here is a partial list:

Character	Code
á	&aacute;
Á	&Aacute;
â	&acirc;
Â	&Acirc;
à	&agrave;
À	&Agrave;
å	&aring;
Å	&Aring;
ã	&atilde;
Ã	&Atilde;
ä	&auml;
Ä	&Auml;
æ	&aelig;
Æ	&AElig;
ç	&ccedil;
Ç	&Ccedil;
ð	&eth;
Ð	&ETH;
é	&eacute;
É	&Eacute;
ê	&ecirc;
Ê	&Ecirc;
è	&egrave;
È	&Egrave;
ë	&euml;
Ë	&Euml;
í	&iacute;
Í	&Iacute;
î	&icirc;
Î	&Icirc;
ì	&igrave;
Ì	&Igrave;
ï	&iuml;
Ï	&Iuml;
ñ	&ntilde;
Ñ	&Ntilde;

ó	`&oacute;`
Ó	`&Oacute;`
ô	`&ocirc;`
Ô	`&Ocirc;`
ò	`&ograve;`
Ò	`&Ograve;`
ø	`&oslash;`
Ø	`&Oslash;`
õ	`&otilde;`
Õ	`&Otilde;`
ö	`&ouml;`
Ö	`&Ouml;`
ß	`&szlig;`
þ	`&thorn;`
Þ	`&THORN;`
ú	`&uacute;`
Ú	`&Uacute;`
û	`&ucirc;`
Û	`&Ucirc;`
ù	`&ugrave;`
Ù	`&Ugrave;`
ü	`&uuml;`
Ü	`&Uuml;`
ý	`&yacute;`
Ý	`&Yacute;`
ÿ	`&yuml;`
©	`&copy;`
®	`&reg;`
&	`&amp;`
>	`&gt;`
<	`&lt;`
"	`&quot;`
(non-breaking space)	` `
`&trade;`	`&trade;`
(soft hyphen)	`&shy;`
(thin space)	` `
(em space)	` `
(en space)	` `
—	`&mdash;`
–	`&ndash;`
(zero-width non-joiner)	`&zwnj;`
(zero-width joiner)	`&zwj;`
(left-to-right mark)	`&lrm;`
(right-to-left mark)	`&rlm;`

A *non-breaking space* is exactly like a normal space, except that it will never be broken at the end of a line. A *soft hyphen* is an invisible mark in the text that indicates that a line may be broken at that point if needed, in which case it will expand to the appropriate type of hyphen to indicate that the word continues on the next line. A *thin space* is a space that is about half as wide as a normal space and that doesn't break between two lines (a common use is between a number and a percent sign). An *em space* is a space that is as wide as the em of the current font and that doesn't break a line. An *en space* is half the width of an em space.

A *zero-width non-joiner* is an invisible mark between two letters to indicate that the two letters should not be combined visually. It can be used to avoid a ligature. In western languages it is almost never necessary. In some oriental languages it is more common. A *zero-width joiner* is the opposite. It combines two letters into a ligature that would otherwise not be combined.

The *left-to-right mark* and the *right-to-left mark* are occasionally useful in texts that combine left-to-right text with right-to-left text, such as an Arabic text with English words. The marks are invisible, but cause the following character to be interpreted as a left-to-right, respectively right-to-left character, in cases where the direction is not clear from the context.

OBSOLETE AND DEPRECATED ELEMENTS

In some old HTML documents (from before HTML 2.0), you may find elements XMP, LISTING and PLAINTEXT. They have been replaced by PRE and should not be used anymore. They are not part of HTML.

Some other elements have been introduced over time in various browsers, and are still allowed in HTML, but are now deprecated. The functionality of APPLET is now included in OBJECT. Some attempts at introducing stylistic information are now deprecated in favor of style sheets. These elements are BASEFONT, BIG, SMALL, CENTER, S, TT, FONT and U.

DIR and MENU are alternatives for UL. They are also deprecated.

CSS software resources

This appendix describes software that supports CSS. The list is likely to increase quickly in 1997, and you should therefore be sure to check this book's Web site (http://www.awl.com/css/) for an updated list. Also, the Web site will describe the browsers in more detail, including documentation on bugs and unimplemented features.

On the Web, a new technical specification will not get far if it doesn't work with the major browsers. Part of the work on CSS has therefore been to ensure that CSS1 is supported by common browsers: in 1997 this means Microsoft Internet Explorer and Netscape Navigator. Together, the two browsers have more than 90% of the market – although "market" may be a misnomer all the time the browsers can be downloaded free of charge.

Microsoft Internet Explorer 3.0 (MSIE3) was the first commercial browser to support CSS when it was released in August 1996. This was before the CSS1 specification had been finalized and Microsoft's early support contributed to the acceptance of CSS. At the time of writing, MSIE3 is the most accessible among the browsers that support CSS, and we encourage you to experiment with it. It supports a significant subset of the current CSS1 specification: the Web site of this book will point you to the details.

Just before this book went to press, Netscape released a beta version of Navigator that supports CSS. This is very good news for style sheets on the web. At the time of writing, we have not been able to evaluate the Netscape implementation of CSS1. On the book's Web site, you can read the latest about Navigator's CSS support.

Before we could promote CSS to the commercial Web software vendors, we had to make sure CSS was a solid specification. The best way to find out is to implement the specification. The process is similar to crash-testing new automobile models before they hit the show rooms. Several testbed CSS1 implementations were therefore available before CSS was supported in the first commercial browsers. Experience gathered from the testbed implementations helped us improve the specification, and gave people a chance to experiment with style sheets at an early stage. Two of the initial testbed browser implementations are Arena and Emacs-W3.

From 1994 to 1996, Arena was W3C's testbed browser (Figure B.1). A number of features that were introduced onto the Web during that period were pioneered in Arena, among them HTML tables and style sheets. Dave Raggett, Henrik Frystyk Nielsen, Yves Lafon and Håkon Lie worked on Arena. When Amaya (see below) became a testbed authoring environment for W3C, development on Arena was taken over by Yggdrasil (http://www.ysgdrasil.com).

Figure B.1 Screenshot from Arena.

Emacs is a legendary editor whose offerings stretch well beyond editing documents. Since Emacs has its own programming language, people have written applications that will let you read email, play games and surf the Web from within Emacs. Bill Perry, the programmer of Emacs-W3, also known as Gnuscape Navigator, takes pride in being among the first to support new features on the Web. CSS is no exception, and although Emacs does not offer all the features of a modern graphical user interface, Emacs-W3 still sports an impressive list of features.

If browser support is the first hurdle for any new specification on the web, support from HTML editors is next. In the early days of the Web, authors used plain text editors to create HTML pages, but dedicated HTML editors are increasingly being used. Editors offer authors an environment similar to common word processing and desktop publishing applications and thereby hide the underlying HTML. In a similar manner, the editor can generate a CSS style sheet without the author ever seeing the CSS code. Support for CSS is among the features of W3C's testbed authoring environment, Amaya (http://www.w3.org/Amaya) (Figure B.2).

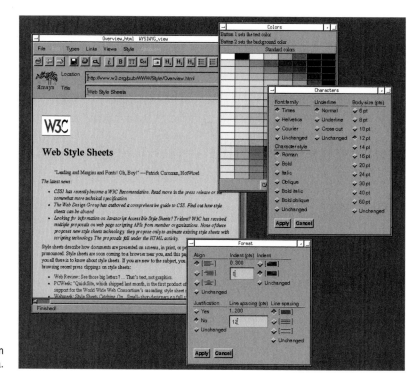

Figure B.2 Screenshot from Amaya.

Instead of using a dedicated HTML editor, many authors would like to continue using editors they have learned to love in pre-Web days. Examples of such editors are Microsoft Word and Adobe FrameMaker. You can find conversion utilities for all popular authoring environments. These programs will take a file written in the editor's preferred storage format and convert it into HTML. Also, with the success of the Web and HTML, many authoring environments have started to support HTML as a storage format selectable from the application itself. No matter how the conversion is done, information will always be lost when HTML is created. HTML can, as we explored in Chapter 1, only represent a very limited part of the information designers would like to put on their pages. The combination of HTML and CSS is able to store a much larger part of that information. Already, Adobe has released an add-on module to FrameMaker – code-named HoTaMaLe – that will save documents as both HTML and CSS. We expect other desktop publishing applications to follow in 1997.

Table B.1 lists CSS software that is either available now or has been announced.

PRODUCT	CATEGORY	AVAILABILITY	PLATFORM
Microsoft Internet Explorer 3 [1]	B	Now	Windows/Mac
Microsoft Internet Explorer 4 [1]	B	First quarter 1997	
Netscape Navigator/Communicator [2]	B	First quarter 1997	All
Arena [3]	B	Now	UNIX
emacs-w3 (aka Gnuscape Navigator) [4]	B	Now	(All platforms with emacs)
Adobe FrameMaker HoTaMaLe [5]	C	(Pre-release now)	All
Amaya [6]	E	(Pre-release now)	UNIX
SoftQuad HotMetal Intranet Publisher	E	Now	
Grif Symposia Pro Web Publisher	E	1997	
Harlequin Webmaker [7]	C	Now	All

Table B.1 Some current and expected products that support CSS. The categories are: B (browser), E (editor), C (converter).

Web addresses at which more information can be found about the products listed above are:

1 http://www.microsoft.com/ie

2 http://home.netscape.com/comprod/products/communicator/guide.html

3 http://www.w3.org/pub/WWW/Arena

4 http://www.cs.indiana.edu/elisp/w3/docs.html

5 http://www.adobe.com/prodindex/framemaker/exportpi

6 http://www.w3.org/pub/WWW/Amaya

7 http://www.harlequin.com/webmaker

Index

default font 68
default style sheet 40, 186, 209, 211, 218–19
default values 197
definition description (DD element) 15, 18, 253–4
definition list (DL element) 15, 16–18, 232, 253–4
definition term (DT element) 15, 18, 253–4, 255
Demi-Bold font 87, 88
deprecated elements (in latest version of HTML) 261
descender (part of letter) 65, 149
design
    to accommodate cascading 226
    CSS arts and crafts 187–94
    CSS makeovers 195–207
    effect 227
    for reusability 225
    for scalability 226
    tips (using type families) 83
designer style sheets 209–16 passim
desktop publishing 1, 2, 4–5, 58–9
Devanagari alphabet 83
device-dependent unit 76
DFN element 255–6
Didot element 64
dingbat font 187
DIR attribute 252, 255–7, 261
display property 133, 164, 241
    basic structures 99–111
DIV element 15, 55–7, 78, 205–7, 221, 252
DL element (definition list) 15, 16–18, 232, 253–4
Document Style Semantics and Specification Language 220, 230–1
documents
    creating (without style sheets) 231–5
    customizing 220–1
    legibility 149, 227
    linking 218–24, 248–9
    reusability 225
    scalability 66, 67, 78–80, 226
    structure 1–2, 26–9, 36–8, 209–12, 227, 250–1
    trees 26–9
dotted line (border style) 123–4

double line (border style) 123–4
download time 7
drop-shadow 247–8
dropcap initial 53, 54–5
DT element (definition term) 15, 18, 253–4, 255

"18 point Helvetica bold italic" 4–5
elements (of HTML)
    block-level, see block-level elements
    BODY, see BODY element
    empty 19–20, 24, 100, 112
    HEAD, see HEAD element inline, see inline element
    invisible 14–15, 31
    LINK 33, 218–19, 224–5, 241, 248, 251
    nested 27–9, 240, 250
    overview (table) 14–15
    parts of 9–10, 13, 15, 43, 250–1
    replaced, see replaced elements
    STRONG, see STRONG elements
    structural 231–3
    STYLE, see STYLE element
    text-level 255–8
    TITLE 10–13, 15, 26–7, 34, 36–7, 251
    within elements 26–7
EM elements 13, 15, 40, 49–50, 95, 121, 255–6
em unit 64, 66–7, 76, 78–9, 92, 201–2, 261
Emacs-W3 262, 263, 265
embedded element 95
emphasis (EM elements) 13, 15, 40, 49–50, 95, 121, 255–6
empty elements 19–20, 24, 100, 112
end tag 9–10, 13, 15, 250–1
Enough is Enough (Stephen Traub) 190
European Laboratory for Particle Physics (CERN) 3
Eurostyle 197
ex unit 64, 66–7, 76, 79, 261
Explorer, see Microsoft Internet Explorer entries
extended expressions 246
extensions (decisions on) 249
external information 51–5